THE MISHNAH
SOCIAL PERSPECTIVES

THE MISHNAH

Social Perspectives

BY

JACOB NEUSNER

BRILL ACADEMIC PUBLISHERS, INC.
BOSTON • LEIDEN
2002

Library of Congress Cataloging-in-Publication Data

Neusner, Jacob, 1932–
    The Mishnah : social perspectives / by Jacob Neusner.
      p. cm.
    Originally published: Leiden : Boston : Brill, 1999. Handbuch der
Orientalistik. Erste Abteilung, Der Nahe und Mittlere Osten ; 46. Bd.
    Includes bibliographical references and index.
    ISBN 0–391–04159–2
      1. Mishnah—Criticism, interpretation, etc. 2. Judaism—Essence, genius,
nature. 3. Mishnah—Philosophy. 4. Economics—Religious aspects—Judaism.
5. Politics in rabbinical literature. 6. Aristotle. I. Title.

BM497.8 .N478385 2002
296.1'2306—dc21

                                                              2001056692

ISBN 0–391–04159–2

PRINTED IN THE UNITED STATES OF AMERICA

TABLE OF CONTENTS

PREFACE

The world-construction set forth by the Mishnah, the second century philosophical law code that lays the foundation, after Scripture, of normative Judaism, encompasses all subjects that pertain to the life of an entire nation. The complete system of the code establishes its Israel's social order. Such a program of social construction by its nature involves three principal intellectual tasks of theoretical thought, politics, economics, and science or learning: definition of the social entity characterized by a comprehensive world view and way of life of one sort, rather than some other. A system that proposes to set forth the main frame and structure of a society will commonly make its statement in what it says about all three matters, establishing the same fundamental principle or viewpoint or attitude in treating each critical component of its theory of the social system. That basic harmony and coherence in what is said by a system about economics, politics, and science will ordinarily characterize a well-composed theory of world-construction, such as the Mishnah's of ca. 200 C.E.

Accordingly, the thesis of this reprise of established research is that the Mishnah sets forth a systematic statement of Israel's social order. The document encompasses the philosophy, economics, and politics of the Israelite world for which it legislates, defined here. That statement finds its correct context for interpretation in the philosophy, economics, and politics of Aristotle, to which in method and message we discern particular matters of correspondence. Specifically, at critical and indicative turnings, the Mishnah's mode of thought about the order of nature and society, and its specific message concerning the politics and economics that define the social order recapitulate those of Aristotle.

Let me briefly describe the document under study in these pages. In the form of a law code, the Mishnah sets forth a theoretical statement of a Judaism or Judaic system—a way of life and world view addressed to a particular "Israel." The document was produced under the sponsorship of Judah the Patriarch, ethnarch of the Jews of the Land of Israel ("Palestine") under Roman authority and sponsorship. The document, absorbing within its systematic statement whatever of Scripture its authorship found urgent, served as the basic law of the Jews of the holy land. It rapidly was adopted as the constitution, also, of the Jews in Babylonia and other of the western satrapies of the Iranian empire of the Sasanians.[1] The Mishnah is divided into six divisions, Agriculture (producing crops and handing over God's share in them to the scheduled castes), Seasons (holy days, conduct of the cult and the village on appointed times), Women (laws of the family, personal status, betrothal, marriage, divorce, also vows and some special problems), Damages (civil and criminal law, the organization and procedures of the courts), Holy Things (the temple, conduct of the sacrificial rites on an everyday basis, the upkeep of the temple buildings), and Purities (taboos affecting the temple cult, uncleanness in respect to persons, and cultic cleanness effected, also, in the home).

These six divisions viewed over all cover six principal topics: sanctification of the agricultural economy by conduct of farming in accord with the taboos of Scripture and support of the priesthood, the holy caste; sanctification of time, with reference to special occasions, appointed times and the Sabbath; sanctification of the family and the individual; the proper conduct of points of social conflict, the political life of the people and the regulation of the economy in regard to trade, commerce, real estate, labor relations, and the like; the sanctification of the Temple and its offerings, with special emphasis on the everyday and the routine occasions; and, finally, the protection of the Temple from uncleanness and the preservation of cultic cleanness. The six principal subjects form the center of the Mishnah's six divisions and, all together, cover the everyday life of the holy people in the here and now. The Mishnah generated systematic study and commentary in both the land of Israel and Babylonia, with two Talmuds, or systematic amplifications of the Mishnah, emerging.

---

[1] We have no evidence known to me of how Jews in other parts of the Roman and Iranian empires governed themselves. While ample comparative study of the Mishnah's law in relationship to that of Rome has gone forward for nearly a century, we have no study at all of the comparison of the Mishnah's and the Talmuds' law to that of the Sasanians, though the *Matigan-i hazar datastan* ("collection of a thousand decisions") has been available, in English, for a century, and is now in hand in a critical edition as well. Nearly thirty years ago. for three years, 1960-1, 1962-4, I studied Pahlavi with the intention of working on the comparison of talmudic and Iranian law-codes and law, but at that time the definition of the task, if it were to involve anything more than the collecting and arranging of essentially uninterpreted "parallels," eluded me. I now know how the work is to be done, but without a systemic study of the counterparts on the Iranian side, it still seems to me not an entirely promising inquiry. Before we can compare, we have to know what we are comparing, and what we are encompassing but also omitting.

Among the six divisions of the Mishnah, Talmud of the Land of Israel or Yerushalmi addresses four, Agriculture, Women, Seasons, and Damages, and the Talmud of Babylonia or Bavli treats four, Women, Seasons, Damages, and Holy Things. The Mishnah is a systemic, and not a traditional, statement and document. While using received facts from Scripture and other sources,[2] the Mishnah in no way forms a traditional document. Rather, it constitutes a cogent and autonomous statement, using received materials for its authorship's own purposes, rather than merely handing on the increment of an inherited set of sayings or rules. The Mishnah in form and system alike emerged as a whole and complete statement, deriving but using for its own purposes information from earlier generations that had been preserved in a variety of ways.

The importance of the systemic, not traditional, character of the Mishnah for the study of the economics, politics, and philosophy of the Mishnah is simple. It is only in the context of the system as a whole that the economics of the Judaism of the Mishnah is to be described. Like all other important topics of the system, therefore, economics or politics or philosophy will in its detail speak for the system as a whole and therefore will have to be read in the context, and as exemplary, of the system as a whole. In more general terms, the point pertains to every topic in the document. Specifically, the system of philosophy expressed through concrete and detailed law presented by the Mishnah, consists of a coherent logic and topic, a cogent world view and comprehensive way of living. Any subject addressed by the authorship of the Mishnah will permit the restatement of essentially the same fundamental proposition. That is the upshot of the Mishnah's character as a systematic statement, not a mere agglutination of received information.

The Mishnah's is a world view which speaks of transcendent things, a way of life in response to the supernatural meaning of what

---

[2] Because the Mishnah's authorship reaches its own judgments on the system it proposes to state, no good is served by surveying, out of all systemic context, sayings in Scripture pertinent in a general way to economic topics. No Judaism simply opened Scripture and paraphrased or restated what it found there; all Judaisms made their own choices. That is why I do not survey biblical statements. For such a survey, see Henry William Spiegel, *The Growth of Economic Thought* (Durham, 1971: Duke University Press), pp. 1-6. At the same time, we shall note in due course, facts of Scripture play a crucial role in the economic program and theory of the Mishnah, e.g., the Sabbath, slavery, the sabbatical and jubilee years, the protection of the weak, and the dignity of labor.

is done, a heightened and deepened perception of the sanctification of Israel in deed and in deliberation. Sanctification means two things, first, distinguishing Israel in all its dimensions from the world in all its ways; second, establishing the stability, order, regularity, predictability, and reliability of Israel in the world of nature and supernature in particular at moments and in contexts of danger. Danger means instability, disorder, irregularity, uncertainty, and betrayal. Each topic of the system as a whole takes up a critical and indispensable moment or context of social being. Through what is said in regard to each of the Mishnah's principal topics, what the halakhic system as a whole wishes to declare is fully expressed. Yet if the parts severally and jointly give the message of the whole, the whole cannot exist without all of the parts, so well joined and carefully crafted are they all. In defining the Mishnah, we lay stress upon the document's topical program, because the document in excruciating detail presents a sustained exegesis of a single theme, and that is, as noted, the sanctification of Israel, the people, in its everyday life. Indeed, in the history of Judaism(s), after the book of Leviticus but even including the Essenic library of Qumran and the New Testament Letter to the Hebrews, the Mishnah provides the single most extreme statement of the centrality of sanctification. Sanctification bears a specific meaning. It is the ordering of all things on earth in conformity with, and in relationship to, the model and pattern of Heaven, meaning, God's realm. To the authorship of the Mishnah,[3] the here and now of every day life, in the natural world, forms the counterpart and opposite of the supernatural world of God in heaven, and the ordering and regularizing of the one in line with the main outlines of the other constitutes, for the system of the Mishnah, the labor of sanctification. That is the overriding topic, and the Mishnah's system finds cogency in the exegesis of that topic.

---

[3] The document has no named author and contains no story of its own origins. As I shall presently point out, it starts in the middle of nowhere and ends in no determinate place. It represents a collectivity of authors, a consensus, and hence I speak of its authorship. I have demonstrated that the final formulation of all materials coincides with the penultimate processes of redaction, since a single system of forms and mnemonics is imposed on all passages uniformly. Not only so, but the document follows a carefully calibrated topical program, in which each given subject is spelled out in accord with a rigidly logical thematic program, with more important aspects of a topic treated first, less important ones later on, and, as is clear, all things treated within a single syntactic pattern. That makes unlikely the possibility that the document took shape in an incremental process, lasting over many generations, in which each generation left its deposit on the unfolding writing.

The Mishnah's topical program throughout thus focuses upon the sanctification of the life of holy Israel, the Jewish people.[4] No wonder, then, that the economics of the Priestly Code, an idiomatic statement of the absolutely standard and established distributive economic theory of temples from Sumerian times onward, dominated in the economics of the Judaism that the Mishnah would set forth. Just as the authorship of the Mishnah invoked the priestly conceptions of the holiness of Israel in answering the question of the age, so it adopted for its own use, with only negligible adaptation, the economic theory of the priesthood behind the pentateuchal Priestly Code and related writings. The question taken up by the authorship of the Mishnah, in the aftermath of the destruction of the Temple, is simple. It concerns whether and—more to the point—how Israel is still holy. And the (to the authorship, self-evidently valid) answer is that Israel indeed is holy, and so far as the media of sanctification persist beyond the destruction of the holy place—and they do endure—the task of holy Israel is to continue to conduct that life of sanctification that had centered upon the Temple. Where now does holiness reside? It is in the life of the people, Israel, there above all. So the Mishnah may speak of the holiness of the Temple, but the premise is that the people—that kingdom of priests and holy people of Leviticus—constitutes the center and focus of the sacred. The land retains its holiness too, and in raising the crops, the farmer is expected to adhere to the rules of order and structure laid down in Leviticus, keeping each thing in its proper classification, observing the laws of the sabbatical year, for instance. The priesthood retains its holiness, even without the task of carrying out the sacrificial cult. Therefore priests must continue to observe the caste rules governing marriage, such as are specified in Leviticus.

Four of the six principal parts of the Mishnah deal with the cult and its officers. These are, first, Holy Things, which addresses the everyday conduct of the sacrificial cult; second, Purities, which takes up the protection of the cult from the sources of uncleanness specified in the book of Leviticus (particularly Leviticus Chapters Twelve through Fifteen); third, Agriculture, which centers on the designation

---

[4] But the Talmuds refocus matters in their topical programs, laying far greater stress on the study and application of the civil code, the fourth of the six divisions of the Mishnah, omitting all reference to the code of purities, and in other ways reframing the composition through choices within and among the given repertoire of topics.

of portions of the crop for the use of the priesthood (and others in the same classification of a holy caste, such as the poor), and so provides for the support of the Temple staff; and, fourth, Appointed Times, the larger part of which concerns the conduct of the cult on such special occasions as the Day of Atonement, Passover, Tabernacles, and the like (and the rest of which concerns the conduct in the village on those same days, with the basic conception that what you do in the cult forms the mirror image of what you do in the village).[5]

In its quest for the rules of order and regularity such as Heaven has laid down and a truly sanctified earth will follow, the authorship of the Mishnah classifies and compares, finding the right rule for each matter, each important situation, by determining whether one case is like another or not like another. If it is like another, it follows the rule governing that other, and if not, it follows the opposite of that rule.[6] In this way an orderly and logical way to sort out chaos and discover the inner order of being generates the balanced and stable, secure world described by the Mishnah. Historical events, when they enter at all, lose their one-time and unprecedented character and are shown to follow, even to generate, a fixed rule; events therefore are the opposite of eventful. This age and the age to come, history and the end of history—these categories play little role. Even the figure of the Messiah serves as a taxon, that is, a classification,

---

[5] Of these four parts, the Talmud of the Land of Israel or Yerushalmi attends to three and the Talmud of Babylonia or Bavli to three, both of them omitting Purities. Two further divisions of the document as a whole deal with every day affairs, one, Damages, concerning civil law and government, the other, Women, taking up issues of family, home, and personal status. That, sum and substance, is the program of the Mishnah. Both Talmuds take a keen interest in these divisions.

[6] I had reached that reading of the logic of the Mishnah in various volumes of my History of the Mishnaic Law, in complete ignorance of the wonderful work of G. E. R. Lloyd, *Polarity and Analogy. Two Types of Argumentation in Early Greek Thought* (Cambridge, 1966: At the University Press). I came upon the work only in my interest in modes of thought in the Judaism of the dual Torah, which I called "the logics," and in comparing those logics with others. Lloyd stresses the interest, in Greek thought, of relationships of "same," "like," "other," "different," "contrary," and "contradictory," and, in my work on the Mishnah, I was able to show, stage by stage, how reflection on these relationships can have generated laws built from Scripture to the statement now contained within the Mishnah, e.g., in Zabim and in Niddah. I might note that the frequently-cited judgment of Saul Lieberman that the rabbinic literature contains no evidence of knowledge of Greco-Roman philosophy may be correct as to the utilization of key-words or phrases but is false as to the utilization of received and established modes of thought. Full bibliography and discussion of that issue will be found in the forth-coming study of "philosophy and 'the rabbis'" by Robert Berchman, and I need not pursue it here.

namely, designation or anointment (as the word *mashiah* means) distinguishes one priest from another. An anointed priest—a messiah-priest—is a priest of one kind or classification, not of some other. So, in all, the Mishnah's method and process dictate the results of its authorship's thought on any given topic, including the one of salvation, which is the proposition before us.

The dominant stylistic trait of the Mishnah, imposed in the process of ultimate closure and redaction, is the acute formalization of its syntactical structure, specifically in its intermediate divisions ("chapters" or composites of two or more paragraphs on exactly the same theme and problem and principle), which are so organized that the limits of a theme correspond to those of a formulaic pattern. Stress on the formalization of language corresponds to the Mishnah's inner structure, based as it is on regularization and order in the logic of being. The balance and order of the Mishnah are particular to the Mishnah.[7] A remarkably coherent, cogent, and exceedingly limited corpus of literary-formulaic devices and redactional conventions characterizes the document throughout. A significant single norm of agglutination predominates, which is reliance upon distinctive formulaic traits imposed on a sequence of sentences and upon distinctive thematic substance expressed by these same patterned sentences. That is how intermediate units were put together and accounts also for the formalization of small ones—without reference to the diversity of authorities cited therein. Four distinctive syntactical patterns characterize all, with the fifth, the "simple declarative sentence" itself so shaped as to yield its own distinctive traits. The Mishnah forms a closed and completed system in both topical program and inner, cogent logic, but also in language and syntax.[8]

---

[7] The Tosefta, ca. A.D. 300, a collection of complementary materials for the Mishnah, does not sustainedly reveal equivalent traits.

[8] The relevance of grammar and syntax to the argument that the Mishnah forms a closed system is simple. If there are traces of diverse theories of formulation and redaction of materials in our division, which would reflect the individual preferences and styles of diverse circles over two hundred years, we cannot point to them. The unified and cogent formal character of the Mishnah testifies in particular to the program and plan of its ultimate tradent-redactors. We learn in the Mishnah about the intention of that last generation of Mishnaic authorities, who gave us the document as we have it. It is their way of saying things which we know for certain. The language of the Mishnah and its grammatically formalized rhetoric create a world of discourse quite separate from the concrete realities of a given time, place, or society. The exceedingly limited repertoire of grammatical patterns by which all things on all matters are said gives symbolic expression to the notion that beneath the accidents of

The remainder of this book elaborates the reading of the Mishnah just now set forth and spells the matter out in vast detail. Specifically, I have devoted monographs to the social construction set forth by the Mishnah, its politics, philosophy, and economics. I chose those principal building blocks because any account of a theory of the social order is going to spell out a world view (here: philosophy), a way of life (here: economics), and a theory of the social entity that explains itself by appeal to the one and embodies the other (here: politics). The Mishnah's account of its Israel's politics, philosophy, and economics would undergo transformation in the documents that received the Mishnah, interpreted it, and mediated it to later generations. But, to begin with formidable components of that theory of the social order reworked, in the context of Israel and its Torah, important elements of the Aristotelian system.

These statements concerning the philosophy (science), economics, and politics of the Mishnah—therefore of Judaism—will not surprise persons familiar with my *Judaism as Philosophy, The Economics of the Mishnah,* and *Rabbinic Political Theory.* But beyond the circle of specialists likely to devote themselves to the reading of current academic literature in the small field at hand are many who may find stimulating the issues raised here. That is why, having spelled out the foundations for that reading of the Mishnah in a variety of works, I now state the whole all together, in severely condensed form, to make the case for those interested readers who are not going to read the protracted presentations of the present thesis. The works that are abbreviated here are as follows:

> *Judaism as Philosophy. The Method and Message of the Mishnah.* Columbia, 1991: University of South Carolina Press. Paperback edition: Baltimore, 1999: The Johns Hopkins University Press.
> *The Economics of the Mishnah.* Chicago, 1989: The University of Chicago Press. Reprint: Atlanta, 1999: Scholars Press for South Florida Studies in the History of Judaism.
> *Rabbinic Political Theory: Religion and Politics in the Mishnah.* Chicago, 1991: The University of Chicago Press.

My research has gone forward in the years following the completion of the initial trilogy. Critics rightly required a systematic statement of

---

life are a few, comprehensive relationships: unchanging and enduring patterns lie deep in the inner structure of reality and impose structure upon the accidents of the world.

the entire repertoire of passages of the Mishnah that take issues of an explicitly philosophical character; this I provided in *The Philosophical Mishnah*. My account of matters, beginning with *Judaism. The Evidence of the Mishnah*,[9] raised the question of what further matters of law and theology, beyond those treated in the Mishnah, animated the system set forth by the Mishnah. That is why I did the systematic survey, *The Judaism behind the Texts*. There I asked the question, what is taken for granted, what are principles that form the premise of thought, in the various explicit discussions of the Rabbinic literature of late antiquity. Finally, having concluded that Formengeschichte in the classic, New Testament model was not feasible in the Rabbinic literature, I challenged that assumption by a reconsideration of the matter within the limits of the documentary hypothesis of the Rabbinic writings. That produced *The Documentary Form-History* project. Other inquiries have brought me back to the Mishnah and to systematic work thereon, in particular my *Religious Commentary to the Halakhah* and the now-beginning *Comparative Hermeneutics of Rabbinic Judaism*.

That is why, in addition, I pursued further research, responding to questions raised by critics of the thesis spelled out here, in these monographs:

The Philosophical Mishnah. Volume I. *The Initial Probe*. Atlanta, 1989: Scholars Press for Brown Judaic Studies.

The Philosophical Mishnah. Volume II. *The Tractates' Agenda. From Abodah Zarah to Moed Qatan*. Atlanta, 1989: Scholars Press for Brown Judaic Studies.

The Philosophical Mishnah. Volume III. *The Tractates' Agenda. From Nazir to Zebahim*. Atlanta, 1989: Scholars Press for Brown Judaic Studies.

The Philosophical Mishnah. Volume IV. *The Repertoire*. Atlanta, 1989: Scholars Press for Brown Judaic Studies.

The Judaism Behind the Texts. The Generative Premises of Rabbinic Literature. I. *The Mishnah*. A. *The Division of Agriculture*. Atlanta, 1993: Scholars Press for South Florida Studies in the History of Judaism.

The Judaism Behind the Texts. The Generative Premises of Rabbinic Literature. I. *The Mishnah*. B. *The Divisions of Appointed Times, Women, and Damages (through Sanhedrin)*. Atlanta, 1993: Scholars Press for South Florida Studies in the History of Judaism.

The Judaism Behind the Texts. The Generative Premises of Rabbinic Literature. I. *The Mishnah*. C. *The Divisions of Damages (from Makkot), Holy Things and Purities*. Atlanta, 1993: Scholars Press for South Florida Studies in the History of Judaism.

---

[9] Chicago, 1981: University of Chicago Press.

The Judaism Behind the Texts. The Generative Premises of Rabbinic Literature. II. *The Tosefta, Tractate Abot, and the Earlier Midrash-Compilations: Sifra, Sifré to Numbers, and Sifré to Deuteronomy.* Atlanta, 1993.: Scholars Press for South Florida Studies in the History of Judaism.

The Judaism Behind the Texts. The Generative Premises of Rabbinic Literature. III. *The Later Midrash-Compilations: Genesis Rabbah, Leviticus Rabbah and Pesiqta deRab Kahana.* Atlanta, 1994: Scholars Press for South Florida Studies in the History of Judaism.

The Judaism Behind the Texts. The Generative Premises of Rabbinic Literature. IV. *The Latest Midrash-Compilations: Song of Songs Rabbah, Ruth Rabbah, Esther Rabbah I, and Lamentations Rabbati. And The Fathers According to Rabbi Nathan.* Atlanta, 1994: Scholars Press for South Florida Studies in the History of Judaism.

The Judaism Behind the Texts. The Generative Premises of Rabbinic Literature. V. *The Talmuds of the Land of Israel and Babylonia.* Atlanta, 1994: Scholars Press for South Florida Studies in the History of Judaism.

The Judaism the Rabbis Take for Granted. Atlanta, 1995: Scholars Press for South Florida Studies in the History of Judaism.

The Documentary Form-History of Rabbinic Literature. I. *The Documentary Forms of the Mishnah.* Atlanta, 1998: Scholars Press for USF Academic Commentary Series.

The Documentary Form-History of Rabbinic Literature II. *The Aggadic Sector: Tractate Abot, Abot deRabbi Natan, Sifra, Sifré to Numbers, and Sifré to Deuteronomy.* Atlanta, 1998: Scholars Press for USF Academic Commentary Series.

The Documentary Form-History of Rabbinic Literature III. *The Aggadic Sector:.Mekhilta Attributed to R. Ishmael and Genesis Rabbah.* Atlanta, 1998: Scholars Press for USF Academic Commentary Series.

The Documentary Form-History of Rabbinic Literature IV. *The Aggadic Sector:.Leviticus Rabbah, and Pesiqta deRab Kahana.* Atlanta, 1998: Scholars Press for USF Academic Commentary Series.

The Documentary Form-History of Rabbinic Literature V. *The Aggadic Sector: Song of Songs Rabbah, Ruth Rabbah, Lamentations Rabbati, and Esther Rabbah I.* Atlanta, 1998: Scholars Press for USF Academic Commentary Series.

The Documentary Form-History of Rabbinic Literature. VI. *The Halakhic Sector. The Talmud of the Land of Israel. A. Berakhot and Shabbat through Taanit.* Atlanta, 1998: Scholars Press for USF Academic Commentary Series.

The Documentary Form-History of Rabbinic Literature. VI. *The Halakhic Sector. The Talmud of the Land of Israel. B. Megillah through Qiddushin.* Atlanta, 1998: Scholars Press for USF Academic Commentary Series.

The Documentary Form-History of Rabbinic Literature. VI. *The Halakhic Sector. The Talmud of the Land of Israel. C. Sotah through Horayot and Niddah.* Atlanta, 1998: Scholars Press for USF Academic Commentary Series.

The Documentary Form-History of Rabbinic Literature. VII. *The Halakhic Sector. The Talmud of Babylonia. A. Tractates Berakhot and Shabbat through Pesa-*

him. Atlanta, 1998: Scholars Press for USF Academic Commentary
  Series.
The Documentary Form-History of Rabbinic Literature. VII. *The Halakhic Sector.*
  The Talmud of Babylonia. B. *Tractates Yoma through Ketubot.* Atlanta,
  1998: Scholars Press for USF Academic Commentary Series.
The Documentary Form-History of Rabbinic Literature. VII. *The Halakhic Sector.*
  The Talmud of Babylonia. C. *Tractates Nedarim through Baba Mesia.* At-
  lanta, 1998: Scholars Press for USF Academic Commentary Series.
The Documentary Form-History of Rabbinic Literature. VII. *The Halakhic Sector.*
  The Talmud of Babylonia. D. *Tractates Baba Batra through Horayot.* At-
  lanta, 1998: Scholars Press for USF Academic Commentary Series.
The Documentary Form-History of Rabbinic Literature. VII. *The Halakhic Sector.*
  The Talmud of Babylonia. E. *Tractates Zebahim through Bekhorot.* Atlanta,
  1998: Scholars Press for USF Academic Commentary Series.
The Documentary Form-History of Rabbinic Literature. VII. *The Halakhic Sector.*
  The Talmud of Babylonia. F. *Tractates Arakhin through Niddah. And Conclu-
  sions.* Atlanta, 1998: Scholars Press for USF Academic Commentary
  Series.
The Halakhah of the Oral Torah: A Religious Commentary. Introduction. And
  Volume I. *Between Israel and God.* Part One. *Thanksgiving: Tractate
  Berakhot. Enlandisement: Tractates Kilayim, Shebi'it, and 'Orlah.* Atlanta,
  1997: Scholars Press for South Florida Studies in the History of
  Judaism.

With a corpus of work of these proportions, it is easy to see the value
of condensation and abbreviation, and that is what I mean to provide
in these pages.

Readers familiar with the Oxford University undergraduate program
in Politics, Philosophy, and Economics will immediately recognize
whence my original plan of the 1980s, realized, in the end, in the
books summarized in the three principal chapters of this precis. The
construction, world view, way of life, theory of the social entity, to
which I appeal, is a slight reworking of ideas of Clifford Geertz in
"Religion as a Cultural System," which I read many years ago and
which made a deep impression on me. Clearly, in studying the
formative history and literature, religion and theology of Rabbinic
Judaism, I have adapted a theoretical model that I have found illumi-
nating.

It remains to express my thanks to my editor at Brill, Drs. Elisabeth
Venekamp, who asked for a book from me about the Mishnah and
led me back to the systematic work treated here. I enjoy research
support, both on-going and in the form of annual grants, from the

University of South Florida and Bard College, and I am happy to express my thanks to both centers of higher learning for their generous commitment to my scholarship. I consulted Dean & Professor William Scott Green, University of Rochester, about the plan for this volume and its companions, and as always found him the consummate editor.

Jacob Neusner
University of South Florida & Bard College

CHAPTER ONE

THE MISHNAH AND ARISTOTLE'S NATURAL HISTORY

> A chain of summa genera, genera, species,
> subspecies, and varieties is not itself a chain
> of premises and conclusions. But what is
> more, it cannot in general be deductively
> established or established by reductio ad ab-
> surdum. The work of a Linnaeus cannot be
> done a priori.[1]

I. *Aristotle's Natural History*

Had Aristotle received Scripture, in addition to nature, as a source of
facts that require hierarchical classification in the manner of natural
history and chosen concrete words in place of symbols, he would
have written a document much like the Mishnah. The Mishnah provides an extreme example of how the modes of inquiry of natural
history—classification of genera and species in a hierarchical structure—come to expression but are worked out solely through the
nitty-gritty of ordinary and everyday life. The document does not
define "justice," but it does explain how to sort out conflicting claims
to the same cloak. Its rhetoric, balanced and orderly and proportion-
ate—is testimony to its conception that within the everyday are contained the highest and most abstract truths of not merely wisdom but
knowledge, in our language, natural philosophy or science. If things
are orderly, then out of the chaos of the here and now, we must show
it. Just as in contemporary empirical, experimental science the case
stands for the principle, which is to be inferred and tested, so in the
Mishnah, cases bear the entire burden of analytical and principled
thought.

The Mishnah's mode of making connections—the details of its
practical logic and applied reason—conforms to the rules of natural
history set forth by Aristotle. In that science, the Mishnaic component of the Talmud proposes to investigate science in everyday life,
identifying the data that follow the same rule, excluding those that do

---

[1] Lloyd, p. 136.

not, and setting the whole into a great chain of being. We shall find
ample cause to classify the taxonomic method—premises and rules—
of the sages of the Mishnah in the same category as the method of
Aristotle. As to substance, we shall further identify the fundamental
propositions of the philosophy of the Mishnah with the premises and
points of acute engagement of Plato in the version that would emerge
in the third century as Neo-Platonism. In its indicative traits of message and method, the Mishnah's philosophical system is a version of
one critical proposition of Neo-Platonism, set forth and demonstrated
through a standard Aristotelian method. So the Mishnah is a document of its day, using the methods of Aristotle in the service of the
philosophical program of Plato. But the principal issue is the meth-
odological one.

Making connections means, specifically, investigating the properties of things and classifying like together with like. The method of
natural history formulated by Aristotle rests upon the classification of
things conducted in just that way. Moving from the known to the
unknown, whether in science or in philosophy, requires that we em-
ploy what is known to solve the problem of the unknown, the certain
imparting sense to the uncertain. And that means, we must discover
the pertinent point of comparison, the governing analogy, that allows
us to invoke the principle governing the known in the disposition of
the unknown. If we can determine that to which the unknown is
comparable, then we may impose upon the unknown the rule that
governs the known, so classify the unknown within the larger system
of sense.

For both Aristotle and the framers of the Mishnah, those
taxonomically-indicative traits inhere in the things themselves; that is
why I insist that for our sages of blessed memory classification is
inductive and rests upon description. Owens sets the matter forth in
the following language:[2]

> Since a theoretical science proceeds from first principles that are found
> within the thing under investigation, the initial task of the philosophy of
> nature will be to discover its primary principles in the sensible thing
> themselves.

I cannot imagine a formulation more suited to the method of the
Mishnah than that simple statement. The philosophers whose system
is set forth in the Mishnah appeal to the traits of things, deriving their

---

[2] Owens, pp. 309ff.

genera from the comparison and contrast of those inherent or intrinsic traits. This I take to be precisely what is stated here.

> In accordance with the general directives of the Aristotelian logic, the process of their discovery will be dialectical, not demonstrative.

This distinction is between genuine reasoning and demonstration. Demonstration proceeds from truth known as such, while dialectic deals with reasoning from opinions.

A brief account, based upon the standard textbook literature, of the taxonomic method of Aristotle permits us to compare the philosophical method of the Mishnah with his. We begin with the simple observation that the distinction between genus and species lies at the foundation of all knowledge. A.W.H. Adkins states the matter in the most accessible way, "Aristotle, a systematic biologist, uses his method of classification by genera and species, itself developed from the classificatory interests of the later Plato, to place man among other animals"[3] The point of direct contact and intersection between the Mishnah's philosophy of hierarchical classification and the natural philosophy of Aristotle lies in the shared, and critical, conviction concerning the true nature or character of things. Neither leaves space for taxonomy based on other-than-intrinsic traits of things.[4] The basic conviction on both side maintains that objects are not random but fall into classes and so may be described, analyzed, and explained by appeal to general traits or rules.

What pertains here is "the use of deductive reasoning proceeding from self-evident principles or discovered general truths to conclusions of a more limited import; and syllogistic forms of demonstrative or persuasive arguments."[5] The goal is the classification of things, which is to say, the discovery of general rules that apply to discrete data or instances. Minio-Paluello states,

> "In epistemology...Aristotelianism includes a concentration on knowledge accessible by natural means or accountable for by reason; an inductive, analytical empiricism, or stress on experience in the study of nature...leading from the perception of contingent individual occurrences to the discovery of permanent, universal patterns; and the primacy of the universal, that which is expressed by common or general

---

[3] Adkins, *From the Many to the One*, pp. 170-171.

[4] That point takes on significance when we examine Sifra's critique of the Mishnah's modes of classification.

[5] Minio-Paluello, Lorenzo, "Aristotelianism," *Encyclopaedia Britannica* 1:1155-1161., p. 1155.

terms. In metaphysics, or the theory of Being, Aristotelianism involves belief in the primacy of the individual in the realm of existence; in correlated conceptions allowing an articulate account of reality (e.g., 10 categories; genus-species-individual, matter-form, potentiality-actuality, essential-accidental; the four material elements and their basic qualities; and the four causes-formal, material, efficient and final); in the soul as the inseparable form of each living body in the vegetable and animals kingdoms; in activity as the essence of things; and in the primacy of speculative over practical activity."

The manner in which we accomplish this work is to establish categories of traits, and these will yield the besought rules or generalizations that make possible both classification, and, in the nature of things, therefore also hierarchization. As we shall see, among these categories, for the Mishnah the most important are genus-species, potentiality-actuality, and essential-accidental.[6]

At work is a triple scheme of classification. The first involves causes, the second, substance, and the third, change. As to causes, there are the formal, efficient, and final causes, which can coincide. In physics there are three classifications of substance: things incapable of motion, things that move and are indestructible, and destructible things. In change there is generation and destruction, and there are three kinds of motion: alteration in the category of quality, increase and diminution in the category of quantity, and locomotion in the category of place.[7] While, as a matter of fact, "the world is composed of individuals, no two of whom are precisely alike,"[8] the correlated categories, matter and form allow us to establish categories that encompass individual or distinct items. Allan states:

> The wood which is potentially a table is also the matter upon which the carpenter will impress the form of a table...Matter and form are relative terms, in the sense that a thing which has some degree of form may serve as the matter upon which a new form is imposed...It is Form.. which imparts structural unity to a single individual. Various materials are required in order to build a house...what holds them together is the Form of the house...Form...tends to unity of design, matter to plurality..[9]

---

[6] Elsewhere I have shown that the Mishnah's law differentiates among types of causation, but that is not critical to the argument of this chapter; see my *Rabbinic Judaism. The Documentary History of the Formative Age.*

[7] *ibid.*

[8] Allan, D. J., *The Philosophy of Aristotle*, p. 42.

[9] *op. cit.*, p. 39.

On the matter of form and matter, G. H. Parker further explains, "The Matter is the basic stuff which makes it possible for the Form to have existence at all."[10] The Form represents what is particular to a given instance. Parker proceeds, "Coupled with the concept of Matter and Form in every substance we find that other typically Aristotelian pair, Actual and Potential." Parker continues:

> "Typically Aristotelian" because it is here we see the outlook of one deeply immersed in Natural History, of one who has studied with minute care the development of living organisms from embryo to old age, of one who attempts to oppose a dynamic to a static view of things....Matter is potential, embryo is actual; the embryo in turn is potential, the baby is actual...The Potential is eternally moving, eternally changing into the Actual. Equally, Matter is eternally moved into Form.[11]

What Aristotle seeks to know is causes: "to know that something happens is mere shallowness unless one probes deeper and reveals the reason why."

The answer to the question of why derives from the famous "four causes." Taking as the question, what has "caused" the famous status of Zeus in his temple at Olympia, "made of ivory and gold on a core of wood by Phidias, the foremost sculptor of his time...placed in the central shrine of Olympia...," we have these four causes in play:

1. The material cause: the gold, the ivory, and the wood
2. The efficient cause: the hands and tools of Phidias
3. The formal cause: what the thing represents; in this case the figure of Zeus
4. The final cause: the purpose and meaning of the thing; in this case the greater glory of Zeus and the improvement of man.

We may draw these four causes into relationship with the issue of the potential and the actual: "The whole end and purpose of an acorn is to grow into an oak; the form taken by an acorn as it so develops is that of an oak; and the efficient cause, that which gave an acorn the opportunity of taking on the form of an oak, was a parent oak....Each cause plays its part in the process which makes a thing become what it is."

Points of intersection in detail are of special interest. For instance, while the actual and the potential form critical taxic categories for Aristotle, they prove subsidiary, though pertinent, in the Mishnah.

---

[10] Parker, *A Short Account of Greek Philosophy from Thales to Epicurus*, p. 141.
[11] Parker, p. 142.

While for the Mishnah, the matter of mixtures defines a central and
generative problematic, for Aristotle, the same matter is subsumed
into other compositions altogether. Mixtures form a chapter in the
story of change, which is explained by the passage of elements into
one another. That will help us to account for the destruction of one
element and the creation of another. In this connection Allan says:

> Aristotle does not mean by 'mixture' a mere shuffling of primary parti-
> cles, as if the seeds of wheat and barley were mixed in a heap, but
> genuine change of quality resulting in a new 'form,' towards which each
> component has made a contribution.[12]

The consideration of the classes of mixtures plays its role in Aristotle's account of the sublunary region; it is not—as represented by
Allan—a point at which Aristotle repeatedly uncovers problems that
require solution, in the way in which the issue of mixtures forms the
source for the Mishnah's solution of urgent problems.

But, in more general terms, what I conceive to be the generative
point of comparison lies in two matters. The paramount one draws
attention to the shared principles of formal logic that I find blatant in
the Mishnah and that all presentations of Aristotle's philosophy identify as emblematic. The second, as is clear, is the taxonomic method,
viewed from afar. Let us turn to the former. When we follow a simple
account of the way in which we attain new truth, we find ourselves
quite at home. Allan's account follows:[13]

> Induction...is the advance from the particular to the general. By the
> inspection of examples...in which one characteristic appears conjoined
> with another, we are led to propound a general rule which we suppose
> to be valid for cases not yet examined. Since the rule is of higher
> generality than the instances, this is an advance from a truth 'prior for
> us' toward a truth 'prior in nature.'

My representation of the Mishnaic mode of presentation of cases
that, with our participation, yield a general rule, accords with this
logic, which is inductive. But that impression requires qualification:

> On the other hand, sometimes two general truths, which are self-evi-
> dent or not open to reasonable doubt, necessarily imply a third truth, of
> more limited scope. Such a procedure is deduction or demonstration. It
> advances from what is prior in nature towards which is prior for us,
> and, because it does this, has a completeness and a constraining force

---

[12] D. J. Allan, *The Philosophy of Aristotle*, p. 60.
[13] *op. cit.*, pp. 126ff.

which is always missing in induction. It shows not merely that a fact is true but why it is true.

The theory of deduction forms the centerpiece of Aristotle's logic, so Allan maintains. Have we instances of the same deductive reasoning in the Mishnah? In my judgment, the exemplary case of the comparison of the king and the high priest, which we now review, forms precisely such a deductive and as a matter of fact syllogistic statement. By syllogism is meant "discourse in which, certain things being stated, something other than what is stated follows of necessity from their being so."[14] When we establish the general truths concerning the high priest and the king, we identify a third truth, concerning the priority of the latter over the former, and that truth is one of deduction.

Let us consider a concrete text to see how the Mishnah puts forth a syllogism. In the following passage, drawn from Mishnah-tractate Sanhedrin Chapter Two, the authorship wishes to say that Israel has two heads, one of state, the other of cult, the king and the high priest, respectively, and that these two offices are nearly wholly congruent with one another, with a few differences based on the particular traits of each. The traits associated with the one then are compared with those pertinent to the other, and out of this classification of shared, indicative traits also emerges the hierarchization of the one over the other. Broadly speaking, therefore, our exercise is one of setting forth the genus and the species. The genus is head of holy Israel. The species are king and high priest. Here are the traits in common and those not shared, and the exercise is fully exposed for what it is, an inquiry into the rules that govern, the points of regularity and order, in this minor matter, of political structure. My outline, imposed in BOLD-FACE type, makes the point important in this setting. What follows is Mishnah-tractate Sanhedrin 2:1-2:

    1. THE RULES OF THE HIGH PRIEST: SUBJECT TO THE LAW, MARITAL RITES, CONDUCT IN BEREAVEMENT

2:1 A. A high priest judges, and [others] judge him;

      B. gives testimony, and [others] give testimony about him;

      C. performs the rite of removing the shoe [Deut. 25:7-9], and [others] perform the rite of removing the shoe with his wife.

      D. [Others] enter levirate marriage with his wife, but he does not enter into levirate marriage,

      E. because he is prohibited to marry a widow.

---

[14] Joseph Owens, *A History of Ancient Western Philosophy*, p. 340.

F. [If] he suffers a death [in his family], he does not follow the bier.

G. "But when [the bearers of the bier] are not visible, he is visible; when they are visible, he is not.

H. "And he goes with them to the city gate," the words of R. Meir.

I. R. Judah says, "He never leaves the sanctuary,

J. "since it says, *Nor shall he go out of the sanctuary* (Lev. 21:12)."

K. And when he gives comfort to others

L. the accepted practice is for all the people to pass one after another, and the appointed [prefect of the priests] stands between him and the people.

M. And when he receives consolation from others,

N. all the people say to him, "Let us be your atonement."

O. And he says to them, "May you be blessed by Heaven."

P. And when they provide him with the funeral meal,

Q. all the people sit on the ground, while he sits on a stool.

2. THE RULES OF THE KING: NOT SUBJECT TO THE LAW, MARITAL RITES, CONDUCT IN BEREAVEMENT

2:2 A. The king does not judge, and [others] do not judge him;

B. does not give testimony, and [others] do not give testimony about him;

C. does not perform the rite of removing the shoe, and others do not perform the rite of removing the shoe with his wife;

D. does not enter into levirate marriage, nor [do his brother] enter levirate marriage with his wife.

E. R. Judah says, "If he wanted to perform the rite of removing the shoe or to enter into levirate marriage, his memory is a blessing."

F. They said to him, "They pay no attention to him [if he expressed the wish to do so]."

G. [Others] do not marry his widow.

H. R. Judah says, "A king may marry the widow of a king.

I. "For so we find in the case of David, that he married the widow of Saul,

J. "For it is said, *'And I gave you your master's house and your master's wives into your embrace'* (II Sam. 12:8)."

2:3 A. [If] [the king] suffers a death in his family, he does not leave the gate of his palace.

B. R. Judah says, "If he wants to go out after the bier, he goes out,

C. "for thus we find in the case of David, that he went out after the bier of Abner,

D. "since it is said, *'And King David followed the bier'* (2 Sam. 3:31)."

E. They said to him, "This action was only to appease the people."

F. And when they provide him with the funeral meal, all the people sit on the ground, while he sits on a couch.

3. SPECIAL RULES PERTINENT TO THE KING BECAUSE OF HIS CALLING

2:4   A. [The king] calls out [the army to wage] a war fought by choice
on the instructions of a court of seventy-one.

B. He [may exercise the right to] open a road for himself, and
[others] may not stop him.

C. The royal road has no required measure.

D. All the people plunder and lay before him [what they have
grabbed], and he takes the first portion.

E. *"He should not multiply wives to himself"* (Deut. 17:17)—only eighteen.

F. R Judah says, "He may have as many as he wants, so long as
they *do not entice him* [to abandon the Lord (Deut. 7:4)]."

G. R. Simeon says, "Even if there is only one who entices him [to
abandon the Lord]—lo, this one should not marry her."

H. If so, why is it said, "He should not multiply wives to himself"?

I. Even though they should be like Abigail [1 Sam. 25:3].

J. *"He should not multiply horses to himself"* (Deut. 17:16)—only
enough for his chariot.

K. *"Neither shall he greatly multiply to himself silver and gold"* (Deut.
17:16)—only enough to pay his army.

L. *"And he writes out a scroll of the Torah for himself"* (Deut. 17:17)

M. When he goes to war, he takes it out with him; when he comes
back, he brings it back with him; when he is in session in court,
it is with him; when he is reclining, it is before him,

N. as it is said, *"And it shall be with him, and he shall read in it all the
days of his life"* (Deut. 17:19).

2:5   A. [Others may] not ride on his horse, sit on his throne, handle
his scepter.

B. And [others may] not watch him while he is getting a haircut,
or while he is nude, or in the bath-house,

C. since it is said, *"You shall surely set him as king over you"* (Deut.
17:15)—that reverence for him will be upon you.

MISHNAH-TRACTATE SANHEDRIN CHAPTER TWO

Clearly, Scripture plays a subordinate role here, not a taxonomically-
indicative one. The topic is organized within its own logic, not in
accord with the order or data of Scriptural references.[15] Scripture
supplies facts. What proves decisive in both the ordering of data and
the conclusions drawn from the specific juxtapositions set forth? It is
the traits of things—kings, high priests—that dictate classification-
categories on their own, without Scripture's dictation.

The philosophical cast of mind is amply revealed in this essay,
which in concrete terms effects a taxonomy, a study of the genus,

---

[15] We shall note the contrasting mode of organization chosen by the authors of
Sifra.

national leader, and its two species, [1] king, [2] high priest: how are
they alike, how are they not alike, and what accounts for the differences. The premise is that national leaders are alike and follow the
same rule, except where they differ and follow the opposite rule from
one another. But that premise also is subject to the proof effected by
the survey of the data consisting of concrete rules, those systemically
inert facts that here come to life for the purposes of establishing a
proposition. By itself, the fact that, e.g., others may not ride on his
horse, bears the burden of no systemic proposition. In the context of
an argument constructed for nomothetic, taxonomic purposes, the
same fact is active and weighty. The whole depends upon three
premises: [1] the importance of comparison and contrast, with the
supposition that [2] like follows the like, and the unlike follows the
opposite, rule; and [3] when we classify, we also hierarchize, which
yields the argument from hierarchical classification: if this, which is
the lesser, follows rule X, then that, which is the greater, surely
should follow rule X. And that is the whole sum and substance of the
logic of *Listenwissenschaft* as the Mishnah applies that logic in a practical way.

Now if I had to specify a single mode of thought that established
connections between one fact and another, it is in the search for
points in common and therefore also points of contrast. We seek
connection between fact and fact, sentence and sentence, and this we
find, in the subtle and balanced rhetoric of the Mishnah, by comparing and contrasting two things that are like and not alike. At the
logical level, too, the Mishnah falls into the category of familiar philosophical thought. Once we seek regularities, we propose rules. What
is like another thing falls under its rule, and what is not like the other
falls under the opposite rule. Accordingly, as to the species of the
genus, so far as they are alike, they share the same rule. So far as they
are not alike, each follows a rule contrary to that governing the other.
So the work of analysis is what produces connection, and therefore
the drawing of conclusions derives from comparison and contrast: the
and, the *equal*. The proposition then that forms the conclusion concerns the essential likeness of the two offices, except where they are
different, but the subterranean premise is that we can explain both
likeness and difference by appeal to a principle of fundamental order
and unity. To make these observations concrete, we turn to the case
at hand. The important contrast comes at the outset. The high priest
and king fall into a single genus, but speciation, based on traits par-

ticular to the king, then distinguishes the one from the other. All of this exercise is conducted essentially independently of Scripture; the classifications derive from the system, are viewed as autonomous constructs; traits of things define classifications and dictate what is like and what is unlike.

II. *The Mishnah's List-Making*

My intent when I speak of philosophy, therefore, is very specific. I mean more than that there was a rather general philosophy expressed by the law, that is, "philosophy of law" or of politics or economics, as we shall see in the following chapters of this book. I mean, further, something more particular than that the intellects represented here thought in a manner philosophers respected, e.g., in accord with rules of order and intelligibility. I mean, very concretely, that, in the medium and idiom of rules, the authorship of the Mishnah worked out positions on matters of distinctively philosophical interest. They were not lawyers who had a general philosophy, e.g., of society and the social order. They were philosophers who happened also to produce law. The bulk of their writing, though not all of it, is philosophy set forth in the form of law. The rules of classification and generalization, the issues of mixtures, the resolution of doubts, the relationship of the actual to the potential (chicken, egg), the role of attitude or intention in the assessment of an action and its consequences (a subset of the foregoing), the sorting out of two or more principles that come to bear in a single case, so assigning to one a primary, to another a subordinated role in resolving that case, and the like—these abstract issues of general intelligibility turn out to form an intellectual program of considerable portions for the Mishnah.

When philosophers did philosophy, these are some of the things that concerned them. In philosophical categories, specifically, the issues of the Mishnah concern principles that transcend the subject-matter of the law and that in fact affect themes and topics entirely unrelated to the law, physics (mixtures), metaphysics (the potential and the actual), and ethics (intentionality and action), for example. These important themes are by their fundamental character philosophical: the nature of mixtures; the relationship of the potential to the actual; the relationship of deed to intentionality; and rules for sorting out issues in doubt. But while philosophers invoked cases and examples, they did not limit discourse to details or expect that their encompassing, abstract generalizations would emerge only through an inductive reading of concrete data. But that is exactly what the authorship of the Mishnah did expect, offering generalizations only rarely, but compelling lists throughout.

The sages of the Mishnah investigated the science within, not the science of, every day affairs. Their goal did not require them to form syllogisms on the potential and the actual, only on the general principles that will settle cases of doubt involving the potential and the actual. They were not, then, natural historians in the way in which Aristotle founded that science. They thought like natural historians in solving the cases that came there way, and that is a different matter. Nonetheless, the program of inquiry, particularly into the principles of hierarchical classification and their consequence in the unity of all being in the One, shared by the Mishnah and Aristotle, as to method, and Middle- and Neo-Platonism, as to proposition, manifests the philosophical character of the Mishnah. And that character emerges in the system's *program* of thought, not merely in the *modes* of thought.[16] The program concerns topics, e.g., potentiality and actuality, intention and action, as well as rules of philosophical thought, e.g., the correct manner of classification, that is, assessing mixtures on the one side and hierarchization on the other, or the proper rules governing resolutions of matter of doubt.

Take the physics of mixtures, for example. Here we find ourselves in the realm of Stoic thought. The specific problematic that the Mishnah's framers identify within a given topic very commonly derives from the nature of mixtures. And within an exercise in natural history, that is hardly surprising. If we classify a variety of things, then how do we deal with a case in which two or three or ten classification-schemes intersect. For example, one scheme would classify things as unclean or clean; a second, as certain or doubtful; a third as required or voluntary; a fourth as determinate or indeterminate, and so on, essentially without limit. Then how do these layers of grids so come together that one reaches a decision, and in what way do we identify the decisive taxic indicators? That forms one mixture, that is, the confusion of classification-systems. Another mixture derives from the nature or property of things. Some things so

---

[16] This is spelled out in my *The Philosophical Mishnah*.

mix as to form a wholly integrated new thing. Some so mix as to keep essentially distinct the components of the mixture. And some, finally, mix in varying measures or degrees. Now that issue is susceptible of practical application to any scheme of classification, made up of any categories, whether deriving from nature or supernature. But it is an essentially philosophical, abstract question, one of method, but also, one of doctrine. The method concerns the how of discerning the traits of mixtures. The doctrine concerns the types of mixture and how each type imposes upon its data a rule of a given sort: this, not that.

Indeed, if we stand back from the details of the law and ask, What is it that the second century rabbis regarded (in general terms) as subject to their speculative inquiry, we should describe their agendum as follows: In respect to society, we want to know what people usually do, how various classes of society may be expected to behave. In respect to happenings in the natural world, the world of animals for example, we ask about what are the likely principles by which we may interpret events we do not know have taken place. In respect to material processes, we wish to speculate on the nature of mixtures. If I have a substance of one sort and it is joined to a substance of another, how do the traits of the one combine with the traits of another? Then whence come interesting questions? The answer, of course, is, from the interstitial cases, in the case of human beings, the person bearing sexual traits of both genders, or the one bearing no discernible sexual traits; the person in the transition period, e.g., a boy nine years and one day old, or a girl between one status, as to maturity and marriage, and the next. In the case of beasts, it will be the one that falls between the two established categories, domesticated and wild. In the case of time, it will be dusk. In the case of the sabbatical year, it will be a crop that matures over two or three growing seasons and hence cannot be definitively assigned to any one year. The list of interstitial possibilities is endless. In all case, we find represented mixtures of things: something that falls into two or more classifications within a given system.

This generalized way of stating the traits of mixtures will not have surprised Alexander Aphrodisiensis who wrote:

> Certain mixtures...result in a total interpenetration of substances and their qualities, the original substances and qualities being preserved in this mixture; this he calls specifically *krasis* of the mixed components. It is characteristic of the mixed substances that they can again be sepa-

rated, which is only possible if the components preserve their properties in the mixture.... This interpenetration of the components he assumes to happen in that the substances mixed together interpenetrate each other such that there is not a particle among them that does not contain a share of all the rest. If this were not the case, the result would not be *krasis* but juxtaposition.[17]

Total interpenetration of course produces that complete mixture, a new one, with traits of its own, to which I referred just now. It involves interpenetration such that the new mixture bears traits of its own and requires classification in its own terms. Mixed substances that can be separated fall in the middle. If these can be separated, then, while mixed, they form a new mixture, but when not mixed, the components regain their original taxon. And what is merely juxtaposed is a third kind of mixture altogether, one in which we take account only of the unalloyed traits of the original components of the mixture.

Now how would we frame these same categories not in terms of natural philosophy, e.g., physics, but in terms of supernatural categories as these are taken over by the Mishnah's sages from Scripture? Through a path that we need not explore, our philosophers came to the conclusion that if something touches a source of uncleanness, it is unclean in the first remove; if something touches that, it is unclean in the second; and what touches that which is unclean in the second remove becomes unclean in the third, and so on down the line. Then what happens when we mix something unclean in the first remove with something unclean in the second? When we hold that a substance at the first remove and one at the second remove interpenetrate and are regarded as entirely unclean at the first remove, we say much the same thing as is said of wholly blended mixtures. If they can be separated, then we have a different problem: can they now be separated? And if they are separated, what is the result?

The same issues as we find in Stoic physics (and that, for the moment, is merely an example) inhere, in precisely the same terms, in discourse not in the abstract about mixtures but in the concrete about meat of the altar that has been affected by a thing that is affected by uncleanness at one or another remove from the initial source of uncleanness. The terms of analysis then are remarkably arcane. But the principles that are exposed through the analysis are simply the same as those that are exposed through the analysis of a

---

[17] S. Sambursky, *Physics of the Stoics*, p. 122.

mixture of fluids of different colors, which blend; of a mixture of pebbles of different colors, which are merely juxtaposed; of a mixture of green and white noodles, which blend but also can again be separated. To make this statement stick, I take up a single acutely detailed case. In this case the principles of mixtures set forth in Stoic physics prove to be the same as the principles of mixtures set forth—*mutatis mutandis!*—in the Mishnah's theory of cultic sanctification and uncleanness. That is true both in detail and in general.

We shall now see, specifically, that our authorities raise precisely that issue, in terms of removes of uncleanness to be sure. The matter of connection is of the same order of theoretical interest. Uncleanness affecting all parts of material after they have been connected affects them all when they are separated. But if something is made unclean, then connected to something else, that latter substance is unclean just as is the former. But when it is separated, it is unclean in a lower remove, only by virtue of its contact with that which was originally contaminated. So now we have a mosaic-like mixture, in which each element in the whole preserves its own individuality. The set of pericopes turn out to be remarkably relevant to the Stoic theory of mixture, stated by S. Sambursky in the following terms:

> As far as classification is concerned, the Stoic theory is much clearer. It distinguished between three types of mixture. One of them, mingling or mechanical mixture, is identical with what Aristotle defines by 'composition' (as in the case of the mixture of barley and wheat), and it applies essentially to bodies of a granular structure where a mosaic-like mixture results, each particle of one component being surrounded by particles of the other. The other extreme is fusion, which leads to the creation of a new substance whereby the individual properties of each of the components are lost.... Between these two types lies a third case of 'mixture' proper (*krasis* for liquids, *mixis* for non-liquids), which, from the Stoic point of view, represents the most important category of blending. Here a complete interpenetration of all the components takes place, and any volume of the mixture, down to the smallest parts, is jointly occupied by all the components in the same proportion, each component preserving its own properties under any circumstances, irrespective of the ratio of its share in the mixture. The properties are preserved in all cases where, as opposed to the case of fusion, the components can be separated out by putting a sponge into the mixture....[18]

Certainly an example of fusion is the contamination of liquids. Once unclean, they are unclean always at a single remove; the uncleanness

---

[18] *Ibid.*, pp. 14-15.

affects the whole equally and profoundly. An example of mingling is connection which takes place after uncleanness has affected one part of what is connected. And an example of the middle sort of mixing is the blending of solids unclean in various removes.

Since in expounding the philosophy, encompassing also the science, of everyday affairs the framers of the Mishnah do not talk in abstract terms about the physics of mixtures but only in practical language about material things, readers may well ask how I have made the move from mixtures to the Mishnah. Two entirely unrelated passages of the Mishnah will suffice, for the moment, the demonstrate that exactly the classification of mixtures described by Sambursky is in play in the Mishnah's work of detailed analysis of problems of cultic uncleanness. The first is at Mishnah-tractate Tohorot 1:5-9, where we see in detail that the Mishnah's theory of mixtures corresponds to Stoic philosophy's theory of mixtures as just now spelled out.   Mishnah-tractate Tohorot 1:5-9, introducing removes of uncleanness in relation to food, is formed of three autonomous units, M. 1:5-6, M. 1:7-8, and M. 1:9. M. 1:5-6 present a beautifully formed set of balanced rules, which make the point that when particles of food, unclean at different removes of uncleanness, join together they share in the uncleanness of the more lenient, or further removed, of the two removes of uncleanness. That is the case when either part by itself does not form a sufficient bulk of food to be susceptible to, or to convey, uncleanness on its own. but when we have sufficient bulk of food—an egg's volume—to be susceptible to, or to convey, uncleanness on its own, then of course a mixture of two such bulks is deemed to convey uncleanness at the remove of the more stringent of the two. If we then divide such a quantity, so that we are no longer certain whether, in either part, we have a volume of food sufficient to convey uncleanness at the more stringent remove, we invoke the opening rule. This matter is fully worked out.

M. 1:7-8 exhibit the same careful attention to form and balance of detail. Now we discuss, first, pieces of dough which are stuck together and then made unclean. In this case the whole conglomerate is unclean at the same remove. We deal, second, with pieces of dough, one of which is unclean, and the others of which are then attached to the unclean one. In this case, while joined together, the whole shares in the uncleanness of the original, unclean piece, but, when separated, the parts attached after the original piece became unclean do not. Then the pieces made unclean only through their contact with the originally unclean piece now are unclean at one remove less than the originally unclean piece. This is worked out, as in M. 1:5-6, in sequence, from the first, to the second, and finally to the third remove. M. 1:7 specifies sources of uncleanness at each remove, creeping thing, a Father of uncleanness, liquid, in the first remove, and hands, in the second remove. M. 1:8 speaks only of the ordinals of remove, without giving in detail the already specified sources of uncleanness. M. asks about heave-offering, so T. (T. 1:5) adds the matter of Holy Things.

M. 1:9 is a singleton, not so carefully formulated as the foregoing, but its rule is equally cogent. It present a paradox to stress the point that liquid made unclean even in the second or third removes (in the case of Holy Things), that is, by something unclean in the first, or second removes, in any event falls into uncleanness in the first remove. This rule is worked out with reference to loaves of Holy Things touching one another; these contain water, preserved in cleanness fitting for Holy Things, in hollows of the loaves. If any one of them is made unclean by a Father of uncleanness, all are unclean. Why? Because even the loaf third in sequence contaminates the liquid in a hollow on it, the liquid falls into the first remove and forthwith renders its loaf unclean in the second remove, and the loaf fourth in sequence, because of its contact with the third loaf (which is unclean in the second remove), is in the third remove of uncleanness, and affects its liquid in the same way, and so on to infinity. This is so because we count four removes for Holy Things, so what is unclean in the third affects the fourth and thus conveys uncleanness, also, to the liquid which is on it, which liquid then falls into the first remove. In the case of heave-offering by contrast, that is not the case. To be sure, if loaves of heave-offering, which touch one another, are affected by liquid between the loaves, then the same infinite sequence is reenacted. T. 1:7B states this same rule in still clearer language.

MISHNAH-TRACTATE TOHOROT 1:5-6

A.   The [solid] food which is made unclean by a Father of uncleanness and that which is made unclean by an Offspring of uncleanness join together with one another [to make up the prescribed volume] to convey the lighter degree [remove] of uncleanness of the two. How so?

B.   A half egg's bulk of food which is unclean in the first remove and a half egg's bulk of food which is unclean in the second remove which one mixed with one another − [the consequent mixture is unclean in the] second [remove of uncleanness].

C. A half egg's bulk of food unclean in the second remove of unclean-
    ness and a half egg's of food unclean in the third remove of un-
    cleanness which one mixed together with one another – [it is un-
    clean in the] third [remove of uncleanness].
D. [But] an egg's bulk of food unclean in the first remove of unclean-
    ness and an egg's bulk of food unclean in the second remove of
    uncleanness which one mixed together with one another – it is
    unclean in the first remove of uncleanness.
E. [If] one divided them up – this is unclean in the second remove of
    uncleanness, and this is unclean in the second remove of unclean-
    ness.
    F. This one fell by itself and this one by itself on (K: LTWK) a
    loaf of heave-offering – they have rendered it unfit [= in the third
    remove].
    G. [If] the two of them feel on it simultaneously [at the same time,
    not necessarily on the same spot] – they have made it unclean in
    the second remove of uncleanness.

                                                                    M. 1:5

A. An egg's bulk of food unclean in the second remove and [V, K lack
    W] an egg's bulk of food unclean in the third remove which one
    mixed with one another – it is unclean in the second remove.
B. [If] one divided them – this is unclean in the third remove, and this
    is unclean in the third remove.
C. [If] this one fell by itself and this by itself on (V, K: LTWK) a loaf
    of heave-offering – they have not made it unfit.
D. If the two of them fell simultaneously – they put it into the third
    remove [= render it unfit].
E. An egg's bulk of food unclean in the first remove and an egg's bulk
    of food unclean in the third remove which he mixed with one
    another – it is unclean in the first remove.
F. [If] one divided them – this one is unclean in the second remove,
    and this is unclean in the second remove.
G. For even that which is unclean in the third remove which touched
    something unclean in the first remove becomes unclean in the
    second remove.
H. Two egg's bulk of food unclean in the first remove, two egg's bulks
    of food unclean in the second remove which one mixed with one
    another – it is unclean in the first remove.
I. [If] one divided them – this is unclean in the first remove and this
    one is unclean in the first remove.
J. [If one divided them into] three or four parts – lo, these are un-
    clean in the second remove.
K. Two egg's bulks of food unclean in the second remove, two eggs
    bulks of food unclean in the third remove, which one mixed to-
    gether – it is unclean in the second remove.
L. [If] one divided them – this one is unclean in the second remove,
    and this one is unclean in the second remove.

M. [If one divided them into] three or four parts, lo, these [all] are in the third remove.

M. 1:6

This large and elegant unit is formulated in complete, declarative sentences, with only slight apocopation in the examples. We have four major subdivisions in all, (1) 1:5A-C, (2) 1:5D-G, 1:6A-D, (3) 1:6E-G, and (4) 1:6H-M. The first opens with a generalization, 1:5A, followed by two illustrations, B and C. The former illustration deals with the first and second remove, the latter, the second and third remove. The second subdivision requires but lacks an introductory generalization parallel to A1. The important shift is that we now have food itself of a bulk sufficient to contract and convey uncleanness. It is mixed with another such quantity. The matter of joining together, to which A alludes, is no longer relevant and the consequent rule shifts. No longer do we assign the status of the consequent mixture to the lighter degree of uncleanness of the two. Now we impose the more severe. D states that rule through its example. E, F, and G then deal with complications of the rule, to be explained below. M. 1:6A-D are in exactly the same model. The first set thus presents food in the first remove mixed with food in the second, and the second, food unclean in the second remove mixed with food unclean in the third.

The third division of the composite carries forward this same matter, quantities of food of requisite volume to convey uncleanness which have mixed together. But now the mixture is between food unclean in the first remove with food unclean in the third, thus completing the thought begun at M. 1:5D. What distinguishes the third division is the generalization at G and the absence of the issue of heave-offering after F, that in two parts, each falling by itself, then the two falling simultaneously. The final division again presents two carefully paired rules, *first/second* remove, *second/third* remove, each spelled out in the same way as the other. H-I go over familiar ground, and what is new is J and its parallel at M. In all, it would be difficult to point to a more carefully constructed set of rules. There can be no doubt that the unit, while sizeable, is unitary and harmonious, the work of a single hand. Let us now turn to the substance of the problem.

We first review the matter of removes, that is, sequences of contact with the primary source of uncleanness. A Father of uncleanness which touches something susceptible to uncleanness produces an

Offspring of uncleanness. These are in four removes from the Father.
That which touches the Father is unclean in the first remove. That
which touches that which has touched the Father is unclean in the
second remove. And so for the third and the fourth, which pertain
solely to heave-offering, for the third, and Holy Things, for the
fourth. Heave-offering which has touched something unclean in the
second remove is rendered unfit; and Holy Things which touch
something unclean in the third remove are rendered unfit, a matter
resumed at M. 2:4.

The problem before us is spelled out by Maimonides (*Uncleanness of
Foodstuffs* 4:12) as follows:

> An equal quantity is prescribed for all unclean foodstuffs, since no
> unclean foodstuff conveys uncleanness unless it is an egg's bulk in quan-
> tity; and their uncleanness is alike, since no unclean foodstuff conveys
> uncleanness except by contact; and it conveys uncleanness neither to
> persons nor to utensils; therefore they can be combined to convey the
> lesser uncleanness of the two of them. Thus, if there is a half egg's bulk
> of foodstuff suffering first-grade uncleanness and a half egg's bulk of
> foodstuff suffering second-grade uncleanness and they are combined,
> the whole suffers second-grade uncleanness; and if this touches heave-
> offering, it renders it invalid. If there is a half egg's bulk of foodstuff
> suffering second-grade uncleanness and a half egg's bulk suffering third-
> grade uncleanness and they are combined, the whole suffers third-grade
> uncleanness. And the same applies in every like case. Even if there is a
> half egg's bulk of foodstuff suffering first-grade uncleanness and a half
> egg's bulk suffering fourth-grade uncleanness, as a Hallowed Thing,
> and they are combined, the whole suffers only fourth-grade unclean-
> ness.

With this in mind, the explanation of the first set, A-C is simple.
Since in our combination a half of the requisite quantity is unclean in
the first remove, and a half in the second, the whole mixture is
unclean in the second remove, and so with a mixture of second and
third.

When we come to D, however, our situation changes. Now we
have a sufficient bulk to make up a contaminating quantity of food.
That is, a whole egg's bulk is unclean in the first remove, and a whole
in the second. Do we rule that they convey uncleanness in accord
with the lesser or lighter degree? No, now we say the whole conveys
uncleanness in accord with the more stringent remove, the first.
Why? Because in fact we have in the whole mixture a sufficient
quantity to convey uncleanness in the first remove. There is no reason to impose only the lesser degree of remove of uncleanness. On

the other hand, E says, if we take the mixture and divide it up, the rule of A does apply. We do not know that within either half is a sufficient quantity of unclean food in the first remove to convey uncleanness in that remove. So we rule that the two parts of the mixture, once divided, convey uncleanness in the lighter degree of uncleanness. It follows, F, that if one of the two parts fell on a loaf of heave-offering, since the part is in the second remove of uncleanness, the heave-offering is rendered unfit, that is, it is placed in the third remove. But, G points out, if the two parts simultaneously fall on heave-offering, then we invoke D, and the heave-offering, subject as it is to be food unclean in the first remove, then falls into the second. There is nothing difficult in this rule, which is simply repeated at M. 1:6A-D. Accordingly, M. 1:5C-G and 1:6A-D spell out the implications of M. 1:5A and the unstated generalization serving M. 1:5D.

This brings us to M. 1:6E-G. The important problem is at F. We have a mixture of food unclean in the first and third removes, each sufficient to convey uncleanness. E tells us what we know, which is that the whole is unclean at the first remove. But F, explains how to deal with the division. Both parts are unclean in the second remove. Why? Because what was unclean in the third remove has touched something unclean in the first remove. So we simply invoke the rule of M. 1:5A, the whole, composed of two insufficient parts, is unclean in the lighter of the two removes, the second. This is a logical extension of the opening group. The expected reference to heave-offering is absent. Why? Because it is obvious that if either of the two parts, unclean in the second remove, falls on heave-offering, it is rendered unfit, just as we have already stated at M. 1:5F, and if the two fell on it simultaneously, they make it unclean in the second remove, as M. 1:5G has said, and for the same reason.

H-J and K-M form the concluding set. Now we have two egg's bulks of food unclean in the first remove, two in the second. The reason for the specification of two egg's bulks is in J/M. The point of I and L is the same as given earlier. Since the four egg's bulks, when divided into two, still contain at least one egg's bulk unclean in the first remove, both of the divided parts, each with two egg's bulks, are unclean in the first remove. But, J asks, what if we divide the four egg's bulks into three or four parts? Then we again invoke the rule of M. 1:5A, ignoring what is spelled out at 1:6G. That is, we take account of the fact that the lesser of the two degrees is second, for J. And for M we do the same. M. 1:5A has emphasized that its rule

applies when we have insufficient volume, so that either part by itself
cannot convey uncleanness. While dividing the four eggs into four
parts, we still have a sufficient volume to convey uncleanness, each of
the three or four egg's bulks contains less than a *whole* egg's bulk of
food unclean in the second remove, for K-M (or first, for H-J).
Therefore we hold that the divided part is unclean in the lower, or
more lenient, of the two removes. Accordingly, the point that is
illustrated is not M. 1:5A, but M. 1:5D-E.

MISHNAH-TRACTATE TOHOROT 1:7-8

A. Pieces of dough [of heave-offering] stuck together,
B. and loaves stuck together –
C. [if] one of them is made unclean by a dead creeping thing [a
Father of uncleanness],
D. they all are unclean in the first remove [as if all had touched the
insect, since they are deemed connected to one another].
E. [If] they were separated [from one another], they are all unclean in
the first remove, [since they originally were connected when con-
taminated, so they are all affected equally by the creeping thing].
F. [If they were made unclean by] liquid [which is always unclean in
the first remove], they all are unclean in the second remove.
G. [If] they separated [from one another], they all are unclean in the
second remove.
H. [If they were made unclean by] hands [in the second remove], they
all are unclean in the third remove.
I. [If] they separated [from one another], they all are unclean in the
third remove.

M. 1:7

A. A piece of dough [of heave-offering], which was unclean in the first
remove, and one stuck others to it, – they all are unclean in the
first remove.
B. [If] they separated, it is unclean in the first remove, but all [the
rest] are unclean in the second remove.
C. [If] it was unclean in the second remove and one stuck others to it,
they all are unclean in the second remove.
D. [If] they separated, it is unclean in the second remove, but all [the
rest] are unclean in the third remove.
E. [If] it was unclean in the third remove, and one stuck others to it,
it is unclean in the third remove, but all [the rest] are clean,
F. whether they separated or whether they did not separate.

M. 1:8

The point of M. 1:8F is that the third remove does not cause a
fourth in the case of heave-offering, and this gloss is what necessitates
our interpreting the whole as a matter of heave-offering. The perfection of the formal articulation (except for the minor interpolation at

M. 1:7B) requires little comment. Each clause is modeled in the form of the foregoing, and the whole is exquisitely balanced in form just as it is in substance. M. 1:8 clearly is harmonious with M. 1:7. The latter speaks in general terms—first remove, second, third—while the former specifies the source of uncleanness. Accordingly, the operative difference between M. 1:7 and M. 1:8 is simply the contrast between *stuck together* (NWSKWT) *vs. one stuck others* (HSYK) *to it*. The point of the difference expressed at M. 1:8 is that the original piece remains in the uncleanness to which it was originally subject, but the others, once removed, are unclean only by virtue of their (past) contact with it. In M. 1:7, by contrast, the pieces when made unclean are a unified mass. If made unclean by a Father of uncleanness, they are all in the first remove of uncleanness and remain so.

It remains to observe that the real issue before us is the nature of connection. The principle is that what is connected at the point of contamination shares in the contamination of the whole so long as it is part of the whole, but, once it is separated, it remains unclean only by virtue of its former condition.

MISHNAH-TRACTATE TOHOROT 1:9

A. Loaves of Holy Things [touching one another], *in* the hollows of which is water preserved in cleanness fitting for Holy Things –
B. [if] one of them was made unclean by a creeping thing, they all are unclean. {Since even the loaf third in sequence contaminates the liquid in a hollow on it, the liquid is in the first remove and goes and renders the loaf unclean in the second remove. The loaf fourth in sequence is therefore in the third remove of uncleanness, affects *its* liquid, and so on. Thus all, however many in sequence, are made unclean].
C. In the case of heave-offering, it [the creeping thing] renders unclean at two removes and renders unfit [but not unclean] at one [third remove]. [And liquid *on* the third is not unclean, so is not in the first remove, and the fourth loaf in sequence is unaffected.]
D. If there is *between* them dripping liquid, even in the case of heave-offering, the whole is unclean. [The liquid is made unclean and all loaves are in the second remove.]

M. 1:9 (y. Hag. 3:2)

The case is parallel to the foregoing. Now we have loaves of Holy Things. In the hollows of the loaves is water which is preserved in cleanness fitting for Holy Things ("sanctified water"). We take for granted we have many loaves touching one another. If a creeping thing, a Father of uncleanness, touches one of the loaves, all are made unclean. Why is this so? I cannot improve on Slotki's explanation of the matter:[19]

> Since the first loaf that was touched by the creeping thing contracted a first grade of uncleanness; the second loaf contracted from the first one a second grade of uncleanness; the third loaf contracts from the second a third grade of uncleanness, and, since in the case of holy things a third grade may cause a fourth grade of uncleanness, it also imparts uncleanness to the water on it which (in accordance with the uncleanness of liquids) becomes unclean in the first grade and causes the [next] loaf to contract second grade of uncleanness and so impart to the next loaf third grade of uncleanness. The next loaf, for the same reason, imparts second grade of uncleanness to the one next to it, and so on *ad infinitum*.

In other words, the water on a loaf raises the degree of uncleanness affecting that loaf, once the water is made unclean, and so each loaf in succession affects the next.

Heave-offering, however, is subject to a different rule. The dead creeping thing makes the first loaf unclean in the first remove, and the loaf unclean in the first remove makes the next loaf unclean in the second, and the one unclean in the second remove makes the third loaf unfit as heave-offering. Here Slotki explains:

> Since in heave-offering a third cannot make a fourth it becomes only invalid but not unclean. As the loaf in the third grade cannot convey uncleanness, the water on it remains clean, so that neither it nor the water can convey uncleanness to the next loaf that touched it, which (like the next loaf that touched it and the one that touched the next, and so on) consequently remains clean.[20]

If we have dripping water *between* the loaves of heave-offering (D), however, all become unclean, Again Slotki:

> The liquid between the first loaf and second becomes, in accordance with the law of unclean liquids, unclean in the first grade and consequently conveys uncleanness of the second grade to the second loaf that touched it. Similarly the water between the second and the third loaves becomes unclean in the first grade and causes the third loaf to be unclean in the second grade, and so on *ad infinitum*.

In other words, the difference between the first case, A-B, and the second, C, is negligible, since the presence of liquid *on* heave-offering, D, imposes on heave-offering exactly the same rule as we had for A-B. However, if we had dry loaves at A, then B would read, *renders*

---

[19] J. Slotki, trans., *The Babylonian Talmud. Seder Tohorot* (London, 1948) p. 367, n.4.
[20] p. 367, no. 7.

unclean at three removes and unfit at one (the fourth), or some such language. Accordingly, A-B and C by no means contrast to one another. If C had matched A, *loaves of heave-offering between which is water preserved in cleanness fitting for heave-offering* (or, all the more so, for Holy Things), then we should have the same rule as in B – *they all are unclean.* And the point of the rule would have been exactly as at B, which is, liquid made unclean in the second remove is unclean in the first remove and conveys uncleanness accordingly, without limit. This is, therefore, an exceedingly complex way of expressing the simple rule governing contamination of liquid: whatever remove of uncleanness affects water, water, once made unclean, is always unclean in the first remove.

At this point I can offer no more persuasive argument than simply to restate what Stoic physics has already said. In my view, we have in hand nothing less, and nothing more, than a statement, in a strange idiom, of precisely the same theory of mixtures as the following:

> Certain mixtures...result in a total interpenetration of substances and their qualities, the original substances and qualities being preserved in this mixture; this he calls specifically *krasis* of the mixed components. It is characteristic of the mixed substances that they can again be separated, which is only possible if the components preserve their properties in the mixture.... This interpenetration of the components he assumes to happen in that the substances mixed together interpenetrate each other such that there is not a particle among them that does not contain a share of all the rest. If this were not the case, the result would not be *krasis* but juxtaposition.

Now readers may judge for themselves whether the issues set forth in the Stoic theory of mixtures and those analyzed by the Mishnah's theory of mixtures are as I claim: the same principles, expressed in different terms. What distinguishes the philosophers of Judaism from the Stoic philosophers is the medium of expression of the former, which is to set forth the results of reason through application to cases, the consequences of logic in practical ways. But as to the principles of logic and the self-evident results of reason, these form a single corpus of thought.

III. *The Mishnah's Principles of Classification*

I see three basic principles that the system repeatedly invokes. The first is to identify the correct definition or character of something and to preserve that essence. So we begin with the thing itself. Our premise is that we can identify the intrinsic or true or inherent traits of a thing, once more, the thing seen by itself. But, having our answer, we then ask in what way something is like something else, and in what way it differs. Our premise is that in some ways things are like other things, traits may be shared. So we proceed to the comparison of things. That requires us to identify the important traits that impart the definitive character or classification to a variety of distinct things. So we proceed to a labor of comparison and contrast. The third principle is that like things fall into a single classification, with its rule, and unlike things into a different classification, with the opposite rule. That conception, simple on the surface, defines the prevailing logic throughout the entire philosophy. At no point do we find any other logic in play.

The system of ordering all things in proper place and under the proper rule maintained that like belongs with the like and conforms to the rule governing the like, the unlike goes over to the opposite and conforms to the opposite rule. When we make lists of the like, we also know the rule governing all the items on those lists, respectively. We know that and one other thing, namely, the opposite rule, governing all items sufficiently like to belong on those lists, but sufficiently unlike to be placed on other lists. That rigorously philosophical logic of analysis, comparison and contrast, served because—so it would seem—in that context it was the only logic deemed able to sustain a system that proposed to make the statement concerning the social order.

Natural philosophy, out of which natural science has evolved, dictates the labor of classification in accord with a simple procedure. Faced with a mass of facts, we are able [1] to bring order—that is to say, to determine the nature of things—by finding out which items resemble others and, [2] determining the taxic indicator that forms of the lot a single classification, and then [3] determining the single rule to which all cases conform. That method of bringing structure and order out of the chaos of indeterminate facts pertains, on the very surface, to persons, places, things; to actions and attitudes; to the natural world of animals, minerals, vegetables, the social world of castes and peoples, actions and functions, and the supernatural world of the holy and the unclean, the possession of Heaven and the possession of earth, the sanctified and the common. A necessary principle of classification is that things are always what they are, never anything else. It comes second in logical order because, once we maintain that taxic indicators are inherent and intrinsic, only then the complementary principle emerges. One way of expressing that conception of the *Ding an Sich* is the notion of intrinsic classification. Something bears intrinsic and inherent traits, which are not relative to the traits of other things and furthermore are not imputed by function or extrinsic considerations of any other kind.

How then do we actually conduct a classification of diverse facts in accord with intrinsic indicative traits? Let us consider a simple case of how those principles operate and what they accomplish. Every tractate of the Mishnah can supply us with examples of hierarchical classification based on intrinsic taxic indicators; the one I have chosen derives from Mishnah-tractate Bikkurim, which deals with firstfruits and their presentation in the temple in Jerusalem. The problem addressed, the solution proposed, the medium of logic by which the one is identified and the other accorded the status of self-evident truth—these emerge in the case that follows.

The facts are not complicated. Mishnah-tractate Bikkurim deals with the disposition of firstfruits, in line with Dt. 26:1-11. There are two principal issues. First, there is the concern for bringing firstfruits, second, for making the required declaration specified in Scripture. So the facts are entirely scriptural. But a considerable program concerning classification and connection comes into play. The concern of M. Bikkurim 1:1-2 is to set up a taxonomic grid to cover three possibilities as specified, [1] do not bring first fruits at all, [2] bring but do not recite, [3] bring and recite. The criterion is ownership of the land on which the firstfruits have grown. Status and circumstance are held together. The farmer must own the land, and those who do not bring firstfruits do not own the land. If someone owns the land but is not entitled to inherit a portion of the land, if someone buys trees without buying the ground on which they grow, and the like, they do not recite. All of these amplifications of the base-verse of Scripture in fact hold together diverse indicators in a single well-crafted taxic construction—therefore also proposition. I give only excerpts of the complete discussion.

MISHNAH-TRACTATE BIKKURIM 1:1-2, 4, 10-11

1:1   A.   There are [those who] bring [the] firstfruits [of the produce of their land] and recite [the confession, "I declare this day . . ." (Dt. 26:3-10)].

B.   those who bring [firstfruits] but do not recite,

C. and there are [those] who do not bring [firstfruits at all].

D. These are the [people] who do not bring [firstfruits]:

E. (1) he who plants [a tree] on his own [property] and bends [a branch of the tree and sinks it into the ground so that it grows on private [property] or on public [property, as an independent plant];

F. (2) [as well as] he who bends [a branch of a tree which is growing] on private [property] or on public [property, and sinks the branch into the ground so that it grows] on his own [property];

G. (3) he who plants [a tree] on his own [property] and bends [a branch of the tree and sinks it in the ground so that it still grows) on his own [property], but a private road or a public road [runs] in between [the tree and its offshoot],

H. lo, this one does not bring [firstfruits from the offshoot]—

I. R. Judah says: "Such a one does bring [them] ."

1:2 A. For what reason does he not bring [them]?

B. Because it is written, "[You shall bring] the first of the firstfruits of your land" (Dt. 26:2).

C. [You may not bring firstfruits] unless all of their growth [takes place] on your land.

D. (1) Sharecroppers, (2) tenant farmers, (3) a holder of confiscated property, and (4) a robber

E. do not bring firstfruits,

F. for the same reason:

G. because it is written, "the first of the firstfruits of your land."

1:4 A. These [people] bring [firstfruits] but do not recite:

B. a proselyte brings but does not recite,

C. because he is not able to say, "[I have come into the land] which the Lord swore to our fathers to give us," (Dt. 26:3).

D. But if his mother was an Israelite, he brings and recites.

E. And when he [the proselyte] prays in private, he says, "God of the fathers of Israel."

F. And when he prays in the synagogue, he says, "God of your fathers."

G. [But] if his mother was an Israelite, he says, "God of our fathers."

1:10 A. And these [people] bring [firstfruits] and recite:

B. [Those who bring firstfruits] (1) from Pentecost until the Festival [of Sukkot], (2) from the seven kinds [of produce native to the Land of Israel], (3) from fruit of the hill country, (4) from dates of the valley, [and] (5) from olives [used] for oil [that grow] in Transjordan.

C. R. Yosé the Galilean says, "They do not bring firstfruits from [produce grown in] Transjordan, for [Transjordan] is not a land flowing with milk and honey [Dt. 26:15]."

1:11 A. He who buys three trees [that are growing] on [the property] of his fellow brings [firstfruits from those trees] and recites.

B. R. Meir says, "Even if [he buys only] two [trees, he brings and recites]."

C. [If] he bought a tree and the ground [on which it grows], he brings and recites.

D. R. Judah says, "Even sharecroppers and tenant farmers, [who do not own the land on which their produce grows], bring [firstfruits] and recite."

The composition does more than assemble a mass of information in a simple arrangement, though that is our first impression of what is at hand. In fact, the authorship has generated a problem—how different classes of persons fall under a single rule, that is to say, the relationship of species to genus. The information that is adduced rests upon premises that each class of persons has its indicative traits, which afford the possibility of comparison and contrast with other classes of persons subject to the rule at hand. In this way the law concerning firstfruits, which Scripture has supplied, forms the foundation for the organization of a taxonomic grid. The concern of M. Bik. 1:1-2 then is to set up a taxonomic grid to cover four possibilities as specified, do not bring first fruits at all, bring but do not recite, bring and recite. M. Bik. 1:10-11 complete the program.

I may now generalize on the foregoing to answer the question, precisely what are the principles of classification? To state the obvious: the answer is, first identify the pertinent taxic indicators, then apply those indicators to the relevant data, seeking out interstitial cases in which two or more contradictory indicators are present. In such cases they determine either which of the indicators takes priority or how a case in the excluded middle is to be disposed of. Here in a very simple case we see that the taxic indicators derive from the facts of the case, which Scripture (in the reading of the philosophers) has defined. The criterion is ownership of the land on which the firstfruits have grown. Status and circumstance are held together. The farmer must own the land, and those who do not bring firstfruits do not own the land. If someone owns the land but is not entitled to inherit a portion of the land, if someone buys trees without buying the ground on which they grow, and the like, they do not recite. On that basis the diverse cases are formed into a few simple classes, and the rule governing each is firmly set.

Since the traits of a thing, which are intrinsic, indicate the classification to which the thing belongs, we must ask, are these traits always concrete? Can we now show that traits also may refer to an abstract, intangible aspect of the thing? Mishnah-tractate Besah sets forth the now-familiar conception that something has an intrinsic character, and our task is to identify, or define, that character. We do so when we can identify the correct taxic indicators, which dictate the classification to which the thing is to be assigned. What is fresh is the abstract nature of the taxic indicator. It concerns what is actual as against what is potential. Do I take account of the traits of a thing as they presently are or as they will inevitably evolve? That conception, clearly an advance over the simple notion that things bear intrinsic traits, is set forth in a debate on the classification of the egg that is in a chicken. Is it part of the chicken, hence within its classification? Or is it distinct from the chicken, hence within a classification of its own?

MISHNAH-TRACTATE BESAH 1:1

A. An egg which is born on the festival-day –
B. the House of Shammai say, "It may be eaten [on that day]."
C. And the House of Hillel say, "It may not be eaten."
D. The House of Shammai say, "[A minimum of] leaven in the volume of an olive's bulk, and [a minimum of] what is leavened in the volume of a date's bulk [are prohibited on Passover (Ex. 13:7)]."
E. And the House of Hillel say, "This and that are [prohibited in the volume of] an olive's bulk."

Now what is the inside issue at hand? In classifying the egg, we identify the principal taxic indicator: is it distinct from the chicken or part of it? And the variable derives from our assessment of the relationship between the potential and the actual. At stake in the matter of the chicken, M. Bes. 1:1, is whether we regard what is going to happen as though it already has happened, or whether we interpret a potentiality as tantamount to an actuality. The House of Shammai take the latter position, the House of Hillel, the former.

What is at stake of course will be concrete, even while the conceptions are highly abstract. But that is characteristic of the discourse of the philosophy, as distinct from its issues, methods, results, and general principles and propositions. For this philosophy of classification works out its conceptions through practical reason and applied logic. The problem is simple. It is permitted on the festival-day to slaughter a chicken and to prepare it for eating on that same day. What is the law having to do with an egg born on the festival-day? The House of Shammai classify the egg under the rule governing the dam. The dam is deemed ready, so is the egg. The House of Hillel regard the egg as distinct from the dam. When it is born, it follows its own rule. The egg was not available prior to the festival, so, it is not permitted

on the festival itself. There was no prior act of designation or preparation of the egg for use on the holy day. These secondary concerns
do not obscure the primary philosophical method at hand, but they
show us how, in a case of applied logic, we sort out our issues.

To show how applied reason and practical logic accomplish the
abstract goals of the system, finally, we address the issue of saying
blessings for the benefits of this world. The reason is that here was see
the full power of the principles of classification on which the philosophy rests. As to the facts, when someone derives a benefit from this
world, eating a given species of produce, for instance, then that person is supposed to acknowledge the benefit by saying a blessing.
There is no limit to the kinds of produce. But this philosophy wishes
to show how many things are really one thing, and, in this case, it
does so by demonstrating that, among all the varieties of nourishing
food, only a few blessings pertain. Then the labor of intellect is to
classify within a given genus the species that fall therein; the upshot is
that a given formulation of the blessing will apply to all the species of
produce within a common genus. As a matter of fact, the whole of
Mishnah-tractate Berakhot forms an essay on the principles of classification as these apply to, and are illustrated by, issues of liturgy. The
working of speciation in matters involving everyday liturgy is shown
in the following:

MISHNAH-TRACTATE BERAKHOT 6:1-5

6:1 A. What blessing does one recite over produce?
   B . Over fruit of a tree he says, "[Blessed are you, 0 Lord, our
       God, King of the Universe] Creator of the fruit of the tree,"
   C. except for wine.
   D. For over wine he says, "Creator of the fruit of the vine."
   E. And over produce of the earth [vegetables] he says, "Creator
      of fruit of the ground,"
   F. except for loaves [of bread].
   G. For over the loaf he says, "Who brings forth bread from the
      earth,"
   H. And over greens he says, "Creator of the fruit of the ground."
   I. R. Judah says, "Creator of kinds of herbs."
6:2 A. If one recited over fruit of trees the blessing "Creator of the
       fruit of the ground'" he has [anyway] fulfilled his obligation.
   B. But [if one said] over produce of the ground, "Creator of the
      fruit of the tree," he did not fulfill his obligation.
   C. [As regards] any [kinds of produce] if one says, "[Blessed are
      you, Lord, our God, King of the Universe] for all was created
      according to his word," he fulfilled his obligation.

6:3 A. Over something which does not grow from the earth one says, "For all [was created according to his word]."

B. Over vinegar, unripe fruit, and edible locusts one says "For all [was created at his word] ."

C. Over milk, cheese, and eggs one says, "For all...."

D. R. Judah says, "Over anything which is a curse, one does not recite a blessing."

6:4 A. If one had before him many different types [of food]—

B. R. Judah says, "If there are among them [foodstuffs] of the seven types [of foods of the Land of Israel], he recites a blessing over that [particular foodstuff]."

C. But sages say, "[He recites a blessing] over whichever type he desires."

6:5 A. If one recited a blessing over the wine before the meal, he exempted the wine after the meal [he need not bless again].

B. If one recited a blessing over the appetizer before the meal, he exempted the appetizer after the meal.

C. If one recited a blessing over the loaf [of bread], he exempted the appetizer.

D. [If one recited a blessing] over the appetizer, he did not exempt the loaf.

E. The House of Shammai say, "[A blessing over the appetizer exempts] not even that [cooked food] made in a pot."

The protracted account at M. Berakhot 6:1-5 goes over the classification of foods. A blessing appropriate to each classification is prescribed, which means that we have to determine the correct category of various types of edibles. The taxonomy involves produce of trees and of the ground, fruit and vegetables, respectively. Bread and wine are treated as unique. Other foods, milk, cheese, eggs, fall into a third, more general category. So the principal categories are fruit and vegetables, distinguished by the locus of their cultivation, and then each yields a distinctive item of its own. The practical reason makes the theoretical point in yet another way, as the system endlessly returns to the same problem and solves it in the same way: many varieties form only a few species, and these of course comprise the common genus: subject to the recitation of a blessing.

By way of conclusion, let me repeat what is abundantly obvious. We have uncovered these basic principles of classification:

[1] All things bear intrinsic traits, inherent and definitive qualities,

[2] But all things stand in relationship to all other things, with the result that nothing is *sui generis*.

[3] It follows that the work of definition, which is to say, identifying the thing-ness of a thing, its true value for economic purposes, its

right place in the order of nature and supernature for metaphysical ones, requires the comparison and contrast of one thing with other things.

[4] This we accomplish by finding how things are alike one another, so establishing a genus that encompasses more than a single thing, and how they contrast with one another, so defining the species of a common genus. But at this point we note how the work of identifying a genus and accomplishing the speciation of a genus is done.

[5] That is by analyzing the traits of things and identifying those traits that are principal and so definitive, those that are subsidiary and not definitive.

[6] Then, among these traits, taxic indicators serve to define the classification into which things are assigned. What is at stake in this work? It is a nomothetic process, in which we uncover among the chaos of things the order stated by the rules that things conform to or reveal. And process then produces both the besought result in any given case and also the philosophy's ultimate proposition, which is that things are orderly, conform to rules, make sense, exhibit a rationality that we can uncover. The process rests on these further propositions, upon all of which our initial foray has touched.

[7] Things that bear like taxic indicators fall into the same classifications and come under the same rule; things that bear unlike taxic indicators fall into the contrary classifications and come under the opposite rule.

[8] Taxic indicators appeal to abstractions, not only to concrete matters, and very commonly derive from fixed relationships, rather than from intrinsic and palpable traits of things.

But these eight principles only introduce the philosophical system and its positions on the nature of things. They do not show us how the system works. And even though in rough and suggestive form they furthermore introduce the main propositions and show that the philosophy does comprise propositions, not merely methods but results of reflection. Our task is now to spell out in appropriate detail and with considerable care how, in exact texts and precise terms, the philosophy in method conducts its intellectual enterprise and so not only states but in proposition makes its points.

IV. *Polythetic and Hierarchical Classification*

The principles of classification require two important refinements, each in response to a considerable problem. The first problem is that species do not always correspond in every way, so appeal for taxonomic purposes to all shared taxic indicators is not feasible. Some supply the wrong signals. The second is that merely classifying things yields no interesting results, no principles susceptible of extension and generalization. The Mishnah's system of classification, within its larger theory of *Listenwissenschaft*, encompasses solutions to these two problems, the first through polythetic, the second through hierarchical, classification. And together, these two principles inform the whole and lead to the principal conclusions that the document, and the system it attests, wish to put forth. The modes of thought, as much as the medium of discourse, in every line express the systemic message.

To understand the former, we have to recall how the work of classification is carried on. Specifically, when things match, so that their indicative traits make possible that required comparison and contrast that permits us to reach conclusions about the like and the unlike, then a simple process of classification gets under way. We can compare one or three or six traits of one thing with corresponding types of traits of some other. If the six in both cases are the same, we classify both things under a single rule. If not, then one thing follows one rule, the other the opposite. But, of course, not much in the here and the now to which practical logic and applied reason apply conforms to such a neat pattern. When we compare species of what we think, as a matter of hypothesis, form a common genus, we find that things are alike in some ways, unlike in others. Then do we have a common genus at all? And how are we to compare what is not precisely comparable with anything else? These two problems find solution in the conception of polythetic classification, the first of two fundamental complications of the basic principles of classification we have identified.

Why does a system of classification find it necessary to accommodate polythetic comparison? The reason is in the nature of things. We can easily demonstrate, things have so many and such diverse and contradictory indicative traits that, comparing one thing to something else, we can always distinguish one species from another. Even though we find something in common, we also can discern some other trait characteristic of one thing but not the other. If on the basis of one set of traits which yield a given classification, we place into order two or more items, on the basis of a different set of traits, we have a different classification altogether. But the formation of classifications based on monothetic taxonomy, that is to say, traits that are not only common to both items but that are shared throughout both items subject to comparison and contrast, simply will not serve. For at every point at which someone alleges uniform, that is to say, monothetic likeness, one can and will demonstrate difference. Then how to proceed? Appeal to some shared traits as a basis for classification: this is not like that, and that is not like this, but the indicative trait that both exhibit is such and so, that is to say, polythetic taxonomy.

The self-evident problem in accepting differences among things and insisting, nonetheless, on their monomorphic character for purposes of comparison and contrast, cannot be set aside: who says? That is, if I can adduce in evidence for a shared classification of things only a few traits among many characteristic of each thing, then what stops me from treating all the things alike? Polythetic taxonomy opens the way to an unlimited exercise in finding what diverse things have in common and imposing, for that reason, one rule on everything. Then the very working of *Listenwissenschaft* as a tool of analysis, differentiation, comparison, contrast, and the descriptive determination of rules yields the opposite of what is desired. Chaos, not order, a mass of exceptions, no rules, a world of examples, each subject to its own regulation, instead of a world of order and proportion, composition and stability, will result. That is the power of the present matter.

Polythetic classification therefore identifies among different species of a hypothetically-common genus some comparable traits, even while admitting the presence of other traits that are not comparable. We then compare like to like, in full knowledge that the whole of the one does not conform to the model of the whole of the other to permit that decision—wholly like, therefore one rule, wholly unlike, therefore the opposite rule—that the system finds the deepest and most satisfying logic of all. The method of polythetic classification rests upon the premise that things may intersect partially, and that that partial intersection suffices for analysis of the like and the unlike. It suffices because it yields, at points of commonality, the same law for different things. And the philosophy as a whole aims throughout at the discovery of regularities and modalities of order, an order that is exhibited by the way things are.

Mishnah-tractate Baba Qamma 1:1-3 form a stunning exercise in polythetic classification, indeed shows precisely what is the discipline of such a taxonomical principle. Specifically, we recognize that there is a variety of indicative traits that characterize a given set of classes of objects or actions. If, then, we wish to form a single taxon to encompass them all, we may not be able to identify indicative traits that equally characterize all the items. So we find some few traits that are present throughout, and on the basis of these, we uncover the law common to all the items, hence not monothetic but polythetic classification. Before proceeding, let us examine the text itself.

Mishnah-tractate Baba Qamma 1:1-3

1:1 A. [There are] four generative causes of damages: (1) ox [Ex. 21:35-36], (2) pit [Ex. 21:33], (3) crop-destroying beast [Ex. 22:4], and (4) conflagration [Ex. 22:5].

B. [The definitive characteristic] of the ox is not equivalent to that of the crop-destroying beast;

C. nor is that of the crop-destroying beast equivalent to that of the ox;

D. nor are this one and that one, which are animate, equivalent to fire, which is not animate;

E. nor are this one and that one, which usually [get up and] go and do damage, equivalent to a pit, which does not usually [get up and] go and do damage.

F. What they have in common is that they customarily do damage and taking care of them is your responsibility.

G. And when one [of them] has caused damage, the [owner] of that which causes the damage is liable to pay compensation for damage out of the best of his land [Ex. 22:4].

1:2 A. In the case of anything of which I am liable to take care, I am deemed to render possible whatever damage it may do.

B. [If] I am deemed to have rendered possible part of the damage it may do,

C. I am liable for compensation as if [I have] made possible all of the damage it may do.

D. (1) Property which is not subject to the law of Sacrilege, (2) property belonging to members of the covenant [Israelites], (3) property that is held in ownership,

E. and that is located in any place other than in the domain which is in the ownership of the one who has caused the damage,

F. or in the domain which is shared by the one who suffers injury and the one who causes injury—

> G. when one has caused damage [under any of the afore-listed circumstances],
>
> H. [the owner of] that one which has caused the damage is liable to pay compensation for damage out of the best of his land [= M.1:16].
>
> 1:3 A. Assessment [of the compensation for an injury to be paid] is in terms of ready cash [but is paid in kind—that is,] in what is worth money,
>
> B. before a court,
>
> C. on the basis of evidence given by witnesses who are freemen and members of the covenant.
>
> D. Women fall into the category of [parties to suits concerning] damages.
>
> E. And the one who suffers damages and the one who causes damages [may share] in the compensation.

I need hardly make explicit the way in which the passage exhibits the traits of polythetic classification, since the matter is made explicit, the result being self-evident. Things are not alike, but they have traits in common, and the common traits then draw within a single rule diverse things (here: actions).

Let us proceed to the continuation of the foregoing, which shows us how the framers of a sizable portion of a tractate have taught the rules of polythetic classification through a sequence of topically related cases. The work of organization and exposition of the materials indeed is classificatory, in the sense that a vast amount of information is set forth in a simple and clear pattern. The grid of the distinction between half and full damages, on the horizontal plane, and the distinctions among leg, tooth, and the like, on the vertical accounts for the whole, a fine piece of taxonomic thought in that the classification of one set of variables within the limits of a second and intersecting set of variables is what is accomplished.

MISHNAH-TRACTATE BABA QAMMA 1:4

> 1:4 A. [There are] five [deemed] harmless, and five [deemed] attested dangers.
>
> B. A domesticated beast is not regarded as an attested danger in regard to butting, (2) pushing, (3) biting, (4) lying down, or (5) kicking.
>
> C. (1) A tooth is deemed an attested danger in regard to eating what is suitable for [eating].
>
> D. (2) The leg is deemed an attested danger in regard to breaking something as it walks along.
>
> E. (3) And an ox which is an attested danger [so far as goring is concerned];

E. (4) and an ox which causes damage in the domain of the one who is injured;

G. and (5) man.

H. (1) A wolf, (2) lion, (3) bear, (4) leopard, (5) panther, and (6) a serpent—lo, these are attested dangers.

1. R. Eliezer says, "When they are trained, they are not attested dangers.

J. "But the serpent is always an attested danger"

K. What is the difference between what is deemed harmless and an attested danger?

L. But if that which is deemed harmless [causes damage], [the owner] pays half of the value of the damage which has been caused,

M. [with liability limited to the value of the] carcass [of the beast which has caused the damage].

N. But [if that which is] an attested danger [causes damage], [the owner] pays the whole of the value of the damage which has been caused from the best property [he may own, and his liability is by no means limited to the value of the animal which has done the damage].

M. Baba Qamma 1:4, expanded and explained at M. 2:1, 2-4, 2:5, 6, classifies and organizes the diverse causes of damages within the grid defined by Scripture that injury done by what has been deemed harmless and causes damages is compensated at only half of the damages done, while injury done by an attested danger is compensated at the full estimate of the damages done. So much for polythetic classification, the less important of the two complicating principles of method.

Hierarchical classification embodies the purpose of the philosophy as a whole: not only to classify diverse things, which yields mere information. It is to establish a hierarchy of classes. That serves to make the point that things are not only orderly, but stand in hierarchical sequence to one another, everything in a single frame of order. This is worked out by showing that the rule applying in one class relates to the rule applying in some other: *all the more so*, in the case of what is of a higher station in the hierarchy to what is of a lower station, for example. The medium by which we move from *this*, to *why this, not that*, is through the argument, *if this, then surely that*, or *if this, then obviously not that.* On its own, that medium presents a mere point of logic. But the medium should not obscure the message, for here the system makes its real point, I shall make abundantly clear.

What is at stake in classification? The answer points us toward the source of the philosophy's dynamic. If we draw no conclusions, then nothing—by definition—happens. We have organized information. But if we do draw conclusions, then much happens, and we have so framed information as to produce conclusions of consequence. When we contemplate the Mishnah's conception of the realm of reality, the social order of humanity, the metaphysical order of nature and supernature, we ask, what makes all things move? How do we account not for a steady-state tableau, in which nothing happens, but for the realm of activity, in which, rightly ordered, everything happens the way it should happen? The answer to that question derives from the point at which classification is accomplished. That is when we must ask, so what? And the point is, from classification we must draw conclusions, the rule that animates all rules. Then what conclusions are we to draw from our power to classify? They derive from hierarchization of the classes of things, as I said at the outset.

Let me say what is at stake in this question of the system's dynamic first in simple, syllogistic terms. In such an argument, we take two facts and produce a third not contained within the prior facts but through right logic generated by them. And that drawing of conclusions, that making of two things into a sum greater than the parts, defines the stakes of classification. For the philosophy we examine in its most concrete expressions serves not only to describe but to explain, not only to classify but to draw conclusions. How is this done? It is by moving from the classification to the comparison of classes of things: which stands lower, which higher? which imposes its rule upon another class altogether—or the opposite rule? To the method of *Listenwissenschaft,* for the Mishnah's mode of thought and argument, the source of power and compelling proof is hierarchization. Things are not merely like or unlike, therefore following one rule or its opposite. Things also are weightier or less weighty, and that particular point of likeness of difference generates the logical force of *Listenwissenschaft.*

V. *The Genus and the Species*

The Mishnah's framers' principle of speciation—like that of natural history as defined by Aristotle—appealed to the intrinsic traits, the nature, of things. The first step in method of hierarchical classification is the simplest: showing that two or more things are one thing, and then demonstrating what difference it makes that one thing en-

compasses different things. This then shows us that species form a
genus. (Later on, the same method will serve to tell us that all things
are really one thing, and that constitutes a philosophy, not merely a
mode of thought.) At M. Nedarim 6:1ff. we have an exercise in
showing the relationships between a genus and its species and also
two species of a common genus. The matter is worked out over and
over again, with a single result. We have to identify what is subject to
a common genus, e.g., cooking covers roasting and seething, but also
what is not within that genus. If one denies himself cooked food, he
cannot eat what is loosely cooked in a pot but may eat what is solidly
cooked in a pot, and so throughout.

Mishnah-tractate Nedarim 6:1-6, 8-10

6:1   A. He who takes a vow not to eat what is cooked is permitted
          [to eat what is] roasted or seethed.
       B. [If] he said, "Qonam if I taste cooked food," he is prohibited
          from eating what is loosely cooked in a pot but permitted to
          eat which is solidly cooked in a pot.
       C. And he is permitted to eat a lightly boiled egg or gourds
          prepared in hot ashes.
6:2   A. He who takes a vow not to eat what is cooked in a pot is
          prohibited only from what is boiled [therein].
       B. [If] he said, "Qonam if I taste anything which goes down
          into a pot'" he is prohibited from eating anything which is
          cooked in a pot.
6:3   A. [He who takes a vow not to eat] what is pickled is prohibited
          only from eating pickled vegetables.
       B. [If he said, "Qonam] if I taste anything pickled," he is pro-
          hibited from eating anything which is pickled.
       C. [If he took a vow not to eat what is] seethed, he is forbidden
          only from eating seethed meat.
       D. [If he said, "Qonam] if I taste anything seethed," he is pro-
          hibited from eating anything which is seethed.
       E. "[He who takes a vow not to eat] what is roasted is prohib-
          ited only from eating roasted meat," the words of R. Judah.
       F. [If he said, "Qonam] if I taste anything roasted," he is pro-
          hibited from eating anything which is roasted.
       G. [He who takes a vow not to eat] what is salted is prohibited
          only from eating salted fish.
       H. [If he said, "Qonam] if I eat anything salted," then he is
          prohibited from eating anything at all which is salted.
6:4   A. [He who says, "Qonam] if I taste fish or fishes," is prohib-
          ited [to eat) them, whether large or small, salted or unsalted,
          raw or cooked.
       B. But he is permitted to eat pickled chopped fish and brine.

C. He who vows not to eat small fish is prohibited from eating pickled chopped fish. But he is permitted to eat brine and fish brine.

D. He who vowed [not to eat] pickled chopped fish is prohibited from eating brine and fish brine.

6:5   A. He who vows not to have milk is permitted to eat curds.

B. And R. Yosé prohibits [eating curds].

C. [If he vowed not to eat] curds, he is permitted to have milk.

D. Abba Saul says, "He who vows not to eat cheese is prohibited to eat it whether it is salted or unsalted."

6:6   A. He who takes a vow not to eat meat is permitted to eat broth and meat sediment.

B. And R. Judah prohibits [him from eating broth and meat sediment].

C. Said R. Judah, M'SH W: "R. Tarfon prohibited me from eating eggs which were roasted with it [meat]."

D. They said to him, "And that is the point! Under what circumstances? When he will say, 'This meat is prohibited to me.'

E. "For he who vows not to eat something which is mixed with something else, if there is sufficient [of the prohibited substance] to impart a flavor, is prohibited [from eating the mixture]."

6:6   A. He who takes a vow not to eat meat is permitted to eat broth and meat sediment.

B. And R. Judah prohibits [him from eating broth and meat sediment].

C. Said R. Judah, "R. Tarfon prohibited me from eating eggs which were roasted with it [meat]."

D. They said to him, "And that is the point! Under what circumstances? When he will say, 'This meat is prohibited to me.'

E. "For he who vows not to eat something which is mixed with something else, if there is sufficient [of the prohibited substance] to impart a flavor, is prohibited [from eating the mixture]."

6:8   A. He who takes a vow not to eat dates is permitted to have date honey.

B. [He who takes a vow not to eat] winter grapes is permitted to have the vinegar made from winter grapes.

C. R. Judah b. Beterah says, "Anything which is called after the name of that which is made from it, and one takes a vow not to have it-he is prohibited also from eating that which comes from it."

D. But sages permit.

6:9   A. He who takes a vow not to have wine is permitted to have apple wine.

B. [He who takes a vow not to have] oil is permitted to have sesame oil.

> C. He who takes a vow not to have honey is permitted to have
> date honey.
>
> D. He who takes a vow not to have vinegar is permitted to have
> the vinegar of winter grapes.
>
> E. He who takes a vow not to have leeks is permitted to have
> shallots.
>
> F. He who takes a vow not to have vegetables is permitted to
> have wild vegetables,
>
> G. since they have a special name.

6:10 1 A. [He who takes a vow not to eat] cabbage is forbidden from
asparagus [deemed a species of the cabbage genus].

> B. [He who takes a vow not to eat] asparagus is permitted to
> have cabbage.
>
> C. [He who takes a vow not to have] grits is forbidden to have
> grits pottage.
>
> D. And R. Yosé permits it.
>
> E. [He who takes a vow not to eat] grits pottage is permitted to
> have grits.
>
> F. [He who takes a vow not to eat] grits pottage is forbidden to
> eat garlic.
>
> G. And R. Yosé permits it.
>
> H. [He who takes a vow not to eat] garlic is permitted to eat
> grits pottage.
>
> I. [He who takes a vow not to eat] lentils is forbidden from
> eating lentil cakes.
>
> J. And R. Yosé permits.
>
> K. [He who takes a vow not to eat] lentil cakes is permitted to
> eat lentils.
>
> L. [He who says, "Qonam] if I taste [a grain of] wheat or
> wheat [ground up in any form]" is forbidden from eating it,
> whether it is ground up or in the form of bread.
>
> M. [If he said, "Qonam if I eat] a grit [or] grits in any form," he
> is forbidden from eating them whether raw or cooked.
>
> N. R. Judah says, "[If he said,] 'Qonam if I eat either a grit or
> a [grain of] wheat,' he is permitted to chew them raw."

The matter is worked out over and over again, with a single result.
We have to identify what is subject to a common genus, e.g., cooking
covers roasting and seething, but also what is not within that genus.
If one denies himself cooked food, he cannot eat what is loosely
cooked in a pot but may eat what is solidly cooked in a pot, and so
throughout. The upshot of these materials, continued at M. 6:4-5, is
carefully to show how the genus defines its species. M. Nedarim 6:6,
8-10 review matters of the genus and the species. If I wanted to make
up a rule book for students' study of the rules of forming a genus,
identifying the species, and then drawing conclusions from the work,

I cannot imagine a more effective mode of teaching than the case at hand.

Mishnah-tractate Niddah 6:2-10 present what I conceive to be a climactic exercise of taxonomy: the specification of species and their exceptions (sub-speciation). The unit is so well composed that I present nearly the whole of it, since I think it provides fine evidence that philosophical the lesson that the framers which to teach concerns the issue of sub-speciation and how it plays itself out. Now to our case

Mishnah-tractate Nedarim 6:2-10

6:2 A. Similarly:

     B. Any clay utensil that will let in a liquid will let it out.

     C. But there is one which lets out a liquid and does not let it in.

     D. Every limb which has a claw on it has a bone on it, but there is that which has a bone on it and does not have a claw on it.

6:3 A. Whatever is susceptible to midras uncleanness is susceptible to corpse uncleanness, but there is that which is susceptible to corpse uncleanness and is not susceptible to midras uncleanness.

6:4 A. Whoever is worthy to judge capital cases is worthy to judge property cases and there is one who is worthy to judge property cases and is not worthy to judge capital cases.

     B. Whoever is suitable to judge is suitable to give testimony, but there is one who is suitable to give testimony but is not suitable to judge.

6:5 A. Whatever is liable for tithes is susceptible to the uncleanness pertaining to foods, but there is that which is susceptible to the uncleanness pertaining to foods and is not liable for tithes.

6:6 A. Whatever is liable for peah is liable for tithes, but there is that which is liable for tithes and is not liable for peah.

6:7 A. Whatever is liable for the law of the first of the fleece is liable for the priestly gifts, but there is that which is liable for the priestly gifts and is not liable for the first of the fleece.

6:8 A. Whatever is subject to the requirement of removal is subject to the law of the Seventh Year and there is that which is subject to the law of the Seventh Year and is not subject to the requirement of removal.

6:9 A. Whatever has scales has fins, but there is that which has fins and does not have scales.

     B. Whatever has horns has hooves, and there is that which has hooves and does not have horns,

6:10 A. Whatever requires a blessing after it requires a blessing before it, but there is that which requires a blessing before it and does not require a blessing after it.

The cases are so immediately accessible that we may turn forthwith to the question: what do we learn about the genus and the species?

First, a genus may encompass species that differ in some ways from one another, but that, nonetheless, fall within the common genus. This implicit affirmation of polythetic taxonomy fully responds to the critique of Sifra's authorship of the principles of identifying genera by appeal to the traits of things, not to the classifications imposed by Scripture. Indeed, if I had to point to a single effective reply in the form of a case, it is to this case. Then we see, in the speciation, what is at stake. All bear one trait, there is one exception. It is the exception, within the genus, that provokes us to recognize the speciation of the genus. And that is the simple point that the authorship of this exquisite composition wishes to make.

VI. *Principles of Speciation*

A well-crafted philosophy finds a useful, if subordinate, place for a variety of encompassing and autonomous principles, each of them capable of forming the foundation for a system on its own. In this way the philosophy enlists in its cause of explaining many things in one way a variety of powerful validating conceptions. Each of these supplies its own points of self-evidence to reinforce the structure as a whole. Claiming that all things find their proper place in the order and composition of a well-formed world, the framers of the Mishnah appealed to differentiating principles with no necessary bearing upon problems of classification. They assigned to them subsidiary positions within the world-ordering system under construction.

In this way the system-builders set in array arguments in favor of the classification of all things by appeal to intrinsic traits. In behalf of the conception of a true and sole character of each thing and of the comparison and contrast of one thing and something else, the document's authorship thereby enlisted the force of such differentiating notions as distinction between the actual and the potential, the deed and the intention, reality and appearance, function and form, and the like. These, of course, form perennial issues in philosophy, East and West alike. In a word, conceptions of a world-ordering potential are transformed into contingent and subsidiary principles of systemic speciation. They reinforce the philosophy formed on the foundation of classification, aimed at showing how many things are one thing.

For that is how the system at hand required their services—that way, and in no other.

Principles of speciation accordingly drew upon principled issues that can have enjoyed autonomous standing. For instance, conceptions of the physical world drew heavily on the distinction between the real and the manifest, on the one side, and those of psychology built upon the distinction between the deed and intentionality, on the other. Four of these here-subordinated principles then are readily specified. The first concerns the formal or merely manifest as against the intrinsic or real traits of things, that is to say, the relationship between appearance and reality. The second derives from the definitive power of the function of things, as against their mere form, that is, not what they are but how they work. The third addresses reality now and reality then, which is to say, the relationship of the actual and the potential. And the fourth, and a very common one in the Mishnah's system, therefore held to be quite useful for the Mishnah's own systemic program, addresses the interplay between what one wants to have happen and what actually does happen.

The reason that these four principles require detailed and protracted attention and are best shown to be subordinate and contingent upon the main task of the system, hierarchical classification, is simple. All four possess disruptive power within a system centered upon classification. Each can on its own serve as an argument against the entirety of the taxonomic structure. I say so because any one of these four distinctions of weight and ubiquity provides a variable, on the one side, and an unanswerable doubt, on the other. Let me explain what I mean by asking a sequence of exceedingly difficult questions.

How can I classify anything, if I cannot distinguish appearance from reality? And what takes precedence, what something is or what it does? And is the now definitive, or the becoming the main thing? Shall I dismiss teleology in all its forms? And, finally, where is there place, in a static account of things, for my wishes and intentionality?

All four of these principles thus serve to introduce movement into a philosophy of classification that wishes to account for the static order of things and to show how everything remains at rest in a well-composed universe. The solution to the problem of movement and disorder represented by imponderables and variables of course drew upon the system's own capacities. That is a mark of the power of the philosophy itself, just as—so we just noticed—the answer to the chal-

lenge of the fundamental taxic principle that the taxon derives from
the things own qualities came from the system itself. The system-
builders represented by the Mishnah solved their problem by trans-
forming (potentially) destabilizing considerations into subordinated
taxic indicators, that is to say, into principles of speciation. Let us
now see in unusually rich detail how this was accomplished.

Showing how great issues found a subordinated place as principles
of speciation begins with the simplest. It is the conception that appearance and reality have to be sorted out. The issue arises, of
course, in the practicalities of applied reason, and that brings us to
one among numerous cases in which our task is to determine
whether how things really are or what they appear to be is the indicative variable. One such case derives from Mishnah-tractate Kilayim,
the greater part of which serves to make the point that we speciate
through resemblance. As with prior inquiries, served by entire
tractates, here too we shall review a whole tractate and show the
cogency that derives from a philosophical reading of it.

With reference to the biblical prohibition of hybridization, Lev.
19:19, "You shall not let your cattle breed with a different kind, you
shall not sow your field with two kinds of seed," and its parallel in Dt.
22:9-11, Mishnah-tractate Kilayim works on two philosophical problems. The first and paramount is the comparison and contrast of the
species of a genus. The second is the consideration of attitude or
intentionality, "It is man who both defines what constitutes a class
and determines how to keep different classes distinct from one
another...what appears to man as orderly becomes identified with the
objective order of the world."[21]

MISHNAH-TRACTATE KILAYIM 1:1, 4

1:1   A. (1) Wheat and tares
      B. are not [considered] diverse kinds with one another.
      C. (2) Barley and two-rowed barley,
         (3) rice wheat and spelt,
         (4) a broad bean and a French vetch,
         (5) a red grass-pea and a grass-pea,
         (6) and a hyacinth bean and a Nile cow-pea,
      D. are not [considered] diverse kinds with one another.
1:4   A. And in [regard to] the tree:
      B. (1) Pears and crustaminum pears,
         (2) and quinces and hawthorns,
      C. are not [considered] diverse kinds with one another.

---

[21] Mandelbaum, *A History of the Mishnaic Law of Agriculture: Kilayim*, p. 1.

D. (1) An apple and a Syrian pear,
   (2) peaches and almonds,
   (3) jujubes and wild jujubes,
E. even though they are similar to one another,
F. they are [considered] diverse kinds with one another.

Mishnah-tractate Kilayim from 1:1 through 7:8 considers plants and the rule governing cultivating together different species of plants. The first consideration is resemblance. But it is not decisive when there are other traits of speciation. These items resemble one another and are not considered diverse kinds with one another, M. Kil. 1:1-4C. Other items, M. Kil. 1:4C-6 even though they resemble each other, are considered diverse kinds. M. 1:7-9 proceed to grafting one kind of plant onto another. M. 1:9E-3:7 proceed to sowing together different kinds of crops, first in the same space, then in adjacent spaces, and then. M.3:4-7, different kinds of crops in adjacent spaces.

MISHNAH-TRACTATE KILAYIM 2:6-7

2:6 A. He who wishes to lay out his field [in] narrow beds of every kind [with each bed containing a different kind]—
B. The House of Shammai say, "[He makes the beds as wide as the width of] three furrows of 'opening' [furrows ploughed for the purpose of 'opening' the field in order to collect rainwater],
C. And the House of Hillel say, "[He makes the beds as wide as] the width of the Sharon yoke."
D. And the words of these [one House] are near the words of those [the other House; there is little difference between the two measurements].
2:7 A. [If] the point of the angle of the field of wheat entered into [a field] of barley,
B. it is permitted [to grow the wheat in the field of barley];
C. for it [the point of the angle of the wheat field] looks like the end of his field.
D. If [his field] was [sown with] wheat, and his neighbor's [field] was [sown with] another kind,
E. it is permitted to flank it [his neighbor's field] [with some] of the same kind [as that of his neighbor's field].
F. [If] his [field] was [sown with] wheat, and his neighbor's [field] was [also sown with] wheat,
G. it is permitted to flank it [his field] [with] a furrow of flax but not [with] a furrow of another kind.
H. R. Simeon says, "It is all the same whether [a furrow of] flax seeds or [a furrow of] any kind [flanks the field]."
I. R. Yosé says, "Even in the middle of his field it is permitted to test [the suitability of the soil for growing flax] with a furrow of flax."

At stake at M. Kil. 2:6-7 is not whether we actually are mixing crops, but whether it looks as though we are doing so. This is made explicit at M. Kil. 2:7C, for example: "for it [the point of the angle of the wheat field] looks like the end of his field." So long as each bed can be readily distinguished from another, different kinds may grow in the same field without producing the appearance of violating the law against diverse-kinds. So in this matter the law depends upon attitude and not upon actuality. The same considerations are operative through M. Kil. 3:7, e.g., M. 3:4: It is permitted to plant two rows each of chate melons or gourds, but not only one, since if it is only one, they do not appear to be planted in autonomous fields (Mandelbaum, p. 8). So too M. Kil. 3:3: "[If] the point of the angle of a field of vegetables entered a field of another [kind of] vegetables, it is permitted [to grow one kind of vegetables in the field of the other kind, for the point of the angle of the vegetable field looks like the end of his field, in line with M. 3:5D: "for whatever the sages prohibited, they [so] decreed only on account of appearances.

Mishnah-tractate Kilayim 4:1

4:1 A. [The] bald spot of the vineyard—
   B. House of Shammai say, '[It] need measure twenty-four cubits."
   C. House of Hillel say, "[It need measure only] sixteen amah [square],"
   D. [The] outer space of the vineyard—
   E. House of Shammai say, "[It need measure] sixteen amah."
   E House of Hillel say, "[It need measure only] twelve amah."
   G. And what is [the] bald spot of the vineyard?
   H. A vineyard which is bare in its middle.
   I. If there are not there [in the bald spot] sixteen amah [square of space], [then) he shall not put seed into it.
   J. [If] there were there [in the bald spot] sixteen amah [square of space], [then] they allow it [the vineyard] its area of tillage and he sows the rest.

We proceed, M. Kil. 4:1-7:8 to the issue of sowing crops in a vineyard. This is permitted if within or around a vineyard is an open space of the specified dimensions. If there is ample space between the vines, that space may be used. But if the appearance is such that the vines appeared mixed with grain, then the grain must be uprooted. The basic consideration is that grain or vegetables not create the appearance of confusion in the vineyard. Everything in the long sequence of rules derives from that single concern.

9:1 A. Nothing is prohibited on account of [the laws of] diverse kinds
except [a garment composed of a mixture of] wool and linen.

B. Nor is anything susceptible to uncleanness through plagues except [a garment composed of either] wool or linen.

C. Nor do priests wear anything to serve in the Temple except
[garments composed of either] wool or linen,

D. Camel's hair and sheep's wool which one hackled [combed]
together—

E. if the greater part is from the camels, it is permitted.

F. But if the greater part is from the sheep, it is prohibited [to mix
the fibers with flax].

G. [If the quantity of camel's hair and sheep's wool is divided] half
and half—it is prohibited [to mix the fibers with flax].

H. And so [is the rule for] flax and hemp which one hackled together [if at least half of the hackled fibers are of flax, it is
prohibited to mix them with wool].

9:2 A. Silk and bast silk are not subject to [the laws of] diverse kinds,

B. but are prohibited for appearance's sake.

C. Mattresses and cushions [composed of a mixture of wool and
linen] are not subject to [the laws of] diverse kinds,

D. provided that one's flesh not be touching them [while one sits
or lies on them].

E. There is no [rule permitting] temporary use in respect to diverse kinds [of garments].

F. And one shall not wear [a garment of] diverse kinds even on
top of ten [garments], even to avoid [paying] customs duty.

9:8 A. Nothing is prohibited on account of [the laws of] diverse kinds
except [wool and flax which are] spun or woven [together],

B. as it is written, "You shall not wear *shaatnez*" (Dt. 22:11)—
something which is hackled, spun, or woven.

C. R. Simeon b. Eleazar says, "It is turned away, and turns his
Father in Heaven against him."

9:9 A. Felted stuffs [composed of wool and linen] are prohibited,

B. because they are hackled [their fibers are hackled together].

C. A fringe of wool [fastened] onto [a garment of] flax is prohibited,

D. because [the threads of the fringe] interlace the web [of the
garment].

E. R. Yosé says, "Cords composed of purple wool are prohibited
[to be worn on a garment of flax],

F. "because one bastes the cord to the garment before tying [the
ends of the cord together."

G. One shall not tie a strip of wool to one of linen in order to gird
his loins, even though a [leather] strap is between them.

Here the concern is to affirm the consideration of reality over appearance. The prohibition of mingling fibers of different species, with

particular attention to wool and linen, occupies M. Kil. 9:1-10. Scripture's basic rule is amplified with special attention to mixtures, e.g., camel's hair and sheep's wool hackled together. Here we assign the traits of the dominant component of the mix to the entire mixture. Items that resemble wool and linen but are not of wool and linen, or that are not intended to serve as garments, are not subject to the prohibition.

The issue of intention is explicitly excluded. Even if one does not intend permanently to use a piece of cloth as a garment, it still may not be used at all if it is a mixture of diverse kinds, and so too at M. 9:2F. M. 9:4-10 complete the matter. Of special interest is M. 9:9, where the issue of connection is addressed. Here we have various mixtures that are prohibited because they are hackled together or interlaced. The entire tractate thus concerns the problem of appearance as against reality in connection with the mixture (commingling) of diverse species of plants, animals, and garments. The consideration of human attitude or intentionality enters in. There is no pericope that ignores one or another of these matters.

We recall that while some philosophical issues characterize the document overall, as the paramount ones of classification, mixture, and rules for hierarchical taxonomy has shown., others occur only episodically. A good example of the latter derives from the issue of the potential as against the actual. I resort to a less-than-felicitous neologism and call this philosophical principle merely "subject-specific," in that the document over all has not identified such principles as the source of its recurrent, generative problematic. One can learn a great deal about principles of classification, whatever particular topic comes to hand; one can learn something about the relationship of the potential to the actual—egg and chicken, acorn and oak—when certain highly particular issues arise. But there is no sustained effort to explore that philosophical problem as a problem of generalization with principles subject to generalization.

The matter of the potential and the actual, the considerations of the form and function of things, the conception of intentionality as a heuristic principle—all of them autonomous and free-standing modes for ordering what was not at rest but in motion and for explaining things or persons or actions—in the philosophy of this Judaism thus answered the call of classification. The uniform task assigned to each is readily determined. It was to serve as a taxic indicator or within the process of classification. Thus whether or not we consider the potential or only the actual character of a thing would determine the classification of that thing. The function, not only the form, of a thing would define its classification. The attitude or intentionality of an actor would take part in the classification of the act or its consequences. While each of these considerations can have formed on its own the foundation for a vast structure and system of explanation, none did. All of them contributed to the system's claim to self-evidence by showing that the system found a place for every conceivable variable and point of differentiation. And that implicit and tacit judgment, the utilization of great conceptions for the system's small purposes in taxonomy, showed the power of this philosophy to encompass all things—even other philosophies altogether. That is how generative conceptions of thought were absorbed within the system and made to contribute to its plausibility. None of these conceptions made the system work. All of them prove episodic and local.

The center and power of the system locates itself in that principle that occurs everywhere, not only in some few places, and that is solely the consideration of classification: the right ordering of everything in accord with some few things, the demonstration of the taxonomic unity of all things. To put matters in a less compelling way, stepping outside of the philosophy for the moment, what was shown was that all things could be unified through taxonomy, which is not what the system claimed, but what it accomplished to its framers' satisfaction at least. So much for the subordinated principles of speciation, to which the system chose not to turn for primary role in the philosophy. The points of stress occur at the identification of problems requiring solution, recurrent issues that pose questions of an urgent sort. In the systemic center is that, just as the philosophy centers upon what is regular, orderly, predictable, autonomous of the uncertainties of human attitude and will, so the philosophy's capacity to concede doubt and uncertainty in the end centers upon what is certain and regular. That is to say, a philosophy of classification repeatedly wants to sort out cases of mixture, crises of taxonomy precipitated by the proximity of two or more taxic principles

VII. *The Many and the One, The One and the Many*

The telos of thought in the Mishnah is such that many things are made to say one thing, which concerns the nature of being. So the

Mishnah's system must be deemed ontological. For it is a statement of an ontological order that the document's system makes when it claims that all things are not only orderly, but ordered in such wise that many things fall into one classification, and one thing may hold together many things of a diverse classifications. These two matched and complementary propositions—many things are one, one thing encompasses many—complement each other, because, in forming matched opposites, the two provide a single, complete and final judgment of the whole of being, social, natural, supernatural alike. Rationality consists in that sense of hierarchy that orders all things in one and the same way. That rationality appeals, moreover, to the nature of things for its demonstration. For it is revealed time and again, as we have seen at tedious length, by the possibility always of effecting the hierarchical classification of all things: each thing in its taxon, all taxa in correct sequence, from least to greatest.

Showing that all things can be ordered, and that all orders can be set into relationship with one another, we of course transform method into message. The message of hierarchical classification is that many things really form a single thing, the many species a single genus, the many genera an encompassing and well-crafted, cogent whole. Every time we speciate, we affirm that position. Each successful labor of forming relationships among species, e.g., making them into a genus, or identifying the hierarchy of the species, proves it again. Not only so, but when we can show that many things are really one, or that one thing yields many (the reverse and confirmation of the former), we say in a fresh way a single immutable truth, the one of this philosophy concerning the unity of all being in an orderly composition of all things within a single taxon. Exegesis always is repetitive—and a sound exegesis of the systemic exegesis must then be equally so, everywhere explaining the same thing in the same way.

We now turn to the sustained effort to demonstrate how many classes of things—actions, relationships, circumstances, persons, places—are demonstrated really to form one class. Just as God, in creation, ordered all things, each in its class under its name, so in the Mishnah classification works its way through the potentialities of chaos to explicit order. As in the miracle of God's creation of the world in six days, here too is classification transformed from the *how* of intellection to the *why* and the *what for* and, above all, the *what-does-it-all-mean*. Recognition that one thing may fall into several categories and many things into a single one comes to expression, for the authorship of the Mishnah, in secular ways. One of the interesting ones is the analysis of the several taxa into which a single action may fall, with an account of the multiple consequences, e.g., as to sanctions that are called into play, for a single action. The right taxonomy of persons, actions, and things will show the unity of all being by finding many things in one thing, and that forms the first of the two components of what I take to be the philosophy's teleology.

MISHNAH-TRACTATE KERITOT 3:9

A. There is one who ploughs a single furrow and is liable on eight counts of violating a negative commandment:

B. [specifically, it is] he who (1) ploughs with an ox and an ass [Deut. 22:10], which are (2,3) both Holy Things, in the case of (4) [ploughing] Mixed Seeds in a vineyard [Deut. 22:9], (5) in the Seventh Year [Lev. 25:4], (6) on a festival [Lev. 23:7] and who was both a (7) priest [Lev. 21:1] and (8) a Nazirite [Num. 6:6] [ploughing] in a grave-yard.

C. Hananiah b. Hakhinai says, "Also: He is [ploughing while] wearing a garment of diverse kinds" [Lev. 19:19, Deut. 22:11].

D. They said to him, "This is not within the same class."

E. He said to them, "Also the Nazir [B8] is not within the same class [as the other transgressions]."

Here is a case in which more than a single set of flogging is called for. B's felon is liable to 312 stripes, on the listed counts. The ox is sanctified to the altar, the ass to the Temple upkeep (B2,3). Hananiah's contribution is rejected since it has nothing to do with ploughing, and sages' position is equally flawed. The main point, for our inquiry, is simple. The one action draws in its wake multiple consequences. Classifying a single thing as a mixture of many things then forms a part of the larger intellectual address to the nature of mixtures. But it yields a result that, in the analysis of an action, far transcends the metaphysical problem of mixtures, because it moves us toward the ontological solution of the unity of being.

So much for actions. How about substances? Can we say that diverse things, each in its own classification, form a single thing? Indeed so. Here is one example, among a great many candidates, taken from Mishnah-tractate Hallah. The tractate takes as its theme the dough-offering to which the framers assume Num. 15:17-21 refers: "of the first of your coarse meal you shall present a cake as an offering." The tractate deals with the definition of dough liable to the dough offering, defining the bread, the process of separating dough-offering, and the liability of mixtures.

MISHNAH-TRACTATE HALLAH 1:1, 3

1:1 A. [Loaves of bread made from] five types [of grain] are subject to dough offering:

   B. (1) wheat, (2) barley, (3) spelt, (4) oats, and (5) rye;

   C. lo, [loaves of bread made from] these [species] are subject to dough offering,

   D. and combine with each other [for the purpose of reckoning whether or not a batch of dough comprises the minimum volume subject to dough offering (M. Hal. 1:4, 2:6, M. Ed. 1:2)].

   E. and products of these species are forbidden for common use until Passover under the category of new produce [produce harvested before the waving of the first sheaf (Lev. 23:14)].

   F. And grasses of these species may not be reaped until the reaping of the first sheaf.

   G. And if they took root prior to the waving of the first sheaf, the waving of the first sheaf releases them for common use;

   H. but if they did not take root prior to the waving of the omer, they are forbidden for common use until the next omer.

1:3 A. Grain in the following categories is liable to dough-offering when made into dough but exempt from tithes:

   B. Gleanings, forgotten sheaves, produce in the corner of a field, that which has been abandoned, first tithe from which heave offering of the tithe has been removed, second tithe, and that which is dedicated to the temple which has been redeemed, the left over portion of grain which was harvested for the offering of the first sheaf, and grain which has not reached a third of its anticipated growth.

   C. R. Eliezer says, "Grain which has not reached one third of its growth is exempt from dough offering when made into dough."

M. Hal. 1:1 addresses the issuing of whether or not five species of grain join together to produce dough of sufficient volume to incur liability to the dough-offering. Since they share in common the trait that they are capable of being leavened (*himus*), they do. So the genus encompasses all of the species, with the result that the classification-process is neatly illustrated. "Joining together" or connection then forms a statement that these many things are one thing. M. 1:2 makes the same point about the five species. The interstitial cases at M. Hal. 1:3 are subject to ownership other than that of the farmer. But that fact does not change their status as to dough offering. We take no account of the status with regard to ownership, past or present use as another type of offering, or the stage of growth of the grain whence the dough derives. This then forms the other side of the taxonomic labor: indicators that do not register distinguish. The upshot is as I said: many things are one thing; one rule applies to a variety of classes of grains.

The real interest in demonstrating the unity of being lies not in things but in abstractions, and, among abstractions, as we have already seen in other connections, types of actions take the center-stage. As before, I present in evidence not episodic compositions, but the better part of a complete composite, a tractate, which, I maintain, is formulated to address the issue of method that I deem critical. For that purpose I point to Mishnah-tractate Keritot, because its governing purpose is to work out how many things are really one thing. This is accomplished by showing that the end or consequence of diverse actions to be always one and the same. The issue of the tractate is the definition of occasions on which one is obligated to bring a sin-offering and a suspensive guilt-offering. The tractate lists those sins that are classified together by the differentiating criterion of intention. If one deliberately commits those sins, he is punished through extirpation. If it is done inadvertently, he brings a sin-offering. In case of doubt as to whether or not a sin has been committed (hence: inadvertently), he brings a suspensive guilt offering. Lev. 5:17-19 specifies that if one sins but does not know it, he brings a sin-offering or a guilt offering. Then if he does, a different penalty is invoked, with the suspensive guilt offering at stake as well. While we have a sustained exposition of implications of facts that Scripture has provided, the tractate also covers problems of classification of many things as one thing, in the form of a single-sin-offering for multiple sins, and that problem fills the bulk of the tractate.

MISHNAH-TRACTATE KERITOT 1:1, 2, 7, 3:2, 4

1:1 A. Thirty-six transgressions subject to extirpation are in the Torah...

1:2 A. For those [transgressions] are people liable, for deliberately doing them, to the punishment of extirpation,

B. and for accidentally doing them, to the bringing of a sin offering,

C. and for not being certain of whether or not one has done them, to a suspensive guilt offering [Lev. 5:17]—

D. "except for the one who imparts uncleanness to the sanctuary and its Holy Things,

E. "because he is subject to bringing a sliding scale offering (Lev. 5:6-7, 11)," the words of R. Meir.

F. And sages say, "Also: [except for] the one who blasphemes, as it is said, 'You shall have one law for him that does anything unwittingly' (Num. 15:29)—excluding the blasphemer, who does no concrete deed."

1:7 A. The woman who is subject to a doubt concerning [the appearance of] five fluxes,

B. or the one who is subject to a doubt concerning five miscarriages

C. brings a single offering.

D. And she [then is deemed clean so that she] eats animal sacrifices.

E. And the remainder [of the offerings, A, B] are not an obligation for her.

F. [If she is subject to] five confirmed miscarriages,

G. or five confirmed fluxes,

H. she brings a single offering.

1. And she eats animal sacrifices.

J. But the rest [of the offerings, the other four] remain as an obligation for her [to bring at some later time]—

K. M'SH S: A pair of birds in Jerusalem went up in price to a golden denar.

L. Said Rabban Simeon b. Gamaliel, "By this sanctuary! I shall not rest tonight until they shall be at [silver] denars."

M. He entered the court and taught [the following law]:

N. "The woman who is subject to five confirmed miscarriages [or] five confirmed fluxes brings a single offering.

0. "And she eats animal sacrifices.

P. "And the rest [of the offerings] do not remain as an obligation for her."

0. And pairs of birds stood on that very day at a quarter-denar each [one one-hundredth of the former price].

3:2 A. [If] he ate [forbidden] fat and [again ate] fat in a single spell of inadvertence, he is liable only for a single sin offering,

B. [If] he ate forbidden fat and blood and remnant and refuse [of an offering] in a single spell of inadvertence, he is liable for each and every one of them.

C. This rule is more strict in the case of many kinds [of forbidden food] than of one kind.

D. And more strict is the rule in [the case of] one kind than in many kinds:

E. For if he ate a half—olive's bulk and went and ate a half—olive's bulk of a single kind, he is liable.

F. [But if he ate two half-olive's bulks] of two [different] kinds, he is exempt.

3:4 A. There is he who carries out a single act of eating and is liable on its account for four sin offerings and one guilt offering:

B. An unclean [lay] person who ate (1) forbidden fat, and it was (2) remnant (3) of Holy Things, and (4) it was on the Day of Atonement.

C. R. Meir says, "If it was the Sabbath and he took it out [from one domain to another] in his mouth, he is liable [for another sin offering]."

D. They said to him, "That is not of the same sort [of transgression of which we have spoken heretofore since it is not caused by eating (A)]."

M. Ker. 1:7 introduces the case of classifying several incidents within
a single taxon, so that one incident encompasses a variety of cases
and therefore one penalty or sanction covers a variety of instances.
There we have lists of five who bring a single offering for many
transgressions, five who bring a sliding scale offering for many incidents, and the like, so M. 2:3-6. Then M. 3:1-3 we deal with diverse
situations in which a man is accused of having eaten forbidden fat
and therefore of owing a sin-offering. At M. 3:1 the issue is one of
disjoined testimony. Do we treat as one the evidence of two witnesses. The debate concerns whether two cases form a single category. Sages hold that the case are hardly the same, because there
are differentiating traits. M. 3:2-3 show us how we differentiate or
unify several acts. We have several acts of transgression in a single
spell of inadvertence; we classify them all as one action for purposes
of the penalty. That at stake is the problem of classification and how
we invoke diverse taxic indicators is shown vividly at M. 3:2 in particular. Along these same lines are the issues of M. Ker. 3:3, 4-6:
"There is he who carries out a single act of eating and is liable on its
account for four sin-offerings and one guilt-offering; there is he who
carries out a single act of sexual intercourse and becomes liable on its
account for six sin-offerings," with the first shown at M. 3:4.

I have repeatedly claimed that the recognition that one thing becomes many does not challenge the philosophy of the unity of all
being, but confirms the main point. Why do I insist on that proposition? The reason is simple. If we can show that differentiation flows
from within what is differentiated,—that is, from the intrinsic or
inherent traits of things—then we confirm that at the heart of things
is a fundamental ontological being, single, cogent, simple, that is
capable of diversification, yielding complexity and diversity. The upshot is to be stated with emphasis. *That diversity in species or diversification
in actions follows orderly lines confirms the claim that there is that single point
from which many lines come forth.* Carried out in proper order—[1] the
many form one thing, and [2] one thing yields many—the demonstration then leaves no doubt as to the truth of the matter. Ideally,
therefore, we shall argue from the simple to the complex, showing
that the one yields the many, one thing, many things, two, four.

MISHNAH-TRACTATE SHABBAT 1:1
1:1 A. [Acts of] transporting objects from one domain to another,
[which violate] the Sabbath, (1) are two, which [indeed] are
four [for one who is] inside, (2) and two which are four [for one
who is] outside,

B. How so?

C. [If on the Sabbath] the beggar stands outside and the house-holder inside,

D. [and] the beggar stuck his hand inside and put [a beggar's bowl] into the hand of the householder,

E. or if he took [something] from inside it and brought it out,

F. the beggar is liable, the householder is exempt.

G. [If] the householder stuck his hand outside and put [something] into the hand of the beggar,

H. or if he took [something] from it and brought it inside,

I. the householder is liable, and the beggar is exempt.

J. [If] the beggar stuck his hand inside, and the householder took [something] from it,

K. or if [the householder] put something in it and he [the beggar] removed

L. both of them are exempt.

M. [If] the householder put his hand outside and the beggar took [something] from it,

N. or if [the beggar] put something into it and [the householder] brought it back inside,

    0. both of them are exempt.

M. Shab. 1:1 classifies diverse circumstances of transporting objects from private to public domain. The purpose is to assess the rules that classify as culpable or exempt from culpability diverse arrangements. The operative point is that a prohibited action is culpable only if one and the same person commits the whole of the violation of the law. If two or more people share in the single action, neither of them is subject to punishment. At stake therefore is the conception that one thing may be many things, and if that is the case, then culpability is not incurred by any one actor.

VIII. *The Mishnah and Hierarchical Classification*

The Mishnah's philosophy as to its basic proposition forms a different quest altogether from that of Aristotle, and that simple contrast moves us from the matter of method, shared with Aristotle in particular, to the issue of message. What we shall now see is that the Mishnah's paramount proposition runs along the lines of important fundamentals of the philosophy that inherited the Classical writings and that came to full expression in the writings of Plotinus (204-270) in the name of Plato, and to that message we have now to turn. The principal proposition of the Mishnah, concerning the ontological unity of being, with many things forming one thing, and one thing yielding many things, proves entirely congruent with one important conception of Middle Platonism, Neo-Platonism, and Plotinus, concerning the unity of all being.

I invoke the Aristotle's method and Plotinus's proposition simply to show that other people—our authorship specifically—who pursued intellection in the manner of the one or set forth a proposition important to the other as to classification were saying philosophical things and saying them in accord with a philosophical method. That is my claim, and I believe I now establish beyond any reasonable doubt. The method, Aristotelian, and the propositions, congruent with the Middle Platonism of Plotinus, were philosophical in the way in which (other) philosophers achieved their results and set forth their propositions.

Let us begin with the most difficult point, deriving from a general description of Middle, or Neo-Platonism. The great Bréhier introduces the philosophy in the following words, which surely call into question the likelihood of the comparison I undertake:

> Neo-Platonism is essentially a means of approaching an intelligible reality and a construction or description of this reality...In Neo-Platonism what matters most is passage from a sphere where knowledge and happiness are impossible to one where they are possible...The philosophy of the age is in a sense a description of the metaphysical landscapes through which the soul is transported as it undergoes what might be described as spiritual training.[22]

On the face of matters, the philosophers of the Mishnah offer not the slightest hint that they concern themselves with such matters; "the soul" for example scarcely appears in the hundreds of chapters of which the Mishnah is composed. But when we speak of ontological unity, we find ourselves at home:

> We can conceive of a unity that increases to the point where the parts of a being fuse and become almost inseparable. For instance, we cannot speak in the same sense of the parts of a living body and of the parts of a science; in a living body the parts are solitary but are locally separated, whereas in a science a part is a theorem and each theorem contains potentially every other theorem. Thus we see how an additional degree of unification takes us from the corporeal to the spiritual.[23]

---

[22] Émile Bréhier, *The History of Philosophy*, p. 182.
[23] ibid, pp. 184.

Here we see, in abstraction, considerations that we locate in very concrete terms in the progress from classification of things to their hierarchization and finally to their unification, shown in the fact that as one thing is made up of—holds together in unity—many things, so many things emerge from one thing. And that, in abstract language, forms the centerpiece of the Mishnaic interest in classification.

So too, as Bréhier says, "But every imperfect reality or union of parts implies a more complete unity beyond itself...In the absence of the higher unity, everything disperses, crumbles and loses its being. Nothing is other than through the One." As to method, what is at hand is "explaining a particular aspect of reality by relating it to a more perfect unity." What we find in the Mishnah is the distinctive definition of those components of reality that are to be taken up in the quest for ontological unity: the this and that of the every day and the here and now, precisely what Plotinus finds of no consequence whatsoever, but what Aristotle in his scientific writings took as the focus of analytical interest. Specifically, Plotinus in the name of Plato set forth a doctrine of the hierarchical order of being, in which many things are subsumed within one thing, and one thing yields many things, from the lowest order, which is diverse, to the highest, which is unified. The doctrine of the One in Plotinus may be best summarized as follows:

> The One is infinite, the others finite; the One is creator, the others creatures; the One is entirely itself, entirely infinite, the others are both finite and infinite...the One has no otherness, the others are other than the One. It is not the case that while the Forms exist, the One does not. Rather the One exists in an infinite way, the others finitely....[24]

The centerpiece of the system then is the conception of the One, and, as we shall now see, the fundamental hierarchical unity of being in the orderly world that descends from the One.

Accordingly, moving from Aristotle to Neo-Platonism opens the way to the rough and ready comparison between the philosophical message of a critical and paramount philosophical system, that which came to full expression only after the closure of the Mishnah, with Plotinus in the middle of the third century, and the philosophical message of the Mishnah, at the end of the second century or beginning of the third. Let me proceed with a simple definition of "Platonism and Neo-Platonism," that supplied by A. H. Armstrong,

---

[24] J. M. Rist, *Plotinus: The Road to Reality*, p. 37.

as follows (with the pertinent points I wish to emphasize given in italics, supplied by me):

> Neoplatonism, the form of Platonism developed by Plotinus in the third century A.D., contains among its leading ideas the following:
> 1. There is plurality of spheres of being, arranged in hierarchical descending order, the last and lowest comprising the universe, which exists in time and space and is perceptible to the senses.
> 2. Each sphere of being is derive from its superior, a derivation that is not a process in time or space.
> 3. Each derived being is established in its own reality by turning back toward its superior in a movement of contemplative desire, which is implicit in the original creative impulse of outgoing that it receives from its superior....
> 4. Each sphere of being is an image or expression on a lower level of the sphere above it.
> 5. Degrees of being are also degrees of unity; in each subsequent sphere of being there is greater multiplicity, more separateness, and increasing limitation,—till the atomic individualization of the spatio-temporal world is reached.
> 6. The supreme sphere of being, and through it all of what in any sense exists, derives from the ultimate principle, which is absolutely free from determinations and limitations and utterly transcends any conceivable reality, so that it may be said to be 'being.' As it has no limitations, so it has no division, attributes, or qualifications; it cannot really be named but may be called 'the One' to designate its complete simplicity. It may also be called 'the Good' as the source of all perfections and the ultimate goal of return; for the impulse of outgoing and return that constitutes the hierarchy of derived reality comes from and leads back to the Good.
> 7. Since this supreme principle is absolutely simple and undetermined (or devoid of specific traits), man's knowledge of it must be radically different from any other kind of knowledge: it is not an object (a separate, determined, limited thing) and no predicates can be applied to it; hence it can be known only if it raises the mind to an immediate union with itself, which cannot be imagined or described. [25]

The point at which I find an important common proposition is, as is surely self-evident, the conviction of a hierarchical order of being, in which, as one ascends, one moves ever toward a more unified realm of being.

This conception here is expressed in the reverse order: as one descends, things become more complex, so the one yields the many.

---

[25] Armstrong, A. H., "Platoism and Neoplatonism," *Encyclopaedia Britannica* 14:539-545

The differences in detail—as any scholar of Middle Platonism must remind us—are stupefying. But I see no fundamental difference between the two positions on the unity of being and subordinated matters I should classify as ontological. Armstrong's points 1 and 5 thus appear to me to coincide with the Mishnah's fundamental and repeatedly demonstrated proposition about the unity of being, attained through the hierarchical classification of all things. Bréhier states the matter in the simplest possible way:

> ...the universe appears as a series of forms each of which depends hierarchically on the preceding, and the universe can be the object of rational thought.[26]

Exactly how this is demonstrated is hardly our problem, since Plotinus's way of showing the ordered hierarchy of being is not the same as Aristotle's, and as to mode of thought it is Aristotle's and not Plotinus's (or Plato's!) that served our philosophers.

It is the proposition of the One that matters, and here I find an identity of viewpoint between the two philosophies, the pagan and the Judaic. A. H. Armstrong's account of the One[27] leaves no doubt of the complexity of what is at stake for Plotinus in thought about that fundamental subject. But the basic point serves our purpose full well: the first aspect of the One" is "as conclusion of the metaphysical and religious search for a primary reality which can act as explanation of the universe." The One of course is transcendent and absolute. The One is "not only self-thinking but self-willing and self-loving." We need not venture into the Neo-Platonic metaphysics and cosmology, with their interest in an astronomical theory of the sensible world.[28] These have no bearing upon our interest. Nor do I appeal to a shared concept of the soul, e.g., as suggested by Plotinus's "If all souls are one,"[29] since in the Mishnah we find no doctrine of the soul or the person or person-hood of the human being. And that is not the only proposition that is not only not shared but, from the perspective of the Judaic philosophy, incomprehensible. Then what is at stake? Once more the answer is the same, but now in greater specificity. It is the proposition that "above this multiple unity, which

---

[26] Bréhier, *Plotinus*, p. 43.

[27] A. H. Armstrong, *The Architecture of the Intelligible Universe in the Philosophy of Plotinus*, pp. 1-48.

[28] ibid, p. 44.

[29] cf. Armstrong, A. Hilary, "The Apprehension of Divinity in Plotinus," *Plotinian and Christian Studies* , paper XVIII.

constitutes the intelligible world, we must posit...the absolute One without distinction and without variety,"[30] that I find pertinent to the simple case at hand—that alone.

The sages of the Mishnah intersect at only a few, very specific points with the philosophical method and message I have identified. The entire medium through which the unity of being was expressed, the system of three hypostases that interested Plotinus for example, not to mention Plotinus's doctrine of the soul, these seem to me remote from the thought-processes and propositions of the Judaic philosophers. But the proposition I have identified as common to the two systems of thought—so I repeat—was the same. And that justifies my calling the one system of thought, the Mishnah's, philosophical, in its proposition as much as in its method and mode of thought. The fundamental argument in favor of the unity of God in the philosophy of the Mishnah is by showing the hierarchical order, therefore the unity, of the world. The world therefore is made to testify to the unity of being, and—to say the obvious with very heavy emphasis—*the power of the philosophy derives from its capacity for hierarchical classification.*

IX. *Sifra's Critique of the Mishnah's* Listenwissenschaft

The authors of Sifra, a third century treatise on the book of Leviticus, appeal to the distinction between similarity and identity to demolish the Mishnah's authors' trust in hierarchical classification based on the traits of things. They maintained that the traits of things on their own never permit reliable classifications to be worked out, because things may be similar but never identical. Hence, they held, Scripture must dictate the valid taxonomies, reason on its own being unable to do so. We have already seen how the compilers of the Mishnah put forth a taxonomy based on inherent traits, not on Scripture's decreed classification, serve. From the viewpoint of the framers of the Mishnah, the subject-matter of a given tractate, viewed autonomously in terms of its own traits, inner tensions, logical progression, contains within itself its own point of interest. The traits of the topic are therefore conceived on their own to precipitate thought about that topic. Whence the authorship of Sifra discovers *its* topical assign-

---

[30] ibid, p. 45.

ment and, more important, how the authorship of Sifra defines what
it wishes to know about a topic, we shall grasp full well the importance of the Mishnah's framers' contrary plan. The framers of the
Mishnah effect their taxonomy through the traits of things. The authorship of Sifra insists that the source of classification is Scripture.
Sifra's authorship time and again demonstrates that classification
without Scripture's data cannot be carried out without Scripture's
data, and, it must follow, hierarchical arguments based on extra-
scriptural taxa always fail.

Let us take with a single, sustained example of how Sifra's authorship rejects the principles of the logic of hierarchical classification *as
these are worked out by the framers of the Mishnah*. I emphasize that the
critique applies to the way in which a shared logic is worked out by
the other authorship. For it is not the principle that like things follow
the same rule, unlike things, the opposite rule, that is at stake. Nor is
the principle of hierarchical classification embodied in the argument
a fortiori at issue. What our authorship disputes is that we can classify
things on our own by appeal to the traits or indicative characteristics,
that is, utterly without reference to Scripture. The argument is simple. On our own, we cannot classify species into genera. Everything is
different from everything else in some way. But Scripture tells us
what things are like what other things for what purposes, hence
Scripture imposes on things the definitive classifications, that and not
traits we discern in the things themselves. When we see the nature of
the critique, we shall have a clear picture of what is at stake when we
examine, in some detail, precisely how the Mishnah's logic does its
work. That is why at the outset I present a complete composition in
which Sifra's authorship tests the modes of classification characteristic of the Mishnah, resting as they do on the traits of things viewed
out of the context of Scripture's categories of things.

5. Parashat Vayyiqra Dibura Denedabah Parashah 3

V:I.1 A. "[If his offering is] a burnt offering [from the herd, he shall
           offer a male without blemish; he shall offer it at the door of
           the tent of meeting, that he may be accepted before the Lord;
           he shall lay his hand upon the head of the burnt offering, and
           it shall be accepted for him to make atonement for him]"
           (Lev. 1:2):
       B. Why does Scripture refer to a burnt offering in particular?
       C. For one might have taken the view that all of the specified
           grounds for the invalidation of an offering should apply only
           to the burnt-offering that is brought as a freewill offering.

D. But how should we know that the same grounds for invalidation apply also to a burnt offering that is brought in
fulfillment of an obligation [for instance, the burnt offering
that is brought for a leper who is going through a rite of
purification, or the bird brought by a woman who has given
birth as part of her purification rite, Lev. 14, 12, respec-
tively]?

E. It is a matter of logic.

F. Bringing a burnt offering as a free will offering and bringing
a burnt offering in fulfillment of an obligation [are parallel to
one another and fall into the same classification].

G. Just as a burnt offering that is brought as a free will offering
is subject to all of the specified grounds for invalidation, so to
a burnt offering brought in fulfillment of an obligation, all the
same grounds for invalidation should apply.

H. No, [that reasoning is not compelling. For the two species of
the genus, burnt offering, are not wholly identical and can be
distinguished, on which basis we may also maintain that the
grounds for invalidation that pertain to the one do not necessarily apply to the other. Specifically:] if you have taken that
position with respect to the burnt offering brought as a free
will offering, for which there is no equivalent, will you take
the same position with regard to the burnt offering brought
in fulfillment of an obligation, for which there is an equivalent? [For if one is obligated to bring a burnt offering by
reason of obligation and cannot afford a beast, one may
bring birds, as at Lev. 14:22, but if one is bringing a free will
offering, a less expensive form of the offering may not serve.]

I. Accordingly, since there is the possibility in the case of the
burnt offering brought in fulfillment of an obligation, in
which case there is an acceptable equivalent [to the more
expensive beast, through the less expensive birds], all of the
specified grounds for invalidation [which apply to the in any
case more expensive burnt offering brought as a free will
offering] should not apply at all.

J. That is why in the present passage, Scripture refers simply to
"burnt offering," [and without further specification, the
meaning is then simple:] all the same are the burnt offering
brought in fulfillment of an obligation and a burnt offering
brought as a free will offering in that all of the same grounds
for invalidation of the beast that pertain to the one pertain
also to the other.

2. A. And how do we know that the same rules of invalidation of a
blemished beast apply also in the case of a beast that is designated in substitution of a beast sanctified for an offering [in
line with Lev. 27:10, so that, if one states that a given,
unconsecrated beast is to take the place of a beast that has
already been consecrated, the already-consecrated beast re-

mains in its holy status, and the beast to which reference is made also becomes consecrated]?

B. The matter of bringing a burnt offering and the matter of bringing a substituted beast fall into the same classification [since both are offerings that in the present instance will be consumed upon the altar, and, consequently, they fall under the same rule as to invalidating blemishes].

C. Just as the entire protocol of blemishes apply to the one, so in the case of the beast that is designated as a substitute, the same invalidating blemishes pertain.

D. No, if you have invoked that rule in the case of the burnt offering, in which case no status of sanctification applies should the beast that is designated as a burnt offering be blemished in some permanent way, will you make the same statement in the case of a beast that is designated as a substitute? For in the case of a substituted beast, the status of sanctification applies even though the beast bears a permanent blemish! [So the two do not fall into the same classification after all, since to begin with one cannot sanctify a permanently blemished beast, which beast can never enter the status of sanctification, but through an act of substitution, a permanent blemished beast can be placed into the status of sanctification.]

E. Since the status of sanctification applies [to a substituted beast] even though the beast bears a permanent blemish, all of the specified grounds for invalidation as a matter of logic should not apply to it.

F. That is why in the present passage, Scripture refers simply to "burnt offering," [and without further specification, the meaning is then simple:] all the same are the burnt offering brought in fulfillment of an obligation and a burnt offering brought as a substitute for an animal designated as holy, in that all of the same grounds for invalidation of the beast that pertain to the one pertain also to the other.

3. A. And how do we know [that the protocol of blemishes that apply to the burnt offering brought as a free will offering apply also to] animals that are subject to the rule of a sacrifice as a peace offering?

B. It is a matter of logic. The matter of bringing a burnt offering and the matter of bringing animals that are subject to the rule of a sacrifice as a peace offering fall into the same classification [since both are offerings and, consequently under the same rule as to invalidating blemishes].

C. Just as the entire protocol of blemishes apply to the one, so in the case of animals that are subject to the rule of a sacrifice as a peace offering, the same invalidating blemishes pertain.

D. And it is furthermore a matter of an argument *a fortiori*, as follows:

E. If to a burnt offering is valid when in the form of a bird, [which is inexpensive], the protocol of invalidating blemishes apply, to peace offerings, which are not valid when brought in the form of a bird, surely the same protocol of invalidating blemishes should also apply!

F. No, if you have applied that rule to a burnt offering, in which case females are not valid for the offering as male beasts are, will you say the same of peace offerings? For female beasts as much as male beasts may be brought for sacrifice in the status of the peace offering. [The two species may be distinguished from one another].

G. Since it is the case that female beasts as much as male beasts may be brought for sacrifice in the status of the peace offering, the protocol of invalidating blemishes should not apply to a beast designated for use as peace offerings.

H. That is why in the present passage, Scripture refers simply to "burnt offering," [and without further specification, the meaning is then simple:] all the same are the burnt offering brought in fulfillment of an obligation and an animal designated under the rule of peace offerings, in that all of the same grounds for invalidation of the beast that pertain to the one pertain also to the other.

The systematic exercise proves for beasts that serve in three classifications of offerings, burnt offerings, substitutes, and peace offerings, that the same rules of invalidation apply throughout. The comparison of the two kinds of burnt offerings, voluntary and obligatory, shows that they are sufficiently different from one another so that as a matter of logic, what pertains to the one need not apply to the other. Then come the differences between an animal that is consecrated and one that is designated as a substitute for one that is consecrated. Finally we distinguish between the applicable rules of the sacrifice; a burnt offering yields no meat for the person in behalf of whom the offering is made, while one sacrificed under the rule of peace offerings does. What is satisfying, therefore, is that we run the changes on three fundamentally different differences and show that in each case, the differences between like things are greater than the similarities I cannot imagine a more perfect exercise in the applied and practical logic of comparison and contrast.

V:II.1 A. "[If his offering is a burnt offering] from the herd, [he shall offer a male without blemish:"

B. The reference to "from the herd" serves to eliminate from consideration a beast that has been torn [and suffers a terminal ailment].

The exposition of the verse is not expanded with the anticipated logical argument. That follows.

V:III.1   A.   "Male:
           B.   And not a female.
2.   A.   When further on, Scripture once more refers to a male, it is only to exclude a beast with undefined sexual characteristics or with the sexual traits of both genders.
           B.   But is that not a matter of logic?
           C.   If animals designated for use as peace offerings, which are valid whether male or female, or not valid should they come with undefined sexual characteristics or with the sexual traits of both genders,
           D.   a burnt offering [under discussion in our base verse], which is not equally valid whether male or female [but only male, as specified], surely should not be valid in the case of an animal with undefined sexual characteristics or with the sexual traits of both genders!
           E.   No, if you have invoked that rule in the case of an animal designated for use as peace offerings, in which instance fowl may not serve, will you invoke that same rule in the case of an animal that is to serve as a burnt offering, in which case fowl may not be used? [So the two are not comparable in the relationship a fortiori such as is proposed at D.]
           F.   A beast designated for use as a sin offering will prove the contrary, for it may come in the form of fowl, but it may not be valid in the case of an animal with undefined sexual characteristics or with the sexual traits of both genders. [The argument of E is not valid, and the proposition of D stands.]
           G.   No, [the animal designated for use as a sin offering is not pertinent in context], for it cannot be brought from any species of male beast [but must be a sheep], while a burnt offering may be either cattle or sheep. [Accordingly, special rules apply, which distinguish the animal designated for use as a sin offering from an animal designated for use as a burnt offering. Will you therefore invoke the same rule for a burnt offering, which is valid in the case of any appropriate male beast.]
           H.   The firstling will prove to the contrary, for it may derive from a male beast of any species, but it is not suitable in the case of an animal with undefined sexual characteristics or with the sexual traits of both genders.
           J.   No, if you have presented the case of the firstling, to which the status of sanctification applies from birth [so that an act of consecration is not required on the part of the farmer], will you say the same for a beast designated as a burnt offering, in which case the status of sanctification does not apply from

the womb [but must be invoked on the beast by an explicit statement on the part of the farmer].

K. An animal designated as a tithe of the herd will prove to the contrary, for such a beast is not held to be sanctified from birth, and yet it is not valid in the case of an animal with undefined sexual characteristics or with the sexual traits of both genders.

L. No, that is not probative. For if you invoke the rule in the case a beast designated as a tithe of the herd, which is one out of ten, will you declare valid a beast designated as a burnt offering, which, by definition, is simply one out of one [namely, the beast specifically chosen by the farmer]? Since it is one out of one, it should be valid in the case of an animal with undefined sexual characteristics or with the sexual traits of both genders.

M. "Male:

N. And not a female.

O. When further on, Scripture once more refers to a male, it is only to exclude a beast with undefined sexual characteristics or with the sexual traits of both genders.

What we accomplished at V:I is now repeated on a still broader scale. We show that each species of sacrifice or sanctified beast is *sui generis* for one reason or another. On that basis we can construct neither analogies, so that a rule that applies to one applies to the other, or arguments a fortiori, with the same consequence. That is the power of polemic that unites and imparts acute interest to what is otherwise simply a set of pointless contrasts.

V:IV.1 A. "...[he shall offer a male] without blemish:"

B. Just as, if it is not unblemished, it is not pleasing, so if it does not accord with other rules in context [and is blemished in some other manner], it also is not pleasing.

2. A. "...he shall offer a male without blemish:"

B. The farmer is to sanctify the beast only if it is unblemished [and it is a violation of the law to sanctify a beast that is blemished, even though no further act of sacrifice applies to that beast (Finkelstein)].

C. R. Yosé says, "'...[he shall offer a male] without blemish:" the officiating priest must examine the beast and offer it up."

D. Said R. Yosé, "I have heard the rule applying to one who slaughters a beast as an obligatory daily whole offering on the Sabbath, that if the beast is not correctly inspected, the priest is liable for a sin-offering and must bring another beast as an obligatory daily whole offering."

We have a phrase by phrase exposition of the base verse, yielding the rules as specified.

V:V.1 A. "...he shall offer it at the door of the tent of meeting:"
      B. The farmer must take care of the beast and bring it to the tent of meeting.

2. A. Why does Scripture repeatedly state, "...he shall offer it..."?
      B. How on the basis of Scripture do we know that if an animal designated as a burnt offering is confused with another animal designated as a burnt offering, or an animal designated as a burnt offering is confused with an animal that has been designated as a substitute [for a sacrificial beast, and so takes on the status of that specified beast, in line with Lev. 27:10], or an animal designated as a burnt offering with an unconsecrated beast, the farmer must offer it up?
      C. Scripture repeatedly states, "...he shall offer it...."

3. A. Might one suppose that if a sanctified beast was confused with blemished animals, [the same rule applies, and one should offer up also the blemished beasts]?
      B. Scripture says, "...he shall offer it...," meaning to exclude the case in which a consecrated beast has become confused with invalid beasts not suitable for being offered up.

4. A. How do we know that even if a beast was confused with animals that elsewhere, but not in the present context, are designated as sin offerings [the beasts are to be sacrificed]?
      B. Indeed I shall exclude [from the present rule, e.g., the bullock of the priest who is to be anointed, or the bullock brought because of a communal transgression that is concealed or a goat that is brought by the prince] those that are confused with animals designated in other contexts as sin offerings, for the blood of these is tossed above the red line around the altar, while the blood of the others is tossed below [so a single rite of sacrifice does not apply to both categories of beasts, and therefore they cannot be sacrificed together].
      C. But how then do I know that even if such a beast has become confused with animals designated in the present context as sin offerings, [the animals should not be sacrificed altogether]?
      D. Indeed I shall exclude [from the present rule] a confusion of beasts designated as sin-offerings in the present context, for these are to be offered within, while the others [animals designated as sin offerings for individuals, as distinct from those that serve communal purposes or officials] are to be sacrificed on the outer altar.
      E. But then how do I know that even if there is a confusion between an animal designated as a firstling, an animal desig-

nated as tithe of the herd, and an animal designated as a Passover offering, [the rule applies, that all three should be sacrificed together]?

F. Indeed I shall exclude from the present rule an animal designated as a firstling, an animal designated as tithe of the herd, and an animal designated as a Passover offering, for in the case of the one, there are four acts of tossing the blood, while in the case of the other, only a single act.

G. And how then do I know that even if there is a confusion between animals designated for sacrifice under the rule of a peace offering and animals designated under the rule of sacrifice of a thanksgiving offering, [the rule applies, that all should be sacrificed together]?

H. I shall indeed exclude the case of confusion between animals designated for sacrifice under the rule of a peace offering and animals designated under the rule of sacrifice of a thanksgiving offering, for the one is in the classification of Most Holy Things, while the other is in the classification of Lesser Holy Things.

I. Might I maintain, then, that even if there is a confusion of some other beast with a beast designated as a guilt offering [which must be a ram, in the status of Most Holy Things, such as a burnt offering, and its blood is tossed below the red line, in two acts of tossing which yield four, also like a burnt offering, the one important difference being that a burnt offering is wholly consumed on the altar fire, while the meat of a guilt offering is eaten by the priests]?

J. Scripture says of that particular case, "...he will offer *it*...," meaning that alone is to be offered, but not in the case of a mixture of the beast designated as a burnt offering given as a free will offering and beasts designated for any other purpose.

4.   A. Why have you then limited the rule to the case of the confusing of a burnt offering confused with another burnt offering, which constitutes a single classification in any event?

B. If it is an animal designated as a burnt offering confused with a beast that has been substituted, the rule also applies, for the beast that has been substituted is offered in the classification of a burnt offering.

C. If it is an animal designated as a burnt offering confused with unconsecrated beasts, the same rule should apply, for the farmer can consecrate the unconsecrated beasts and treat the entire lot as burnt offerings.

The exposition of the base verse in terms of its own language now takes over, with a sequence of *ad hoc* rules. We accomplish an exercise of reason at Nos. 2, 3, however, for what we achieve here is to establish that a variety of species of sacrificial beast fall under a single rule, but then we eliminate one species of beast from the same rule. In No. 3 we systematically show why diverse types of sacrifice are distinct from one another, specifying the particular distinction in a very systematic way. Then No. 4 identifies some categories that may be treated in common, that is, under the rule governing the burnt-offering, and we explain why that is the case. What is important is that no effort to prove on the basis of logic that the same rule applies across the board is even undertaken here. The polemic is quite the opposite. Now we show why the use of mere logic cannot have worked to begin with, namely, the diversity of *genera*, and the grounds for that diversity. No. 4 gives back only a small proportion of what No. 3 has taken away, and then for reasons extrinsic to the issue altogether! That therefore strengthens the basic polemic.

The upshot is very simple. The authorship of Sifra concurs in the fundamental principle that sanctification consists in calling things by their rightful name, or, in philosophical language, discovering the classification of things and determining the rule that governs diverse things. Where that authorship differs from the view of the Mishnah's concerns—I emphasize—*the origins of taxa*: how do we know what diverse things form a single classification of things. Taxa originate in Scripture. Accordingly, at stake in the critique of the Mishnah is not the principles of logic necessary for understanding the construction and inner structure of creation. All parties among sages concurred that the inner structure set forth by a logic of classification alone could sustain the system of ordering all things in proper place and under the proper rule. The like belongs with the like and conforms to the rule governing the like, the unlike goes over to the opposite and conforms to the opposite rule. When we make lists of the like, we also know the rule governing all the items on those lists, respectively. We know that and one other thing, namely, the opposite rule, governing all items sufficiently like to belong on those lists, but sufficiently un-like to be placed on other lists. That rigorously philosophical logic of analysis, comparison and contrast, served because it was the only logic that could serve a system that proposed to make the statement concerning order and right array.

As is now clear, the source of classifications proves decisive. No one denies the principle of hierarchical classification. That is an es-tablished fact, a self-evident trait of mind. The argument of Sifra's authorship is that, by themselves, things do not possess traits that permit us finally to classify species into a common genus. There always are traits distinctive to a classification. Accordingly, it is the argument of Sifra's authorship that without the revelation of the Torah, we are not able to effect any classification at all, are left, that is to say, only with species, no genus, only with cases, no rules. We shall now review a series of specific statements of that general position.

A single example among the countless instances in Sifra in which the authorship encompasses all possibilities in a given context, places them all into hierarchical relationship, demonstrates that each taxon has unique traits exclusive to itself, and then shows how, nonetheless, Scripture makes possible the logically-sound procedure of comparison and contrast. But only through Scripture can we find out what species fall into a single classification, since the traits of things, by themselves, prove too diverse and complex. In the end, it is God, through the revelation of The Torah, who has organized and classified all things, each in its proper place and under its correct name. The power of what follows is its capacious capacity to encompass and place into a single rule and relationship a broad selection of taxa of a single genus.

4. Parashat Vayyiqra Dibura Denedabah Pereq 3

IV:I.1 A. "...you shall bring your offering [of cattle from the herd or from the flock]" (Lev. 1:2) [RSV]:

B. [The use of the plural, you,] teaches that such an offering may be given as a freewill offering on the part of two persons.

C. But does not logic bring us to the same conclusion?

D. The burnt offering made of a bird may be brought either in fulfillment of a vow or as a freewill offering, and the burnt offering made of a beast may be brought either in fulfillment of a vow or as a freewill offering. [So the two are analogous.]

E. Just as the rule governing a burnt offering made of a bird, which may be brought either in fulfillment of a vow or as a freewill offering, is that, lo, it may be offered as the freewill offering of two persons, so too the burnt offering made of a beast, which may be brought either in fulfillment of a vow or as a freewill offering, also should be permitted as a freewill offering of two persons. [Hence since the two fall into the same classification, namely, both bird and beast may be given in fulfillment of a vow or as a free will offering, so too the rule governing the bird pertains also to the beast. The bird may be brought by a partnership, and the same is so of the beast.]

F. Or take this route:

G. A meal-offering may be given either in fulfillment of a vow or as a free will offering, and so too, a burnt offering made of a beast may be given either in fulfillment of a vow or as a free will offering.

H. Just as a meal-offering, which may be given either in fulfillment of a vow or as a free will offering, may be given not as a free will offering of two persons [but only by a single individual], so too the burnt offering may of a beast, may be given either in fulfillment of a vow or as a free will offering, also cannot derive from two persons [but only from one].

I. Let us then see which analogy applies, [that is, the bird made as an offering or the meal made as an offering].

J. We should draw an analogy from something the whole of which is burned up on the altar fire to something the whole of which also is burned up on the altar fire [thus the bird and the beast presented as a burnt-offering],

K. and let us not derive an analogy from the meal-offering, the whole of which is not burned up on the altar fire [but only a handful thereof[.

L. Or take this route:

M. Let us derive an analogy from something that is brought in fulfillment of an obligatory offering owed by the entire community for something that also may be brought in fulfillment of an obligatory offering owed by the entire community,

N. but let a burnt-offering made of a bird prove the case, for it may not be offered in fulfillment of an obligatory offering owed by the entire community.

O. [Since the proposed analogies yield no final solution, it was necessary for the rule to be derived from Scripture, namely:] "...you shall bring your offering of cattle from the herd or from the flock" (Lev. 1:2) [RSV]: [The use of the plural, you,] teaches that such an offering may be given as a freewill offering on the part of two persons.

The freewill offerings under discussion here may be made of fowl, meal, or cattle. May two or more persons bring such an offering in partnership? Indeed so, two or more persons may join in the making of a sacrifice in the classification of a freewill offering, such as is under discussion at Lev. 1:1ff. That is the proposition. But the generative problematic derives from the mode by which we prove that proposition. The mode of argument is classic and shows the range of doubt affecting argument by classification, namely, analogy and contrast.

IV.II.1 A. "...your offering:"

B. This teaches that such an offering made of cattle may serve as a freewill offering of the entire community.

C. But can [the opposite of] that proposition not be proved solely from logic? [And if we can disprove the opposite of that proposition through the same logic, we can also prove the proposition at hand solely through logic and do not require an exegesis to tell us the law.]

D. Specifically, a meal offering is brought in fulfillment of a vow or as a free will offering, and a burnt offering made of a beast may be brought in fulfillment of a vow or as a free will offering.

E. Just as a meal offering, which may be brought in fulfillment of a vow or as a free will offering, may not be brought as a free will offering of the entire community [but only on individual initiative], so the burnt offering made of a beast, which is brought in fulfillment of a vow or as a freewill offering, should not be permitted to be offered as the freewill offering of a community [but only as one of an individual].

F. No, if you have stated that rule in the case of the meal-offering, it is because such an offering may not be brought as a free will offering in behalf of two persons in partnership. But will you apply the same rule to the burnt offering made of a beast, which indeed may be given as a freewill offering of two persons in partnership. [The two are not analogous at all.]

G. The burnt offering made of a bird will prove the case, then, for it indeed may be given as a freewill offering in behalf of two persons, but it may not be offered as a free will offering in behalf of the community at large.

H. No, if you have stated that rule in the case of the burnt-offering made of a bird, which cannot serve in fulfillment of an obligatory offering owed by the entire community, will you apply the rule to the quite different category of a beast, which indeed may be offered in fulfillment of an obligatory offering owed by the entire community?

I. Sacrifices under the rule governing peace-offerings will prove the contrary, for they indeed may be brought in fulfillment of an obligatory offering owed by the entire community, but quite to the contrary, they may not be offered as a free will offering in behalf of the entire community. [That is to say, the free will offering made in behalf of the entire community may not be subjected to the rule governing offerings in the classification of peace offerings. The community's free will offering is governed by the rule that applies to burnt-offerings; the whole is burned up on the altar, and no parts are yielded for eating.]

J. You therefore should not find remarkable the case of the burnt-offering made of a beast, that, even though it may serve in fulfillment of an obligatory offering owed by the community, it may nonetheless not serve as a free will offering given by the entire community.

K. [The several possible analogies yield no firm conclusion, on which account we require the information of Scripture:] "...you shall bring your offering of cattle from the herd or from the flock" (Lev. 1:2). [The use of the plural, you,] teaches that such an offering may be given as a freewill offering on the part of two persons.

2. A. Another mode of reasoning to yield the same conclusion:

B. If in the case of an individual, who may not bring an obligatory burnt offering every single day, may bring a burnt offering made of a beast as a freewill offering [every single day, without limit], the community at large, which indeed does bring an obligatory burnt offering [namely, the daily whole offering, of course] every single day, logically should be able to bring a burnt offering made of a beast as a free will offering [every single day, without limit].

C. No, if you have invoked the rule for the individual, who may bring a meal-offering as a free will offering, will you say the same of the community at large, in behalf of which a meal offering may not serve as a free will offering?

D. Partners will prove the matter, who may not bring a meal offering together as a free will offering, but who may bring a burnt offering of a beast as a free will offering.

E. But the distinctive trait governing the case of partners, who may bring as a free will offering a burnt-offering made of a beast, is that they also may bring as a free will offering a burnt-offering made of a bird. But will you say the same, namely, that the community may bring as a free will offering a burnt offering made of a beast, even though the community at large may not bring as a free will offering a burnt-offering made of a bird?

F. But the distinguishing trait governing the community, which may not bring a burnt offering made of a bird as a free will offering, is that it may not bring such an offering in fulfillment of an obligation at all [for the community must offer up something considerably more costly than a mere bird, and cannot carry out its obligation by offering a pigeon].

G. But will you still maintain that the community may not offer as a free will offering a burnt offering of a beast, for the community may indeed bring such a thing in fulfillment of its obligation.

H. Since the community may indeed bring such a thing in

fulfillment of its obligation, it should also be permitted to bring it, also, as a free will offering.

I. But a meal-offering will prove the contrary [and distinguish the two cases]. For the community indeed may bring a meal offering in fulfillment of an obligation, but it may not bring a meal -offering as a freewill offering.

J. So you should not find remarkable the fact that in the case of a burnt offering made of a beast, even though the community brings it as an obligatory offering, it may not bring it as a free will offering. [We remain in confusion, since argument leads to contradictory results.]

K. [The several possible analogies yield no firm conclusion, on which account we require the information of Scripture:] "...you shall bring your offering of cattle from the herd or from the flock" (Lev. 1:2). [The use of the plural, you,] teaches that such an offering may be given as a freewill offering on the part of the community at large.

The problem governing offering cattle as a free will offering for two or more persons, that is, a partnership, is worked out in respect to the community as well, and that is what holds Nos. 1 and 2 so close together. No. 1 compares the burnt offering of a bird and the burnt offering of a beast. The complicating analogy derives from the meal-offering. We cannot settle the question of the appropriate analogy; each item is sui generis. The same reasoning is worked out at No. 2, with a parallel exegetical, and substantive, result.

IV.III.1 A. Another statement concerning "...your offering:"

B. From the same source from which an individual derives his offering, the community derives its offering [that is, the community's beast, offered in fulfillment of its daily obligation, must be one that would be valid were an individual to designate as his offering that same beast].

The point in common between the individual's and the community's offering has now to be specified, and we remove from the range of possibilities all but the simplest consideration: the same rules of invalidation of a beast by reason of a blemish pertain to the beast designated by the individual and one designated for use by the community.

Time and again, we can easily demonstrate, things have so many and such diverse and contradictory indicative traits that, comparing one thing to something else, we can always distinguish one species from another. Even though we find something in common, we also can discern some other trait characteristic of one thing but not the other. Consequently, we also can show that the hierarchical logic on which we rely, the argument *a fortiori* or *qol vehomer*, will not serve. For if on the basis of one set of traits which yield a given classification, we place into hierarchical order two or more items, on the basis of a different set of traits, we have either a different classification altogether, or, much more commonly, simply a different hierarchy. So the attack on the way in which the Mishnah's authorship has done its work appeals to not merely the limitations of classification solely on the basis of traits of things. The more telling argument addresses what is, to Listenwissenschaft, the source of power and compelling proof: hierarchization. That is why, throughout, we must designate the Mishnah's mode of Listenwissenschaft a logic of hierarchical classification. Things are not merely like or unlike, therefore following one rule or its opposite. Things also are weightier or less weighty, and that particular point of likeness of difference generates the logical force of Listenwissenschaft.

Time and again Sifra's authorship demonstrates that the formation of classifications based on monothetic taxonomy, that is to say, traits that are not only common to both items but that are shared throughout both items subject to comparison and contrast, simply will not serve. For at every point at which someone alleges uniform, that is to say, monothetic likeness, Sifra's authorship will demonstrate difference. Then how to proceed? Appeal to some shared traits as a basis for classification: this is not like that, and that is not like this, but the indicative trait that both exhibit is such and so, that is to say, polythetic taxonomy. The self-evident problem in accepting differences among things and insisting, nonetheless, on their monomorphic character for purposes of comparison and contrast, cannot be set aside: who says? That is, if I can adduce in evidence for a shared classification of things only a few traits among many characteristic of each thing, then what stops me from treating all things alike? Polythetic taxonomy opens the way to an unlimited exercise in finding what diverse things have in common and imposing, for that reason, one rule on everything. Then the very working of Listenwissenschaft as a tool of analysis, differentiation, comparison, contrast, and the descriptive determination of rules yields the opposite of what is desired. Chaos, not order, a mass of exceptions, no rules, a world of examples, each subject to its own regulation, instead of a world of order and proportion, composition and stability, will result.

X. *The Failure of Philosophy and the Beginning of Theology*

Sifra's critique carries us beyond the limits of our topic, which is the Mishnah. But it points us toward the next phase in the intellectual history of Rabbinic Judaism. The Mishnah's God, as a matter of fact, is a God of the philosophers, but the God of the Judaism of the authoritative documents which attached themselves to the Mishnah was, and is, a God of not the philosophers but of religious thinkers. That the God of the Mishnah is philosophical, essentially extrinsic to the world-order, hardly surprises. For the Mishnah presents a philosophical system constructed in a philosophical mode of thought. Its manner of discourse is guided by philosophical principles of natural philosophy. Those principles guide the search for the one thing that explains many things, the rule that governs a variety of cases, that is to say, rational explanation.

Not only so, but the method is secular, in appealing to the indicative traits of things in this world alone. These traits are viewed as subject to orderly rules, and nothing can be conceded to be *sui generis*. Furthermore, the main results of the document's portrait of its philosophical system, repeated over and over again in a variety of propositions concerning a long protocol of topics, are uniform. They concern a reasoned and philosophical reading of matters in the most narrow and specific sense. Indeed, even when proving the essential unity of being, the philosophers of Judaism do not appeal to God, or the idea of One God, to explain that unity, let alone to demonstrate it. But that, of course, is the implicit proposition of their philosophy.

Like eighteenth century Deists, the Mishnah's philosophers focus upon the government by laws, to be discovered by intelligent use of intellect, that God has set forth in the Torah. Taking slight, and then merely episodic, interest in God's particular and ad hoc intervention into the smooth application of the now-paramount regularities of the law, that authorship rarely represented God as an immediate—therefore *ad hoc,* so by definition irregular—presence, let alone person. The Mishnah's authorship rarely decided a rule or a case by appealing to God's presence and choice particular to that rule or case.[31] That is to

---

[31] I say rarely, because there are some very few cases, such as the ordeal inflicted on the wife accused of adultery, in which God or a divine agency is expected to intervene on the spot. But that is very uncommon. Rules establish regularities throughout, and there is no place for God to make up his mind on any particular case.

say, God as not premise but immediate presence does not very often play an everyday and active role in the Mishnah's processes and system of decision-making. The full philosophical character of the Mishnah's portrayal of the role of divinity is best seen in the contrast with the Bavli's. There the contrast between God as essentially a premise of all being and God as an active personality engaged in everyday transactions with specific persons show how profoundly the Mishnah's system adhered to the principles of orderly, this-worldly, philosophical thought, even while affirming God as the foundation of all order and regularity.

Scripture's portrait of God as an active personality finds no counterpart whatsoever in the Mishnah. That fact may be seen in a simple observation. The majestic presence of God in the unfolding of events, which forms the great theme of the scriptural narratives of ancient Israel's history, may define a premise of the Mishnah's world-view. But at no passage in the Mishnah does an action of God serve to explain an event, nor do we find lessons drawn, as to God's purpose or will, from events. Events take place, truths endure, but the two form a merely assumed and implicit relationship. If, moreover, God is conceived as not merely a first principle but a person possessed of specific traits of personality, the Mishnah hardly contains evidence that its authorship could specify what those personal traits might be. A creature of a philosophical system, the Mishnah's God is not portrayed as a distinct and individual personality, walking, talking, caring, acting as people do. True, we may impute such traits and others to the God that serves as premise and even presence. But the authorship of the Mishnah, unlike the diverse scriptural writers, simply did not portray God as a personality. Nor, apart from liturgical settings, does that translate its fixed premise of God as giver of the Torah into the notion of the active presence of God in the everyday and the here and now.

Shall we then compare the creative power of the Mishnah's God to the laws of gravity? I am inclined to think so. For once we recognize that God defines a ubiquitous premise but never an independent variable, we see the aptness of such a metaphor. The laws of gravity, to a systematic account of the ecology of a botanical world, constitute a given and an immutable fact. Without those laws, it goes without saying, in the way in which they now do grass cannot sprout and trees cannot grow. But the laws of gravity, while necessary, are hardly sufficient—or, once conceded, even very urgent. They do not dictate many important systemic facts (though they make possible all facts) and they do not settle many of the system's interesting questions. So the laws of gravity in botany prove at once necessary and insufficient for explanation; implicit and ubiquitous, but not at all generative. Indeed, when we ask about the importance of the laws of gravity in a theory of botany—or biology, or plate-tectonics in geology, for that matter—we see how awry matters have become. The laws are absolutely necessary but, even when sufficient, still not very interesting.

And, to come to the world-view before us, we are therefore constrained to ask ourselves where is the God who acts? where is the God who cares? where is the God who rules "Israel" in accord with the Torah? In this system of philosophers with its law-abiding, philosophically acceptable God, the answer is, no where. Later on, in a system consequent upon the Mishnah's, God would become not only necessary but also sufficient. But while without God the authorship of the Mishnah cannot have constructed their system, to which God is necessary, still, since without God that authorship can have framed all of the system's most compelling propositions, God was hardly sufficient for the explanation of the system. God in the Mishnah's system is everywhere present, the ground of all being, giver and guarantor of the Torah—and a monumental irrelevance.

No wonder, then, that in not diachronic, but synchronic context, the Mishnah's system proves asymmetrical to what would follow.[32] For, within the on-going line of Judaic writing, the Mishnah is the first philosophical system in a thousand years and the last important philosophical system for another thousand years, until Maimonides. Accordingly we see—if only cursorily and in a merely speculative manner—the Mishnah in its diachronic context.

In our diachronic inquiry we turn backward first. Can we find a philosophical cast of mind in Scripture. There we locate, after all, among the modes of thought and inquiry of Scripture processes that yield generalizations. But a second glance shows otherwise. The aphorisms in Qohelet and Proverbs yield no well-crafted arguments, no demonstrations out of data, analysis of the traits of things, of one

---

[32] In my study of the history of the formation of Judaism as a problem in category-formation (the comparison and contrast of categories), *The Transformation of Judaism. From Philosophy to Religion*, I spell out the full sense of this statement. The received categories were left untouched, but counterpart categories were set beside them, and an entirely fresh system unfolded. We need not dwell on this topic.

truth rather than some other. They form wise observations, the raw material for philosophical thought, but no philosophy. Job's author(s) may intend to tell us about the problem of evil, and one can certainly generalize in one way or another on the basis of what they say. But in that book there is scarcely any appeal in a sustained way to thought-processes that work their way in an orderly manner through data, sifted systematically and in a single sieve, to generalizations. Observations are episodic and persuade by compelling example: but of what? As a matter of fact even in the Wisdom literature truth even when it concerns issues familiar from philosophy is established in other than philosophical modes of thought.

And what about prophecy? The appeal not merely to what was, that is, to history viewed as a collection of equally weighty facts, but rather, to a canonical and parochial selection of events deemed probative to begin with, finds justification in one way. Revelation, e.g., to Moses and the prophets, tells us which facts are unique and therefore probative, and which ones are common and inert. The task of the prophet then is to pronounce upon the unique facts and set forth the lessons to be learned from them. The propositions of faith emerge then in other than philosophical modes of thought and methods of inquiry.

So in the setting of the writings of ancient Israel, in which its authorship placed their own work, the Mishnah stands alone. But it is not in that context alone that the Mishnah finds few companions. The sacred scriptures of ancient Israel ("Old Testament," "Tanakh," and, in Judaism, "the written Torah") in due course were joined by a variety of books written by Jews and received by (a component of) Israel as holy. Called apocryphal, because of their status as non-canonical, or pseudepigraphic, because the authorship of some of them was assigned to ancient Israelite figures such as Adam or Abraham or Jacob, rather than to their then-contemporary authors, these writings in one way or another all explore the literary genres of the Hebrew Scriptures. But, among them all, until the Mishnah not a single piece of writing produced in the Land of Israel diverged from those genres or failed to attach itself as amplification and exposition to one of those genres. Starting a new Judaism as a matter of fact, the Mishnah also reached back to Scripture, even while ignoring all the genres of Scripture in presenting the results of a mode of thought and method of inquiry lacking all precedent in the diachronic setting of Israel, writing in Hebrew or in Aramaic, in the Land of Israel.

So when the Mishnah sets forth, in the manner and method of philosophy, a philosophical statement about the program that the Mishnah's authorship has taken for itself, it finds no antecedents among writings of which the authorship of the Mishnah can have been aware.[33] Now I have claimed that that the Mishnah's system of thought in its method and concerns, mode of discourse and manner of framing and solving problems, carries forward the natural philosophy of Aristotle in order to set forth a message remarkably congruent in an important way to that of Middle Platonism. And what if I am right about the Mishnah, and hence about the character of the Judaism that flowed from it? That questions turns attention from past to future. The stakes in this rather substantial program are considerable.

The authorship of the Mishnah proposed to recognize the limits of their range of discourse, set by Scripture, and also to transcend those limits. They knew that a pot was a pot, but they spoke of Ideas and Forms when they talked about pots. They knew that the chicken was a chicken and the egg an egg, and they assuredly kept the law pertaining to the egg born on a festival day. But the chicken and the egg permitted them to speak about the actual and the potential. They knew that one apple plus one apple equals two apples, but they showed that one plus one equals two—whether apples or temples. So too with intentionality and action and a broad range of profound and speculative questions of relationship, comparison and contrast, classification, and the definition of genera and species. The intellects represented in the Mishnah recognized the limitations of discourse that are imposed by restriction to the everyday.

These limitations then defined the challenge, and in response, the philosophy of Judaism—I repeat, mode of thought, medium of expression, message all together—emerged within those limitations to talk only of the here and the now of pots and pans, goring cows and trampled chickens, quarrels over pennies or slivers of useless land, petty rituals about gestures of no consequence, violations of boundaries no one perceived in a world in which no one lived: a geography of the mind in a never-never-land. But then, the whole held together and made its statement *by means of those same limitations*. I repeat: it was not despite, but within and through, their limitations of discourse that the message was delivered through the medium.

---

[33] I obviously mean to exclude Philo and such other Greek-speaking philosophical traditions as Jews had worked out elsewhere than in the Land of Israel.

Now, we have seen, when we study the law of the Mishnah, we
also study philosophy in certain significant dimensions of philosophical (in our language, scientific) method. But when we study the Torah, we study God's word. The one whole Torah given by God to
our rabbi, Moses, at Sinai, encompasses philosophy. But it is not a
philosophical treatise, because God is not bound by those rules of
rationality and order that, in philosophy, lead upward through the
orderly hierarchy of all being to God. Philosophers adduce out of the
world-order evidence for God who governs. But philosophers do not
lead us to love God with all our heart, soul, and might. Only Torah
does. And that is why, though read as philosophy, in the end, the
Mishnah is not philosophy but is taken into and absorbed by the
Torah, the one whole Torah, oral and written, of our rabbi, Moses,
the Torah forever nourishing, forever sustaining, forever sanctifying.

Bibliography

Adkins, A. W. H., *From the Many to the One. A Study of Personality and Views of Human
    Nature in the Context of Ancient Greek Society, Values, and Beliefs* (Ithaca, 1970: Cornell
    University Press).
Allan, D. J., *The Philosophy of Aristotle* (London, New York, Toronto, 1952: Oxford
    University Press/Geoffrey Cumberlege).
Armstrong, A. H., "Platonism and Neoplatonism," *Encyclopaedia Britannica* (Chicago,
    1975) 14:539-545
Armstrong, A. H., "Plotinus," *Encyclopaedia Britannica* (Chicago, 1975) 14:573-4
Bréhier, Émile, *The History of Philosophy. The Hellenistic and Roman Age* (Chicago and
    London, 1965: The University of Chicago Press). Translated by Wade Baskin.
Cherniss, Harold, *Selected Papers* (Leiden, 1977: E. J. Brill). Edited by Leonardo
    Tarán.
Feldman, Louis H., "Philo," *Encyclopaedia Britannica* (Chicago, 1975) 14:245-247
    Goodenough, Erwin R., *An Introduction to Philo Judaeus. Second Edition* (Lanham,
    1986: University Press of America Brown Classics in Judaica).
Merlan, P., "Greek Philosophy from Plato to Plotinus," in A. H. Armstrong, ed., *The
    Cambridge History of Later Greek and Early Medieval Philosophy* (Cambridge, 1967:
    Cambridge University Press), pp. 14-136.
Minio-Paluello, Lorenzo, "Aristotelianism," *Encyclopaedia Britannica* 1:1155-1161.
Owens, Joseph, *A History of Ancient Western Philosophy* (N.Y., 1959: Appleton, Century,
    Crofts Inc.)
Parker G. F., *A Short History of Greek Philosophy from Thales to Epicurus* (London, 1967:
    Edward Arnold (Publishers) Ltd.)
Reale, Giovanni, *A History of Ancient Philosophy*. III. *The Systems of the Hellenistic Age*
    (Albany,1985: State University of New York Press). Edited and translated from
    the third Italian edition by John R. Catan.

CHAPTER TWO

THE MISHNAH AND ARISTOTLE'S ECONOMICS

> "[Aristotle] will be seen as attacking the problem of man's livelihood with a radicalism of which no later writer on the subject was capable—none has ever penetrated deeper into the material organization of man's life. In effect, he posed, in all its breadth, the question of the place occupied by the economy in society"
>
> Karl Polanyi[1]

I. *Economics*

The premise of this study is best expressed by Joseph Schumpeter, when he says, "In economics as elsewhere, most statements of fundamental facts acquire importance only by the superstructures they are made to bear and are commonplace in the absence of such superstructures."[2] For the Mishnah economics is systemically not inert but active and generative, indeed expressive of the basic message of the system of the Mishnah as a whole. What is at stake is how a theory of economics forms an integral and coherent component of the larger theoretical statement of a social system. For no utopian design, such as is given by the Mishnah, a classic political novel or *Staatsroman* in the tradition of Plato's *Republic* and Aristotle's *Politics*, can ignore the material organization of society. True, in modern times we are accustomed to view economics as disembedded from the political and social system, the market, for instance, as unrelated to kinship or to the institutions of culture. But until the eighteenth century economics was understood as a component of the social system, and also a formative constituent of culture. It follows that those religious systems, such as Judaism, Islam, and Christianity in its medieval phase, that propose to prescribe public policy in the earthly city and design

---

[1] "Aristotle Discovers the Economy," in Polanyi et al., eds., *Trade and Market in the Early Empires*, p. 66.

[2] Joseph A. Schumpeter, *History of Economic Analysis*, p. 54.

a social world will integrate into their systems theories of (correct) economic behavior and also accounts of systemically-correct economic policy. Then precisely how does a religion make its systemic statement, also, through its economics?

A useful definition of "economics" directs our attention to the meaning of the word in antiquity and today. In Greek antiquity, *oikonomia* meant a formal administrative art directed toward the minimization of costs and the maximization of returns, with the prime aim of efficient management of resources for the achievement of desired objectives; "it was an administrative, not a market approach, to economic phenomena...*Oikonomia* was an early predecessor of political economy."[3] Economics today is defined as the theory of rational action with regard to scarcity. The economics of the Mishnah was a mode of rational action with regard to scarcity. The document treats subjects ordinarily addressed in antiquity by documents generally deemed to bear upon issues of economics and does so within the economic theory of Aristotle.

When we place the economics, or, more really, the political economics of the Mishnah into the context of Greco-Roman economic thought, we gain a clearer picture of the power of economics to serve in the expression and detailed exposition of a utopian design for society, such as the Mishnah contemplates. For, as Robert Lekachman states, "We see the economics of Plato and Aristotle somewhat differently when we realize that what they were discussing above all was the good life, the just state, and the happy man."[4] They sought a unified science of society. And that serves as a suitable definition, also, for the program of the framers of the Mishnah. The authorship of the Mishnah covered every important problem that any treatise on economics, covering not only the rules of household management covered in an *oikonomikos*, but also the law of money-making, found it necessary to discuss, and on that basis, I claim to describe in some modest detail what I conceive to have been the economics of Judaism as the Mishnah's authorship defined Judaism and as the ancient world understood the science of economics, or, in its context, political economy.

Why do I claim that the Mishnah's statements on topics conven-

---

[3] S. Todd Lowry, ed., *Pre-Classical Economic Thought. From the Greeks to the Scottish Enlightenment* (Boston, Dordrecht, Lancaster: Kluwer Academic Publishers, 1987), p. 12.

[4] Robert Lekachman, *History of Economic Ideas* (N.Y., 1959: Harper & Bros.), p. 4.

tionally classified as economics *is* economics in the classic (though not the modern) sense of the word? Economics from Aristotle to Quesnay and Riqueti, in the eighteenth century, dealt with not the science of wealth but rather "the management of the social household, first the city, then the state."[5] Economics formed a component of the larger sociopolitical order and dealt with the organization and management of the household (*oikos*). The city (*polis*) was conceived as comprising a set of households. Political economy, therefore, presented the theory of the construction of society, the village, town, or city, out of households, a neat and orderly, intensely classical and, of course, utterly fictive conception. One part of that larger political economy confronted issues of the household and its definition as the principal unit of economic production, the market and its function within the larger political structure, and the nature and definition of wealth. The framers of the Mishnah set forth, in acute detail and not as generalities, a theory of the household, the market, and wealth, indeed, that they joined two distinct and incompatible theories of all three. Point by point that the economics of this Judaism conformed in its principles to the economics of Aristotle.

Just as through economics, Aristotle made the larger point that animated his system as a whole, so through economics did the framers of the Mishnah. The theory of both, moreover, falls into the same classification of economic theory, namely, the theory of distributive economics, familiar in the Near and Middle East from Sumerian times down to, but not including, the age of Aristotle himself. Before proceeding, then, let me define market- and distributive economics, since these form the two economic theories at issue in antiquity, and, among them, the far-more-ancient, the distributive, shaped the economic thought of the two important systems of antiquity that made their systemic statement, also, through economics, those of Aristotle and the Mishnah. In market economics merchants transfer goods from place to place in response to the working of the market mechanism, which is expressed in price. In distributive economics, by contrast, traders move goods from point to point in response to political commands. In market economics, merchants make the market work by calculations of profit and loss. In distributive economics, there is

---

[5] Elizabeth Fox-Genovese, *The Origins of Physiocracy. Economic Revolution and Social Order in Eighteenth-Century France* (Ithaca and London, 1977: Cornell University Press), p. 9. See also Karl Polanyi, *The Livelihood of Man*. Edited by Harry W. Pearson (N.Y., San Francisco, and London, 1977: Academic Press), p. 7.

no risk of loss on a transaction.[6] In market economics, money forms an arbitrary measure of value, a unit of account. In distributive economics, money serves as a medium of barter and bears only intrinsic value, as do the goods for which it is exchanged. It is understood as "something that people accept not for its inherent value in use but because of what it will buy."[7] The idea of money requires the transaction to be complete in the exchange not of goods but of coins. The alternative is the barter-transaction, in which, in theory at least, the exchange takes place when goods change hands. Clearly, therefore, in the Mishnah's conception of the market and of wealth, distributive, not market, economics shapes details of all transactions. In distributive economics money is an instrument of direct exchange between buyers and sellers, not the basic resource in the process of production and distribution that it is in market economics.

That distributive mode of economics, rationalized within theology and also fully realized in the detail of law, will not have astonished the framers of social systems from ancient Sumerian times, three thousand years before the time of the Mishnah, onward. For from the beginning of recorded time, temples or governments imposed the economics of distribution, and market economics, where feasible at all, competed with the economics of politics, organization, and administration. From remote antiquity onward, a market economy coexisted with a distributive economy.[8] Distributive economic theory characteristic of ancient temples and governments, which served as the storage-points for an economy conceived to be self-supporting and self-sustaining, involved something other than a simultaneous exchange of legally recognized rights in property and its use; one party gave up scarce goods, the other party did not do so, but re-

---

[6] All: Davisson and Harper, p. 130.

[7] William I. Davisson and James E. Harper, *European Economic History. I. The Ancient World* (N.Y., 1972: Appleton-Century-Crofts), p. 131.

[8] See Morris Silver, *Economic Structures of the Ancient Near East* (London and Sydney: Croom Helm, 1985), and J. Wansbrough's review of that book in *Bulletin of the London School of Oriental and African Studies* 1987: 50-361-2. In this and prior studies Silver has successfully refuted the thesis of Polanyi that "there were not and could not be circumstances conducive to a market economy" (Wansbrough, p. 362). But the distinction between distributive and market economics has no bearing whatsoever upon whether or not, in remote antiquity, there was no such thing as a market in an economic sense, as Polanyi maintained. My argument focuses o only upon economic theory. But, as is clear, I take for granted that Silver and those he represents have established as fact the coexistence of market- and distributive-economics, such as I claim to discern, also, in the system of the Mishnah.

ceived those goods for other than market-considerations. Free disposition of property, in distributive economics, found limitations in
rules of an other-than market character, e.g., taboos with no bearing
upon the rational utilization of resources and individual decisions on
the disposition of assets.

If, for example, the private person who possesses property may not
sell that property to anyone of his choice, or may not sell it permanently, then the possessor of the property does not exercise fully free
choice in response to market conditions. The reason is that he cannot
gain the optimum price for the land at a given moment, set by
considerations of supply and demand for land or (more really) for the
produce of land of a particular character. Another, a co-owner, in
addition to the householder in possession of a piece of property, has
a say. The decisions of that other owner are not governed solely (or
at all) by market considerations. In the case of temple communities or
god-kings, land ownership and control fall into the hands of an entity
other than the private person, whether we call it the temple, priesthood, the government, the gild, or even the poor (!). Then, with
private property and its use placed under limitations and constraints
of an other-than-market origin, market trading is not possible:
"While there could be a considerable development of governmental
status distribution and some marginal barter, there could not develop
a price-making market."[9] Private property in land, not merely in
control of production, was required for the formation of a market-
economics in the conditions of antiquity, when ownership of production derived from ownership of land.

A further mark of the distributive economy—we shall see time and
again—is that transactions take the form of commodities of real
value, that is, barter, and not of symbolic value, that is, money. In
ancient Mesopotamia, with its distributive economics, while silver
was the medium of exchange, it was used in ingots and required
weighing at each transfer.[10] We shall repeatedly notice in our survey
of the working of the market that that conception dominates in the
Mishnah. Finally, in distributive economics, profit is a subordinate
consideration, and, in the hands of so sophisticated a mind as Aristotle's and as the Mishnah's authorship's, profit is treated as unnatural.
We need hardly review the positions already established to claim

---

[9] Davisson and Harper, p. 125.
[10] A. Leo Oppenheim, *Ancient Mesopotamia. Portrait of a Dead Civilization* (Chicago &
London, 1972: The University of Chicago Press), p. 87.

that, competing with market economics in the Mishnah is a fully-developed and amply instantiated, if never articulated, distributive economics. The Mishnah's authorship took over the economics of the Priestly Code, itself a restatement, in the idiom of the Israelite priesthood, of the distributive economics of temples and kings beginning with the Sumerians and Egyptians and coming down to the Greeks. Market-economics was an innovation, its economics not fully understood, at the time of the Priestly Code, and, for reasons of their own, the framers of the Mishnah fully adopted and exhaustively spelled out that distributive economics, even while setting forth a plan for the market life of "Israel" in the market enclaves of the larger society.

That old and well-established theory of economics, in the received Scriptures, is accurately represented by the Priestly Code, spelled out in the rules of the biblical books of Leviticus and Numbers, upon which the Mishnah's authorship drew very heavily. The economic program of the Mishnah, as a matter of fact, derived its values and also its details from the Priestly Code and other priestly writings within the Pentateuchal mosaic. Indeed, at point after point, that authorship clearly intended merely to spin out details of the rules set forth in Scripture in general, and, in economic issues such as the rational use of scarce resources, the Priestly Code in particular. The Priestly Code assigned portions of the crop to the priesthood and Levites as well as to the caste comprising the poor; it intervened in the market-processes affecting real estate by insisting that land could not be permanently alienated but reverted to its "original" ownership every fifty years; it treated some produce as unmarketable even though it was entirely fit; it exacted for the temple a share of the crop; it imposed regulations on the labor force that were not shaped by market-considerations but by religious taboos, e.g., days on which work might not be performed, or might be performed only in a diminished capacity.

In these and numerous other details, the Priestly Code stated in the Israelite-priestly idiom and in matters of detail the long-established principles of distributive economics and so conformed to thousands of years of that distributive economics that treated private property as stipulative and merely conditional and the market as subordinate and subject to close political supervision. Market-economics, coming into being in Greece in the very period—the sixth century B.C.—in which the Priestly Code was composed. Aristotle, as we have seen, theorized about an economics entirely beyond anyone's ken and stated as principle the values of an economics (and a social system, too) long since transcended. Market-economics, moreover, had been conveyed in practice to the Middle East a century and a half or so later by Alexander. By the time of the Mishnah, seven centuries after the Pentateuch was closed, market-economics was well-established as the economics of the world economy in which, as a matter of fact, the land of Israel and Israel, that is, the Jews of Palestine, had been fully incorporated. Theories of fixed value, distribution of scarce resources by appeal to other than the rationality of the market—these represented anachronisms. But, as our encounter with the prohibition against profit called "usury" has already shown us, the framers of the Mishnah developed a dual economics, partly market, partly distributive (but, as we shall see at length, with the distributive in the normative position). That is the fact that permits us to treat as matters of economic theory a range of rules that, in market economics, can have no point of entry whatsoever. Here an important qualification must register. It is an overstatement to claim that the Mishnah (or Scripture) set forth a theory of economics. In the Mishnah what we have is an account of economics in which there was room left for market action, so that the seeds for such a theory were planted; not more than that.

Only when we have grasped the general terms within which those concrete rules are worked out shall we understand the mixed economics characteristic of the Judaism of the Mishnah. A distributive economics, we now realize full well, is one that substitutes for the market as the price-fixing mechanism for the distribution of goods the instrumentality of the state or some other central organization, in the case of Scripture's economics in the Priestly Code of ca. A.D. 500, the Temple. In such an economics, in the words of Davisson and Harper,

> Such an organization will involve people's giving and receiving, producing and consuming, according to their status.[11]

Substituting for the market as a rationing device, the distributive economy dealt with "the actual things that are distributed," while in markets, "purchases and sales are usually made for money, not directly for other commodities or services."[12]

---

[11] Davisson and Harper, p. 115.
[12] Davisson and Harper, p. 123.

The definition of market-economics cited above calls to our attention the contrary traits of distributive economics, in particular, the intervention of authority other than the market in controlling both production and distribution of scarce goods. In the case of the Mishnah, the temple requires the recognition of the status of certain individual participants—in addition to the householder—in the transaction of distributing the material goods of the economy, in particular, portions of the crop. Priests, Levites, and the poor have a claim on the crop independent of their role in the production of the crop, e.g., in labor, in land-ownership, in investment of seed and the like. Not only so, but the market is not the main point of transfer of value. For material goods of the economy are directed to the temple—so in the theory of the Mishnah—without any regard for the working of the market. When it comes to the claim of the temple and priesthood upon the productive economy, there is no consideration of the exchange of material value for material value, let alone of the intervention of considerations of supply and demand, the worth of the goods as against the worth of the services supplied by the temple, and the like.[13] Davisson and Harper state of the market, "Even politically powerful interests and corporations must agree to accept the market decisions whether or not the outcome of a particular market transaction favors a person of high status."[14] But in the Mishnah, that simply is not so. And, we shall further observe, the temple taboos imposed upon the productive economy considerations of a non-market, non-productive character, in consequence of which the maximization of productivity forms only one among several competing considerations, and not the most important one, in the planning of production.

This brings us to the fundamental and necessary trait of market economics, private property. Davisson and Harper further state,

> Private ownership of property...is an essential condition of the market, but its existence does not guarantee that a market will exist or that contractual exchanges will occur [that can reach a conclusion with a simultaneous exchange of legally recognized rights in property and its use]. To be sure, in the absence of private property in the ancient Near

---

[13] True, the ideology of the Priestly Code insisted that payment of the temple taxes insured that God would "bless" the country with ample harvests, large herds, big families, and the like. But these factors in shaping of public opinion, therefore of considerations of demand, on their own do not—and cannot—fall into the classification of economic facts.

[14] Davisson and Harper, p. 123.

East and early medieval Europe, we find a distributive economic order. Is there, then, some relation of cause and effect between private property and the operation of a market? It seems that insofar as there is monolithic ownership and control of property (as in the Sumerian temple communities or with the god-king pharaoh of Egypt) there can be no development of a market. Where private property was so limited, there could be no market trading. While there could be a considerable development of governmental status distribution and some marginal barter, there could not develop a price-making market.[15]

That statement again draws our attention to the datum of the Mishnah, which informs, by the way, its economics as well: that God owns the land and that the household holds the land in joint tenancy with God. Private ownership does not extend to the land at all. That simple fact imposes upon the Mishnah's economic theory the principles of distributive economics, even while the framers of that theory address a world of market economics. It accounts for the mixed economics—market, distributive—of the Mishnah. Not only so, but as we just noted, the mortal owner-partner with God in the management of the household is not free to make decisions based solely on maximizing productivity; other considerations as to the use of land, as much as to the disposition of the crop, intervened.

Both Aristotle and the framers of the Mishnah addressed economic theory not only within the framework of distributive economics. They also acknowledged the facts of market-economics, even while reaffirming (each party in its own terms and context) the higher (Aristotle: "natural," thus more natural, Mishnah-authorship: "holy" and hence holier) value associated with distributive economics. For Aristotle, therefore, the criterion of correct economic action derived from a larger concern to uncover natural, as against unnatural, ways of conducting affairs, and for the sages of the Mishnah, the counterpart criterion appealed to the theology of the Priestly Code, with its conception of the magical character of the land the Jews held as their own, which they called (and still call) "the land of Israel." This land was subject to particular requirements, because God owned this land in particular and through the temple and the priesthood constituted the joint-owner, along with the Israelite householder, of every acre. But in so saying, I have jumped far ahead in my story. It suffices to note, at this point, that in what follows I therefore focus upon how the economics of the Mishnah fits into the larger world-view and way

---

[15] Davisson and Harper, pp. 124-125

of life set forth by the authorship of that document, and, further, how important components of that world-view and way of life in the context of the Mishnah correspond to what we know as economics today, a two-fold inquiry.

II. *The Marketplace*

The framers of the Mishnah understood the market to mean the market place, in which goods were transferred from one to another.[16] But that correct conception has no bearing upon market-economics. For the market as an economic theory finds definition in its function as the price-making mechanism, the system of rationing scarce goods and services, that forms the centerpiece of economics. A price making market regulates the supply of goods in relation to demand and channels demand in relation to supply.[17] The self-regulating market is a closed system; considerations of supply and demand operate without intervention of other matters, e.g., status, non-economic claims upon the supply of goods and services, and the like. To the self-regulating market system personal life is irrelevant: "Religious faith, social status, political belief, family life, loving, hating, gossiping, do not decide what will be done, except as they are part of the complex of motives and emotions creating demand for products."[18] When, however, considerations of caste-status interfere with demand and supply, the self-regulating market can no longer function, and a different economics comes into play. Then we may have a marketplace, but no market, that is to say, no market-economics. In order to understand what is at stake in the Mishnah's economic system seen as a function and aspect of its theological conviction, we have therefore to understand what we mean by market-economics as against distributive economics, in the case of the Mishnah's system, a distribution that takes place from the temple and through the priesthood.

In a (mere) market place (as distinct from a market-economy) the supply-demand-price mechanism is not free to operate. Price may be

---

    [16] Walter C. Neale, "The Market in Theory and History," in Karl Polanyi, Conrad M. Arensberg, and Harry W. Pearson, eds., *Trade and Market in the Early Empires. Economies in History and Theory* (Glencoe, 1957: The Free Press and The Falcon's Wing Press), p. 357.
    [17] Neale, p. 358.
    [18] Neale, p. 364.

fixed, for example, or merely traditional, and hence does not determine either the amount supplied or the amount demanded. It may not
even involve a price; it can be a meeting place for the transfer of goods
from group to group, and even barter is not required, since equivalence may be determined on entirely different principles.[19] Supply is
unaffected by price, demand unregulated, produce distributed by considerations not defined by the supply-demand-price mechanism at all.
When the rights of the priesthood or the poor to a share of the crop
affect the distribution of the crop, then the supply-demand-price
mechanism is no longer in play, and a different one, which we have
called distributive, governs. Neale lays out these choices, therefore:

> [a] Self-Regulating Markets, where demand, price and cost mutually
> and exclusively determined what shall be produced, how it shall be
> produced, and to whom it shall be distributed.
> [b] Market Places, which have nothing in common with Self-regulating
> Markets except that goods move from person to person....[20]
> Between these two types are other markets having some of the char-
> acteristics of Self-Regulating Markets. They may be price-making mar-
> kets in which considerations other than demand, price, and cost affect
> what is produced, how it is produced, and to whom it goes. They may
> be essentially market places which happen to make use of money but fix
> the prices.[21]

A mixed market characterized the economics of Judaism, a conclusion that supports the view that the self-regulating market forms the
exception, rather than the rule: "For most of its span man has lived
with fixed price markets, nonprice making Market Places, and perhaps mostly with economic systems best treated in terms of reciprocal
or redistributive institution whose essential character must be established independently of orthodox economic theory and with the help
of other disciplines more familiar with nonmarket institutions."[22]

This brings us to the distributive economy in its own terms. In
discussing what he calls "marketless trading," Polanyi states that
where we do not have the market, "the lack of functioning markets
calls for a substitute for markets."[23] Babylonia, he says, "possessed

[19] Neale, p. 367.
[20] Neale, pp. 370-1.
[21] Neale, p. 371.
[22] Neale, p. 371.
[23] Karl Polanyi, "Marketless Trading in Hammurabi's Time," in Karl Polanyi,
Conrad M. Arensberg, and Harry W. Pearson, eds., *Trade and Market in the Early
Empires. Economies in History and Theory* (Glencoe, 1957: The Free Press and The
Falcon's Wing Press), p.14.

neither market places nor a functioning market system of any description." Non-market trade, which characterized antiquity, "is in
all essentials different from market trade. This applies to personnel,
goods, prices, but perhaps most emphatically to the nature of the
trading activity itself."[24] The main point is simple: "'Prices' took the
form of equivalencies established by authority of custom, statute, or
proclamation. The necessaries of life were supposed to be subject to
permanent equivalencies...The chief difference between administrative or treaty trade on the one hand and market trade on the other
lies in the trader's activities themselves. In contrast to market trade,
those activities are here risk-free, both in regard to price expectation
and debtor's insolvency. Under such circumstances of no-risk business along administrative lines, the term 'transaction' hardly applies;
we will therefore designate this type of activity as 'dispositional.'"[25]
The determinative economic power lay not in the market but in "the
interaction between the two independent variables, palace and city,
[which] determined the entire course of the economic—and political—history of Babylonia."[26]

Enough has been said even at this initial stage in the exposition so
as to place the Mishnah's economic theory well within the framework
of distributive economics, even while according in concrete terms
with the requirements of market economics. It follows that we must
now recognize the Mishnah's economics as a through-going mixture,
in a single economic theory, of two incompatible theories economics.
For the Mishnah's economic theory introduces principles of distributive economics at odds with the workings of the market, and it does
so in an age in which, in point of fact, market economics prevailed.
Our task therefore is to describe the indications of the mixed character of the theory and to explain, in the Mishnah's details and by
uncovering the Mishnah's system's premises, the relationship between the mixed economics of the system and the larger systemic
principles of politics and social theory. For our ultimate goal is to
explain the relations between the system of production and distribution of scarce resources and other institutions in the society imagined
by the Mishnah's authorship, that is, the workings of the political

---

[24] Polanyi, p. 19.
[25] Polanyi, pp. 20-22, *pass.*
[26] A Leo Oppenheim, "A Bird's Eye View of Mesopotamian Economic History,'
in Karl Polanyi, Conrad M. Arensberg, and Harry W. Pearson, eds., *Trade and Market
in the Early Empires. Economies in History and Theory* (Glencoe, 1957: The Free Press and
The Falcon's Wing Press), p. 33.

economy in the interplay and balance between the market and society, relations of production, investments in capital goods and in consumer goods, and between merchants and producers, as these relationships are set forth in the Mishnah's vision of "Israel." When we can account for these matters, as I claim to be able to do in Chapter Seven, we shall know in its entirety and cogency the economics of Judaism.

If, therefore, we propose to describe, analyze, and interpret the economics of Judaism, we have to invoke the other of the two economics that have shaped the Mishnah's, that is, the economics of the palace- or temple-complex. That other mode of economics organized the rationing of scarce commodities around the palace or temple, which exercised a monopoly on production and trade, and which also organized the economic, military, political, and, of course, religious life of the society.[27] The distributive economics, resting on status and preferment, competed with market-economics because of the advent, in the Near and Middle East, of Greek, then Roman government. The Graeco-Roman world "was essentially and precisely one of private ownership," while the Near Eastern world for many centuries had emphasized not private trade and private manufacture but the organization of affairs by bureaucracy. Whether or not we should appeal for explanation of the difference to the requirement of large-scale social organization to make possible the river-valley civilizations of the Nile, Tigris and Euphrates (not to mention the Indus and Yellow rivers) is not pertinent here.[28]

For our purposes the simple point is that ancient Israel's priesthood set forth in its singular system principles of economic organization familiar for more than two thousand years before ca. 500 B.C., when the priestly conception (attributed to Moses at Sinai) reached written form in the Priestly Code and further drew together and made into a single statement what we now have as the Pentateuch. The conception of the market, the free market, is the innovation and came from without. The economics of the Mishnah, then, is the economics of a temple in a world in which the rules were made by the market, a world in which, indeed, market-economics in fact had predominated and in the aggregate had governed for some seven hundred years—indeed, the economics of a temple that then lay in ruins.

---

[27] Finley, *The Ancient Economy*, p. 28.
[28] Compare for the simplest statement of the matter Finley, p. 31.

III. *Antique Economics*

Before the middle of the fourth century an Athenian philosopher, Xenophon, better known for his *Anabasis*, wrote a treatise called *Oeconomicus*, a discourse on estate management, as Cicero, who admired the work and translated it into Latin, described it.[29] Framing matters in the contemporary mode, as a Socratic dialogue, Xenophon viewed economics as a practical and applied science only. In his economics he simply explained the management of an estate, the rules governing the preservation of wealth in the form of the land, the crafts of the household, land development, and agriculture. The work begins with the claim that estate management is the name of a branch of knowledge, like medicine, smithing, and carpentry: 'the business of a good estate manager is to manage his own estate well" (I.2). One who understands this art, even if he has no property of his own, can "earn money by managing another man's estate...and he would get a good salary if, after taking over an estate, he continued to pay all outgoings and to increase the estate by showing a balance."

Xenophon goes on to ask the abstract questions of theory that, in our world, we regard as economics, e.g., the definition of "estate," which we may render "wealth:"

> "But what do we mean now by an estate? Is it the same thing as a house or is all property that one possesses outside the house also part of the estate?"
> "Well I think that even if the property is situated in different cities, everything a man possesses is part of his estate" (I.5).

Land is wealth if it is worked in such a way as to produce a profit, the same is so of sheep: "The same things are wealth and not wealth, according as one understands or does not understand how to use them" (I.9). Xenophon then proceeds to ask how to increase one's estate (II.1ff.). The way, of course, is to spend less than one's income. And the way to do that is through sound estate management. Xenophon's advice is to keep everything in the right place. The householder (if I may call him that) does his business in town, then

---

[29] I follow E. C. Marchant, trans., *Xenophon. Memorabilia and Oeconomicus* (London, William Heinemann, and New York, G. P. Putnam's Sons, 1923). For a judgment upon Xenophon, note John Fred Bell, *A History of Economic Thought* (N.Y., 1967), p. 25 n. 15: "Economics students will find his essay...a very original work." Finley found less merit in the same work., and the great economics, Schumpeter and Polanyi, saw still less.

superintends the details of the work of the estate: planting, clearing, sowing, harvesting (XI.14-18). In all, one who is to be successful in the management of a farm must learn what to do and how and when to do it (XV:6). Xenophon's observations on economic activity, as distinct from economic analysis, led him also to recognize the division of labor:

> In small towns the same man makes couches, doors, ploughs and tables...and still he is thankful if only he can find enough work to support himself, and it is impossible for a man of many trades to do all of them well. In large cities, however, because many make demands on each trade, one alone is enough to support a man...Of necessity he who pursues a very specialized task will do it best.[30]

Can we deem Xenophon's thought to compare to economic theory as we know it? Hardly. The art of household management is not economics: "though that may involve 'economic' activity, it is misleading, and often flatly wrong, to translate it as 'economics.'"[31] We shall have to await our encounter with Aristotle to find discourse to which "economics" appropriately pertains. Aristotle joins *oikonomia* and *chrematistike*, the art of acquiring property, when he presents us with something we may read as an economic theory. In all, therefore, if we wish to invoke the word "economics," we will have to discuss farming; but farming in a far broader sense than mere agronomics is involved in economics, it is farming as the central action in the production of wealth by the unit of production comprising the household. To put matters simply, in the Greco-Roman world, a doctrine of economics will tell us how to manage wealth so as to increase it. And, since the same is so today, we must conclude that the Greeks and Romans understood economics just as we do: the theory of the management and increase of wealth.

To claim, that either the Mishnah's economics or Xenophon's, when viewed in tandem, corresponds to economics as we know the science exceeds the limits of the evidence. As Finley notes, "In Xenophon...there is not one sentence that expresses an economic principle or offers any economic analysis, nothing on efficiency of production, 'rational' choice, the marketing of crops."[32] But we shall

---

[30] Cyropaedia viii.2.5, quoted by M. I. Finley, "Aristotle and Economic Analysis," in M. I. Finley, ed., *Studies in Ancient Society* (London and Boston: Routledge and Kegan Paul, 1974), p. 27.

[31] Finley, "Aristotle and Economic Analysis," p. 41.

[32] op. cit., p. 19.

see in due course considerable thought, in the Mishnah and related writings, on precisely that: what brings about increased production or causes scarcity. A theory of economics, absent in Xenophon and in other Greco-Roman writers on agronomics,[33] encompasses and makes into a whole diverse observations on the right conduct of the household. Finley explains the absence of economics in a way important for our study. He first cites Erich Roll's definition of economics:

> If then we regard the economic system as an enormous conglomeration of interdependent markets, the central problem of economic enquiry becomes the explanation of the exchanging process, or, more particularly, the explanation of the formation of price.

Finley then states, "But what if a society was not organized for the satisfaction of its material wants by 'an enormous conglomeration of interdependent markets'? It would then not be possible to discover or formulate laws...of economic behavior, without which a concept of 'the economy' is unlike to develop, economic analysis impossible."[34]

The framers of the Mishnah for their part conceived interdependent realms that formed a single, mutually-interacting world of economic activity, in which scarcity found rational explanation, and economic action, reasoned guidance by laws subject to testing and replication. Finley explains that ancient society produced no economic theory because "ancient society did not have an economic system which was an enormous conglomeration of interdependent markets.... There were no business cycles in antiquity; no cities whose growth can be ascribed, even by us, to the establishment of a manufacture; no 'Treasure by Foreign Trade,' to borrow the title of Thomas Mun's famous work stimulated by the depression of 1620-24...."[35] But for their part sages recognized cycles of abundance and scarcity, if they did not call them business cycles; they explained the growth of cities by appeal to what was done in them, and understood a process of exchange between economic entities that by no grand leap of metaphor we may readily identify as foreign trade. Sages most certainly understood the principles of market-economics as they affected the market-mechanism and manipulated those principles to achieve their own goals, as the following story indicates:

---

[33] Finley, pp. 19ff.
[34] Finley, p. 22.
[35] Finley, pp. 22-23.

A pair of birds in Jerusalem went up in price to a gold denar.

Said Rabban Simeon b. Gamaliel, "By this sanctuary! I shall not rest tonight until they shall be sold at silver denars."

He entered the court and taught, "The woman who is subject to five confirmed miscarriages or five confirmed fluxes brings only a single offering, and she eats animal-sacrifices, and the rest of the offerings do not remain as an obligation for her."

And pairs of birds stood on that very day at a quarter-denar each, one hundredth of the former price, the demand having been drastically reduced]."

(M. Keritot 1:7K-Q).

The story shows that sages recognized the affect upon prices of diminished demand and were prepared to intervene in the market. For, as in the present case, cultic rules could create "artificial" demand, demand not related to the production-efficiency of the household. For example, if a rules for the selection of a sacrificial animal laid forth requirements difficult to meet in ordinary beasts, e.g., a particular color, or a beast that had never worked, then such beasts would command a far higher price than otherwise. And that is one way in which the non-economic considerations of the cult intervened in the normal working of the market. Good examples of this phenomenon derive from the red cow, to be burned for the creation of ash for purification-water, Num. 19:1ff.and tractate Parah. The rules are various, e.g. as to age, color, condition, and the cost of such a beast is measured in gold. At the same time, sages legislated for the market in such a way as to intervene and set aside the market-mechanism altogether. They favored one that, in due course, we shall identify as distributive.

There was exchange, the exchange bore concrete economic consequences, and understanding the world as sages portrayed in the Mishnah, we may penetrate into that rationality, that economic rationality, that, in their system, corresponds, point by point, with the rationality of economics as presently understood. To claim that economics takes place only when people invoke our explanations for phenomena of, e.g., trade, perceived by both them and us seems to me to construe economics in a needlessly limited framework.

IV. Aristotle

The only important thinker in economics in antiquity was Aristotle, and we do well by beginning with an account of the fundamental

intellectual context in which economics as Aristotle was to define the
field developed. For that purpose we review Polanyi's introduction to
Aristotle's economics in its larger context, because Polanyi, so it
seems to me, has taken the broadest perspective on Aristotle's economic thought:

> Whenever Aristotle touched on a question of the economy he aimed at
> developing its relationship to society as a whole. The frame of reference
> was the community as such which exists at different levels within all
> functioning human groups. In terms, then, of our modern speech Aris-
> totle's approach to human affairs was sociological. In mapping out a
> field of study he would relate all questions of institutional origin and
> function to the totality of society. Community, self-sufficiency, and jus-
> tice, were the focal concepts. The group as a going concern forms a
> community (*koinonia*) the members of which are linked by the bond of
> good will (*philia*). Whether *oikos* or *polis* [household or village], or else,
> there is a kind of philia specific to that *koinonia,* apart from which the
> group could not remain. *Philia* expresses itself in a behavior of reciproc-
> ity..., that is, readiness to take on burdens in turn and share mutually.
> Anything that is needed to continue and maintain the community, in-
> cluding its self-sufficiency... is "natural" and intrinsically right. Autarchy
> may be said to be the capacity to subsist without dependence on re-
> sources from outside. Justice...implies that the members of the commu-
> nity possess unequal standing. That which ensures justice, whether in
> regard to the distribution of the prizes of life or the adjudication of
> conflicts or the regulation of mutual services is good since it is required
> for the continuance of the group. Normativity, then, is inseparable from
> actuality.[36]

So, Polanyi goes on, for Aristotle trade is "natural" when it contributes to the community's self-sufficiency. The just price derives from
good will, *philia,* as a matter of reciprocity which is of the essence,
Polanyi says, of all human community. "Prices are justly set if they
conform to the standing of the participants in the community,
thereby strengthening the good will on which community rests...In
such exchange no gain is involved; goods have their known prices,
fixed beforehand."[37]

The theory of trade and price therefore elaborate the general theo-
rem of the human community: "Community, self-sufficiency and justice: these pivots of his sociology were the frame of reference of his
thought on all economic matters, whether the nature of the economy

---

[36] Polanyi, "Aristotle Discovers the Economy," p. 79.
[37] Polanyi, p. 80.

or policy issues were at stake."[38] The economy concerns the household in particular, that is, "the relationship of the persons who make up the natural institution of the household." Why the interest, then, in economics at all? The answer of Polanyi is that people had to link the requirements of communal existence and communal self-sufficiency to two matters of policy: trade and price. The fundamental notion was the self-sufficiency of the community, which yielded the principles that trade that served to restore self-sufficiency was in accord with nature, trade that did not was contrary; prices should strengthen the bond of community. That is why Aristotle called commercial trade "hucksterism," since this had no bearing upon the sociology that mattered to him. He had no perception of the price-mechanism of supply and demand. Commerce was administered and institutional.

The strength of Polanyi's reading of Aristotle's economics in the political and sociological context is that he sees Aristotle as composing a system; Polanyi therefore shows us how we for our part must read the economics of the Mishnah's Judaism as a systemic indicator and component, a systemic variable, understood only in context. So I find Polanyi important not only for his results but also his model of sound method. This brings us to the end of the matter: the premise of the analysis. The postulate of self-sufficiency governed all else; such trade as was required to restore self-sufficiency was natural and right, but that alone.[39] The fundamental principle, which will find ample instantiation, also, in the Mishnah's economics, is therefore natural self-sufficiency attained by the *oikos* and the *polis* made up thereof: political economy:

> The institution of equivalency exchange was designed to ensure that all householders had a claim to share in the necessary staples at given rates, in exchange for such staples as they themselves happened to possess. ...barter derived from the institution of sharing of the necessities of life; the purpose of barter was to supply all householders with those necessities up to the level of sufficiency...[40]

Accordingly, Aristotle's economic theory rested on the sociology of the self-sufficient community, made up of self-sufficient, if mutually dependent households—a contradiction in terms, since self-suffi-

---

[38] Polanyi, p. 80.
[39] Polanyi, p. 88.
[40] Polanyi, p. 90. I also consulted Karl Polanyi, *The Lifelihood of Man*, ed. by Harry W. Pearson (N.Y., 1977: Academic Press), see in particular pp. 145-276.

ciency and mutual dependency surely are not compatible as theories
of economic exchange. And all economics would rest on that same
torn, divided premise, as we shall see in the coming chapters.

With Polanyi's overview in hand,[41] let us return to the exposition
of matters in a more systematic way. Taking as our standpoint the
comparison of ancient to contemporary economic theory, we still
shall find no compelling reason to reject Cannan's view.[42] Nonethe-

---

[41] I find especially suggestive the comments of Sally Humphreys, "Thus, what
disturbed the philosophers of the fourth century was not, as Polanyi thought, an
increase in profit-making on price differentials, but the disembedding or structural
differentiation of the economy, leading to the application of 'economic' criteria and
standards of behavior in a wide range of situations recognized as economic above all
by the fact that money was involved; the old civic virtues of generosity and self-
sufficiency were being replaced by the market attitudes of the traders." See Sally C.
Humphreys, "History, Economics, and Anthropology: The Work of Karl Polanyi,"
History & Theory 1969., 8:165-212, p. 211. Note also Otto Erb, *Wirtschaft und Gesell-
schaft im Denken der hellenischen Antike* (Berlin, 1939), cited by her. Humphreys asks an
interesting question: "Would a decrease in the importance of market institutions in a
society which had reached this level of differentiation produce a revival of the attitudes whose loss Aristotle and Polanyi deplored? In the Roman Empire the state
increasingly had to take over the functions of the market system in order to ensure an
adequate supply and distribution of food to the city population. This change was
accompanied by an increase in private redistribution...The process of bureaucratiza-
tion of the economy and the rise under the influence of Christianity of new attitudes
to economic matters has never really been studied." We return to this question in the
concluding chapter.

[42] In addition to the works in the history of economic thought that are cited in the
notes below, I also consulted the following:

John Fred Bell, *A History of Economic Thought* (N.Y., 1967: Ronald Press), pp. 13-32.

Mark Blaug, *Economic Theory in Retrospect* (Cambridge, 1978: Cambridge University
Press).

William F. Campbell, "The Free Market for Goods and the Free Market for Ideas
in the Platonic Dialogues," *History of Political Economy* 1985: 17, 187-97.

Edwin Cannan, *A Review of Economic Theory* (London, 1929: P. S. King and Son),
pp. 1-4.

Henri Denis, *Histoire de la pensée économique* (Paris, 1966: Presses Universitaires de
France), pp. 7-57.

Barry Gordon, "Aristotle and Hesiod: The Economic Problem in Greek
Thought," *Review of Social Economy* 1963, 21-147-56.

idem., "Biblical and Early Judeo-Christian Thought: Genesis to Augustine," in S.
Todd Lowry, ed., *Pre-Classical Economic Thought. From the Greeks to the Scottish Enlightenment* (Boston, Dordrecht, Lancaster: Kluwer Academic Publishers, 1987), pp. 43-67.
This essay on rational action in regard to scarcity seems to me little more than a
paraphrase of ancient writings, with no important analytical side at all What we have
here is not economics but sayings on themes in some way deemed relevant to economics. I find no attention to how people understood the economy to work or even
to the conception, in ancient times, of an economy. All of the issues important to
Finley and Schumpeter, on which I have concentrated in this chapter, are neglected.
What I find is neither "economic analysis" nor any other kind of analysis. This is the

less, in context, we learn much about a system as thinkers work it out when we ask how system-builders think through issues urgent then and now, having to do, in specific and concrete ways, with value,

---

sort of writing that gives economic history a bad name for merely collecting and arranging. But Ohrenstein, cited below, is worse.

idem., *Economic Analysis before Adam Smith: Hesiod to Lessius* (N.Y., 1975: Barnes and Noble).

Alexander Gray, *The Development of Economic Doctrine. An Introductory Survey* (London, 1931: Longmans Green and Co.).

Sally C. Humphreys, "History, Economics, and Anthropology: The Work of Karl Polanyi, " *History and Theory* 1969, 8:165-212.

idem., "Economy and Society in Classical Athens," *Annali della Normale Superiore di Pisa* 1970, 39:1-26.

M. L. W. Laistner, ed., *Greek Economics* (N.Y., 1923).

Robert Lekachman, *A History of Economic Ideas* (N.Y., 1959: Harper & Brothers). This book is delightful reading.

S. Todd Lowry, ed., *Pre-Classical Economic Thought. From the Greeks to the Scottish Enlightenment* (Boston, Dordrecht, Lancaster: Kluwer Academic Publishers, 1987), pp. 7-76.

R. McKeon, *Introduction to Aristotle* (N.Y., 1947).

A. E. Monroe, *Early Economic Thought* (Cambridge, 1924).

Roman A. Ohrenstein, "Commentary: Some Socioeconomic Aspects of Judaic Thought," in S. Todd Lowry, ed., *Pre-Classical Economic Thought. From the Greeks to the Scottish Enlightenment* (Boston, Dordrecht, Lancaster: Kluwer Academic Publishers, 1987), pp. 68-76. This article is entirely uninformed on its subject, as the bibliography by itself proves. I am puzzled by the inclusion of these ramblings in what otherwise appears to me a very competent collection of essays under Lowry's editorship.

Roman A. Ohrenstein, "Economic Thought in Talmudic Literature in the Light of Modern Economics," *American Journal of Economics and Sociology* 1968, 27:185-96;

idem., "Economic Self-Interest and Social Progress in Talmudic Literature," *American Journal of Economics and Sociology* 1970, 29:59-70.

idem., "Economic Analysis in Talmudic Literature: Some Ancient Studies of Value," *American Journal of Economics and Sociology* 1979, 38:00-00.

idem., Some Studies of Value in Talmudic Literature in the Light of Modern Economics," *The Nassau Review* 1981, 4:48-70.

O. Popescu, "On the Historiography of Economic Thought. A Bibliography," *Journal of World History* 1964, 8:1ff.

Kurt Singer, "*Oikonomia*: An Inquiry into the Beginnings of Economic Thought and Language," *Kyklos* 1958, 11:29-54.

C. J. Soudek, "Aristotle's Theory of Exchange," *Proceedings of the American Philosophical Society* 1952, 5:96ff.

Joseph J. Spendler, "Aristotle on Economic Imputation and Related Matters," *Southern Economics Journal* 1955, 21.

Jules Toutain, *The Economic Life of the Ancient World* (N.Y., 1930).

Max Weber, *Economy and Society. An Outline of Interpretive Sociology*. Edited by Guenther Roth and Claus Wittich (Berkeley, 1978: University of California Press).

The bibliography in Lowry, pp. 27-30, seems to me particularly informative. I found very interesting the contrary position to that of Lowry, outlined by William F. Campbell in Lowry, pp. 31-42.

prices, markets, exchange, money and credit, not to mention the definition of wealth and, to revert to our simple definition, rational action in regard to scarcity.

From the time of Thucydides Greeks knew the difference between real wealth, e.g., fixed assets, real estate and the like, which, as a matter of fact, they valued, and liquid capital, that is, money wealth, and movables, which they did not value so highly. The war against Troy, for Thucydides, involved the wealth of the community measured in land and its products, quantities of arms, treasures, utensils, metal, and large houses and slaves. In the time of the Peloponnesian War wealth was in the form of coin, which could command all forms of real wealth.[43] But the economic theory of the important philosophers was primitive and unimportant in their larger work, which concerned politics, not economics. General principles with bearing on economic theory or policy, of course, can be identified, e.g., the recognition of the subjective and relative character of utility by Democritus.[44] Plato's ideas on economic subjects are random.[45] Joseph A. Schumpeter introduces Graeco-Roman economics with these words:[46] "...rudimentary economic analysis is a minor element —a very minor one—in the inheritance that has been left to us by our cultural ancestors, the ancient Greeks."[47] The reason for that fact, many maintain, is that prior to the development of the market, economic activities were insufficiently differentiated to attract particular attention.[48] As we already have observed, when writers such as

---

[43] William I. Davisson and Hames E. Harper, *European Economic History. I. The Ancient World* (N.Y., 1972: Appleton-Century-Crofts), p. 126.

[44] Henry William Spiegel, *The Growth of Economic Thought* (Durham, 1971: Duke University Press), p. 13.

[45] Spiegel, p. 15.

[46] Joseph A. Schumpeter, *History of Economic Analysis* (New York, 1954: Oxford University Press). Edited from Manuscript by Elizabeth Boody Schumpeter, p. 53.

[47] But we should not ignore Polanyi's quite contrary view, "He will be seen as attacking the problem of man's livelihood with a radicalism of which no later writer on the subject was capable—none has ever penetrated deeper into the material organization of man's life. In effect, he posed, in all its breadth, the question of the place occupied by the economy in society." See his "Aristotle Discovers the Economy," in Polanyi et al., eds., *Trade and Market in the Early Empires*, p. 66. He was, Polanyi says, "trying to master theoretically the elements of a new complex social phenomenon in statu nascendi," so p. 67. The debate on the value of Aristotle's economics carries us far from the purpose at hand, which is only to outline the ideas of economic theory in circulation in antiquity so as to place, within that outline, economic ideas found in the Mishnah.

[48] William I. Davisson and Hames E. Harper, p. 122. But that is the very point that Polanyi finds important.

Xenophon, all the more so the Romans later on, spoke about economics, they provided rules for household management, observation
rather than analysis.[49] When Aristotle refers to *Chrematistics*, he discusses pecuniary aspects of business activity.[50] Economic thought
forms a small part of a larger general philosophy of state and society.
Plato envisaged an essentially steady-state economy within a stationary population. In that context each person would have an inalien-
able allotment of land, given to a single heir, so as to keep the family
intact and its property intact as well.[51] He sought in general to preserve a social equilibrium, with a limited, and not increasing, number
of citizens. Plato proposed to describe economics within the context
of the ideal state, which was to be large enough "to allow appropriate
scope for the play of each man's natural talent."[52] That is why a small
state was adequate. In that context, Schumpeter describes Plato's
perfect state:

> Plato's Perfect State was a city-state conceived for a small, and, so far as
> possible, constant number of citizens. As stationary as its population
> was to be its wealth. All economic and non-economic activity was
> strictly regulated—warriors, farmers, artisans...being organized in per-
> manent castes, men and women being treated exactly alike. Govern-
> ment was entrusted to one of these castes, the caste of guardians or
> rulers who were to live together without individual property or family
> ties.[53]

Schumpeter explains the "rigid stationarity" by appealing to Plato's
dislike of "the chaotic changes of his time...Change, economic
change, was at the bottom of the development from oligarchy to
democracy, from democracy to tyranny." (We shall find a remarkable counterpart in the stasis, the steady-state world, which the framers of the Mishnah envision for themselves, in the setting of the
second century, after the catastrophic wars of 66-73 and 132-135.)
Plato's caste system rests upon the perception of the necessity of some
division of labor.[54] The emphasis lies upon the "increase of efficiency
that results from allowing everyone to specialize in what he is by

[49] See M. I. Finley, "Aristotle and Economic Analysis," in M. I. Finley, ed., *Studies in Ancient Society* (London and Boston: Routledge and Kegan Paul, 1974), p. 27.

[50] Schumpeter, p. 53.

[51] Lewis H. Haney, *History of Economic Thought. A Critical Account of the Origin and Development of the Economic Theories of the Leading Thinkers in the Leading Nations* (N.Y., 1920: Macmillan), pp. 51-81. Inheritance: pp. 54-5.

[52] Lekachman, *History of Economic Ideas*, p. 6.

[53] Schumpeter, p. 55.

[54] Schumpeter, p. 56.

nature best fitted for." Plato's theory of money is that the value of money is on principle independent of the stuff it is made of.[55]

Aristotle, the important economic thinker in antiquity,[56] proposed to think through the requirements of the state, and it is in that context, as with Plato, that his economic thought went forward, once more that political economy that characterizes the Mishnah's system as well. In that context, he dealt with property and the art of managing the household that we should find in Greek called by the word economics. The fundamental of Aristotle's economics is the distinction between *oikonomik*, economics, and *chrematistics*, the former involving wealth consumed in the satisfaction of wants and the use of commodities or goods for that purpose, the latter, wealth-getting, money-making, and exchange.[57] As to "chrematistics," there are both unnatural and natural ways of doing things, the former, barter, the latter, through retail trade and money-making. Exchange is natural, therefore. Things have a primary and a secondary use; the primary use of a shoe is for wearing, the secondary, for trading or exchanging. As to value, Plato had maintained that one "should not attempt to raise the price, but simply ask the value," while Aristotle introduces the notion of subjective value and the usefulness of the commodity: "In the truest and most real sense, this standard lies in wants, which is the basis of all association among men."

So Haney: "An exchange is just when each gets exactly as much as he gives the other; yet this equality does not mean equal costs, but equal wants."[58] In Book V of the *Nicomachean Ethics* and Book I of the *Politics*, economic analysis, a subsection of other matters, comes to the fore. In the case of the *Ethics*, Aristotle treats economics in the context of justice. Aristotle concerns himself with distributive justice, e.g., involving honors, goods, and other possessions. Justice means equality. Corrective justice involves private relations between individuals, in which "it may be necessary to 'straighten out' a situation, to rectify an injustice by removing the (unjust) gain and restoring the loss."[59] Aristotle had in mind fraud or breach of contract, not an "unjust"

---

[55] Schumpeter, p. 56.

[56] M. I. Finley, "Aristotle and Economic Analysis," in M. I. Finley, ed., *Studies in Ancient Society* (London and Boston: Routledge and Kegan Paul, 1974), p. 28.

[57] Haney, *History of Economic Thought*, p. 58..

[58] Haney, p. 60.

[59] Finley, "Aristotle and Economic Analysis," p. 30. Hereinafter all references to "Finley" are to this article.

price.[60] In the case of *Politics*, Aristotle addresses as the context in which (fair) exchange is discussed the forms of human association, which are the household and, made of households, the *polis*. Here he deals with issues of authority—dominance and subjection—which form the center of political theory. And in that context, he treats, also, property and acquiring it, asking whether "the art of acquiring" property is the same as "the art of household management," that *oikonomike* which we met earlier.[61] What Aristotle contributed to economic theory covers the economic organization of society, the matter of communal versus private property, and value and exchange.[62] On this latter topic, Spiegel states:

> Aristotle makes the important distinction between use and exchange, which later was to be expanded into the distinction between value in use and value in exchange. The true and proper use of goods...is the satisfaction of natural wants. A secondary or improper use occurs when goods are exchanged for the sake of monetary gain. Thus, all exchanges for monetary gain are labeled as unnatural. This includes specifically commerce and transportation, the employment of skilled and unskilled labor, and lending at interest. The exchange of money for a promise to pay back the principal with interest is considered the most unnatural one.... Lending at interest yields gain from currency itself instead of from another exchange transaction which money as a medium of exchange is designed to facilitate. Money begets no offspring; if nevertheless there is one—interest—this is contrary to all nature.[63]

The essential point, Spiegel notes, is the emphasis on the mutuality of give and take. Each gives to the other something equivalent to what he receives from the other.

Aristotle defines wealth as "a means, necessary for the maintenance of the household and the polis (with self-sufficiency a principle in the background), and, like all means, it is limited by its end."[64] Money makes possible exchange, and, as we just noted, Aristotle regards usury, e.g., consumer-loans, as one who practices the art of money-making in an unnatural way: "interest makes [money] increase," and that violates the purpose of money, which is merely for the sake of exchange. Exchange by itself is natural: "shortages and surpluses...were corrected by mutual exchange...When used in this

---

[60] Finley, p. 30.
[61] Finley, p. 40.
[62] Spiegel, p. 25.
[63] Spiegel, p. 26.
[64] Finley, p. 41.

way, the art if exchange is not contrary to nature, nor in any way a
species of the art of money-making. It simply served to satisfy the
natural requirements of self-sufficiency."[65] Profit is made no according to nature but at the expense of others. Aristotle in general insists
on the "unnaturalness of commercial gain," and Aristotle therefore
does not consider the rules or mechanics of commercial exchange:
"Of economic analysis there is not a trace."[66]

As Finley notes, we cannot translate the abstraction, "the
economy," into Greek—any more than, as we shall see, we can into
the Hebrew of the Mishnah (though we can into contemporary Hebrew). And Finley's judgment of Xenophon as an economist is already before us: "In Xenophon there is not one sentence that expresses an economic principle or offers any economic analysis,
nothing on the efficiency of production, 'rational' choice, the marketing of crops."[67] The argument of Lowry is that "the ancient Greeks
developed many of the analytical formulations basic to modern economic theory and that the discipline of economics is heavily indebted
to them."[68] We need not take up a position on that disagreement. It
is clear that Finley's judgment pertains to what we have in hand, not
what the Enlightenment economic theorists made of what the Greeks
left, which, it would appears, was more than meets the eye.

Aristotle simply divided the art of acquisition into *oikonomia* and
money-making, and what survived was the manual of the household
such as that of Xenophon's, which we noted above. From that kind
of writing, economics could not come, for the reason given by Finley:

> Without the concept of relevant "laws" (or "statistical uniformities" if
> one prefers) it is not possible to have a concept of "the economy."[69]

Finley's explanation for that fact is of interest to us, since it will in
due course provide perspective on the document of our concern. He
sees it is a consequence of the idea of *koinonia,* a perspective already
familiar to us in Polanyi's reading of matters. *Koinonia* was "a heavy
encroachment by political and status demands on the behavior of

---

[65] Finley, citing *Politics* 1257a24-30.

[66] Finley, p. 44.

[67] Finley, *The Ancient Economy*, p. 23. But others differ, for their own reasons, from
Finley's judgment. The issue is not one into which I can enter an opinion.

[68] S. Todd Lowry, ed., *Pre-Classical Economic Thought. From the Greeks to the Scottish
Enlightenment* (Boston, Dordrecht, Lancaster: Kluwer Academic Publishers, 1987), p.
11.

[69] Finley, p. 49.

ordinary Greeks...If we consider investment, for example, we immediately come up against a political division of the population that was
unbridgeable. All Greek states...restricted the right of land ownership
to their citizens...They thereby...erected a wall between the land,
from which the great majority of the population received their livelihood, and that very substantial proportion of the money available for
investment which was in the hands of non-citizens." The upshot was
that money-holding citizens turned to the land "from considerations
of status, not of maximization of profits." The upshot is that "the
non-citizens [kept off the land] of necessity lived by manufacture,
trade and moneylending."[70] The consequence—to abbreviate
Finley's interesting argument—is that "what we call the economy
was properly the exclusive business of outsiders."[71] Aristotle favors
private property over communal property on five grounds: progress,
peace, pleasure, practice, and philanthropy.[72] None of these has any
bearing upon economic theory or policy, except for progress: "Private property is more highly productive than communal
property...Goods that are owned by a large number of people receive
little care. People are inclined to consider chiefly their own interest
and are apt to neglect a duty that they expect others to fulfill."[73]

This rapid review of Aristotle on economics in hand, we turn to
the interesting analysis of Aristotle's economics by Joseph
Schumpeter. Aristotle, for his part, impressed Schumpeter as a figure
of "more than slightly pompous common sense."[74] But the analytic
intention makes him an interesting figure. As to economic problems,
the interest was subordinate; social and political analysis predominated in his program. Schumpeter described Aristotle's general contribution to social science in these words:

> [1] that not only was Aristotle, like a good analyst, very careful about
> his concepts but that he also coordinated his concepts into a conceptual
> apparatus, that is, into a system of tools of analysis that were related to

---

[70] Finley, p. 50. I cannot find an elaboration of this exceedingly interesting idea
elsewhere in Finley's corpus, but I also do not claim to be an expert on that corpus.
We shall want to know who is in, and who is outside of, the economics of the
Mishnah. I am inclined to find a considerable correspondence between Finley's
observation on Greek economics and what we shall presently observe concerning
Judaism's economics.

[71] Finley makes this point in *The Ancient Economy* as well.

[72] Spiegel, p. 28.

[73] Spiegel, p. 28. I bear no brief for the definition of "private property" here or
elsewhere.

[74] Schumpeter, p. 57.

one another and were meant to be used together...; [2] that...he investigated processes of change as well as states; [3] that he tried to distinguish between features of social organisms or of behavior that exist by virtue of universal or inherent necessity and others that are instituted by legislative decision or custom; [4] that he discussed social institutions in terms of purposes and of the advantages and disadvantages they seemed to him to present...[75]

Aristotle's economics, in *Politics* I 8-11 and *Ethics* v,5, present an economic analysis based upon wants and their satisfactions, so Schumpeter: "Starting from the economy of self-sufficient households, he then introduced division of labor, barter, and, as a means of overcoming the difficulties of direct barter, money—the error of confusing wealth with money duly coming in for stricture. There is no theory of 'distribution.'"[76]

As to value, Aristotle distinguished value in use and value in exchange and saw the latter as derivative of the former. But there was no theory of price and the ethics of price. This theory of an intrinsic or fixed value, which will concern us, is treated by Schumpeter in these words:

> Aristotle...sought for a canon of justice in pricing, and he found it in the 'equivalence' of what a man gives and receives. Since both parties to an act of barter or sale must necessarily gain by it in the sense that they must prefer their economic situations after the act to the economic situations in which they found themselves before the act—or else they would not have any motive to perform it—there can be no equivalence between the 'subjective' or utility values of the goods exchanged or between the good and the money paid or received for it.[77]

Schumpeter denies that Aristotle has in mind "some mysterious Objective or Absolute Value of things that is intrinsically inherent in them and independent of circumstances or human valuations or actions. He argues that Aristotle "simply thought of the exchange values of the market, as *expressed* in terms of money, rather than of some mysterious value substance *measured* by those exchange values." Schumpeter sets forth his reading of matters as follows: "...his concept of the just value of a commodity is indeed 'objective,' but only in the sense that no individual can alter it by his own action."

We find ourselves on familiar ground. For example, Schumpeter

---

[75] Schumpeter, p. 58.
[76] Schumpeter, p. 60.
[77] Schumpeter, p. 61.

explains that an equality in every act of exchange or sale involves the following:

> If A barters shoes for B's loaves of bread, Aristotelian justice requires that the shoes equal the loaves when both are multiplied by their normal competitive prices; if A sells the shoes to B for money, the same rule will determine the amount of money he ought to get. Since...A would actually get this amount, we have before us an instructive instance of the relation which, with Aristotle himself and a host of followers, subsists between the logical and the normal ideal and between the 'natural' and the 'just.'[78]

In denying the notion of an objective or absolute or intrinsic value, Schumpeter calls that notion "a metaphysical entity most welcome to people with philosophical propensities and most distasteful to people of a more positive' type of mind." In due course, we shall see how that notion comes to expression in the economics of Judaism. There, the conception of a true value is not murky or obscure but expressed in simple and plain words: concrete rules, which people (merchants in the market) had to observe.

Taking the view of money opposite to that of Plato, Aristotle took the position that the exchange of goods and services in barter is not always possible. People may not have what other people want, and so have to offer in exchange, or accept in exchange, "what one does not want in order to get what one does want by means of a further act of barter (indirect exchange)." But money is not wealth, it is merely a medium of exchange; money does not satisfy the necessities of life.[79] It is merely the inconvenience of barter that yields the development of money as a medium of exchange. Some commodities, such as metals, may serve better than others.

As Schumpeter presents matters, Aristotle's theory of money therefore regards money as principally a medium of exchange. In order to serve as a medium of exchange in markets of goods, money itself must be one of those goods: "it must be a thing that is useful and has exchange value independently of its monetary function,...a value that can be compared with other values:"[80]

> Thus the money commodity goes by weight and quality as do other commodities; for convenience people may decide to put a stamp on it in

---

[78] Schumpeter, p. 62. This is a difficult matter, and Schumpeter has had his critics. It is not an issue to which I can make a contribution.

[79] Spiegel, p. 27.

[80] Schumpeter, pp. 62-3.

order to save the trouble of having to weight it every time, but this stamp only declares and guarantees the quantity and quality of the commodity contained in a coin and is not the cause of its value.[81]

Money then takes the place of barter, but it is a kind of barter (a matter of importance to us presently).[82] Money was a medium of exchange and eliminating the need to barter. That was the natural use of money:

> "There are two sorts of wealth-getting:...one is a part of household management, the other is retail trade. The former necessary and honorable, while that which consists in exchange is justly censured; for it is unnatural, and a made by which men gain from one another. The most hated sort...is usury, which makes a gain out of money itself, and not from the natural object of it. For money was intended to be used in exchange, but not to increase at interest"
>
> (Politics 1258a-b).[83]

Since Plato held, as Schumpeter reads him, that the value of money is independent of the stuff of which it is made, we have here a point of difference to direct to the Mishnah's authorship as well: how do they understand the theory of money, in our terms, intrinsic to the coin, as with Aristotle, or functional and imputed, therefore extrinsic, as with Plato. The third point of interest in Aristotle, besides the question of true value and the theory of money, concerns interest. Schumpeter states, "Aristotle accepted the empirical fact of interest on money loans and saw no problem in it."[84] He made no effort to classify loans by their purposes and saw no difference between a consumer-loan and a producer-loan. He simply condemned interest ("usury" in all cases), "on the ground that there was no justification for money, a mere medium of exchange, to increase in going from hand to hand...But he never asked the question why interest was being paid all the same." Aristotle had no theory of interest."[85]

The Mishnah came forth in a Greek-speaking world, and its framers appear to have known little or no Latin. Lekachman sums up the opinion of all historians of economic theory: "Rome developed nothing new in the sphere of theoretical economics."[86] He goes on to say, "There was much the same relation between their economic writings

---

[81] Schumpeter, p. 63.
[82] Davisson and Harper, p. 128.
[83] Cited by Davisson and Harper, p. 132.
[84] Schumpeter, p. 65.
[85] Schumpeter, p. 65. Contrast Spiegel's account, cited above.
[86] Lekachman, *History of Economic Ideas*, p. 15.

and economic analysis as between the art of business management and the abstruse economic theory of the graduate school." His survey of maxims makes the point full well. Lekachman and others find little of theoretical interest in the economics in the sense of household management left by Cato, Cicero, and others. While well informed as to the facts of the agricultural economy in the narrow sense just now introduced, namely, rules of household management and agronomy, they presumably had no access to technical treatises on the rural economy, e.g., producing wine and oil and grain, such as were written by Cato, Varro, and Columella, in the tradition of Xenophon.[87] When we consider the economic thought upon which the Mishnah's authorship drew, the premises that guided concrete decisions, we shall not find reason to regret their slight knowledge of the then-ruling state and its economics, for, in Schumpeter's judgment, all that has to be explained in Roman economics is the absence of analytic work.[88]

V. *Ancient Israel: The Heritage of Scripture*

In seeing matters in this way, I do not mean to suggest that the sages of the Mishnah knew what Greek philosophers or Roman legislators had to say about economics or about transactions of an economic character, respectively. For it remains to make the simple and obvious observation that the authorship of the Mishnah did not have to go to an academy to study philosophy or to a law school to learn economics, such as the field, in theory, consisted of in Greco-Roman antiquity. They had only to open Scripture to find out a variety or rules and regulations of an economic character.[89] A very brief re-

---

[87] Haney, p. 74.

[88] Schumpeter, pp. 66ff.

[89] Gordon in S. Todd Lowry, ed., *Pre-Classical Economic Thought. From the Greeks to the Scottish Enlightenment* (Boston, Dordrecht, Lancaster: Kluwer Academic Publishers, 1987), pp. 65-67, provides some bibliographical references on the matter. He refers to the following items:

R. Barraclough, *Economic Structure in the Bible* (Canberra, 1980)

Roland deVaux, *Ancient Israel* (London, 1978: Darton, Longman and Todd)

Frederick C. Grant, *The Economic Background of the Gospels* (N.Y., 1973 [1926]: Russell and Russell).

Ben Nelson, *The Idea of Usury* (Chicago, 1969: University of Chicago Press).

Robert North, *Sociology of the Biblical Jubilee* (Rome, 1954: Pontifical Biblical Institute).

minder of the well-known topics calls to the fore recognition of how much, within Scripture, will have found resonance for the Greek and Roman philosophers and legislators. Mosaic law recognized usury and within Israelite life forbade it (Dt. 23:19-20). One might not lend money upon usury nor lend commodities for increase (Lev. 25:37). Usury meant lending things over time and getting back three shekels for two or three bushels for two.[90] Lending was a kind of charity (Dt. 15:7-9). Scripture also provided evidence for the conception of a just price, at least so far as just weights and measures are concerned. A well-regulated market does not permit adulteration of produce. The notion that real wealth meant real estate came to expression, e.g., in the saying, "He who tills the soil will have plenty of food" (Prov. 12:11). Trade and commerce were deemed things outsiders, e.g., Canaanites, did (Hos. 12:7-8).

That economic gain formed only one consideration in the organization of society is shown by the institution of the Sabbath, the Seventh or Sabbatical and the Jubilee Years, on which, in the former instance, people had to cease from productive labor, and, in the latter, the land had to be left fallow. Yet these rules were persistently explained as part of the economic plan governing the world, and, in consequence of keeping these rules, people would prosper, while, not keeping them, they would suffer want. Accordingly, we have to take account of taboos, particularly as these affected production and the organization of units of production, as part of the economics of the system. Take for example the affects of the seventh year, perceived to reduce agricultural production, but not presented as part of the natural economy. In the seventh year the land had a Sabbath; leaving the fields fallow, we know, restored fertility. But in that same year debts were remitted (Dt. 15:4). That had nothing to do with the fertility of the soil, and the social utility of the remission of debts was not self-evident to lenders, who declined to lend money as the seventh year approached, so the Mishnah's authorship claims. Not only so, but, like Plato, the Pentateuchal legislators imagined that land was to remain within its "original" family, so that at the fiftieth year, everyone might return to his possession (Lev. 25:13). Land was to be rented, not permanently sold.

Reflection on these and similar rules, however, viewed as systemically not inert but indicative, will have led to such conceptions as that

---

[90] Haney, p. 37.

"stationarity" of society so important to Plato and, as a matter of fact, also to the framers of the Mishnah, and that broader spectrum of thought about the question of intrinsic or true value that interested Aristotle and his continuators. But these rules did not yield economics, in the sense in which Aristotle presented something very like the economics, as a matter of theory, that such exemplary minds as Schumpeter and Finley take to form a counterpart of interest to modern economic theory. They yielded only ethics, and, as we have seen in our swift glance at the New Testament and Fathers of Christianity, ethics is not the same thing as economics. There was no Christian economics, but as I shall now show, point by point, there assuredly *was* in the initial statement, set forth by the Mishnah's authorship, an economics of Judaism, that is to say, an economic component, of considerable theoretical sophistication, of the Judaism of the dual Torah.

VI. *The Mishnah's Market-Economics: The Household*

Like Aristotle's economics, the Mishnah's system thought in terms of social, not economic, categories and actors, beginning with the integrated social economics of the household. What Polanyi says of Aristotle applies also to the Mishnah-sages:

> In terms, then, of our modern speech Aristotle's approach to human affairs was sociological. In mapping out a field of study he would relate all questions of institutional origin and function to the totality of society.
> Polanyi, "Aristotle Discovers the Economy," p. 79.

The encompassing and ubiquitous householder, a technical classification defined presently, is the Mishnah's authorship's most characteristic invention of social thought. Ancient Israelite thinkers of the same order, e.g., the priestly authorship of Leviticus, the prophetic schools that produced Isaiah's and Amos's conceptions, discerned within, and as, "Israel" classes identified by their sacerdotal and genealogical traits and functions, in relationship to other classes; or a mixed multitude of poor and rich. We look in vain in the imagination of the Deuteronomist writers in their several layers for a conception of an "Israel" composed of neatly arranged farms run by landowners, of families made up of households, an Israel with each such household arrayed in its hierarchy, from householder on top, to slave on bottom. But that is how the authorship of the Mishnah sees things, a

vision quite its own in the context of thought on society and economy
in all Judaic writings of antiquity.

Indeed, while the Pentateuchal composite encompasses issues of
political economy, its focus is not upon those issues. By contrast,
critical to the system of the Mishnah is its principal social entity, the
village, comprising households, and the model, from household to
village to "all Israel," comprehensively describes whatever of "Israel"
the authorship at hand has chosen to describe. We have therefore to
identify as systemically indicative the centrality of political economy
—"community, self-sufficiency, and justice"—within the system of
the Mishnah. It is no surprise, either, that the point of originality of
the political economy of the Mishnah's system is its focus upon the
society organized in relationship to the control of the means of production—the farm, for the household is always the agricultural unit.
I cannot point to any other systemic statement among the Judaisms
of antiquity, to any other Judaism, that, in the pattern of the
Mishnah, takes as its point of departure the definition of an "Israel"
as a political economy, that is, as an aggregation of villages made up
of households.[91] We should look in vain for a counterpart in the Dead
Sea library, for example.

We realize, in the context of social thought of ancient times, that
this systemic focus upon political economy also identifies the
Mishnah's authorship with the prevailing conventions of a long ago
age and a far-away land. For, as we recall from the preceding chapter, it was a world in which thinkers represented by Aristotle took for
granted that society was formed of self-sufficient villages, made up of
self-sufficient farms: households run by householders. But, we know,
in general, nothing can have been further from the facts of the world
of "Israel," that is, the Jews in the land of Israel, made up as it was of
not only villages but cities, not only small but larger holders, and,
most of all, of people who held no land at all and never would.

Let us now turn, in the context of a world of pervasive diversity, to
the Mishnah's authorship's fantastic conception of a simple world of
little blocks formed into big ones: households into villages, no empty
spaces, but also, no vast cities (for a reason characteristic of the
system as a whole, as I shall specify presently). In the conception of
the authorship of the Mishnah, community, or village (*polis*) is made
up of households, and the household (*bayit/oikos*) constituted the

---

[91] And that statement encompasses, as a matter of fact, even the two Talmuds that
took shape around the exegesis of the Mishnah.

building block of both society or community and also economy.[92] It follows that the household forms the fundamental, irreducible, and of course, representative unit of the economy, the means of production, the locus and the unit of production.

We should not confuse the household with class-status, e.g., thinking of the householder as identical with the wealthy. The opposite is suggested on every page of the Mishnah, in which householders vie with craftsmen for ownership of the leavings of the loom and the chips left behind by the adze. The household, rather, forms an economic and a social classification, defined by function, specifically, economic function. A poor household was a household, and (in theory, the Mishnah's authorship knows none such in practice) a rich landholding that did not function as a center for a social and economic unit, e.g., a rural industrial farm, was not a household.[93] The household constituted "the center of the productive economic activities we now handle through the market."[94] Within the household all local, as distinct from cultic, economic, therefore social, activities and functions were held together. For the unit of production comprised also the unit of social organization, and, of greater import still, the building block of all larger social, now also political, units, with special reference to the village.

In the conception at hand, which sees Israel as made up, on earth, of households and villages, the economic unit also framed the social one, and the two together composed, in conglomerates, the political one, hence a political economy (*polis, oekos*), initiated within an economic definition formed out of the elements of production. The Mishnah makes a single cogent statement that the organizing unit of society and politics finds its definition in the irreducible unit of eco-

---

[92] The household is a theoretical construct, not a concrete entity, in Mishnaic discourse. The laws of the Mishnah recognize full well that people lived cheek by jowl in houses set into courtyards in the village, and when it wishes to refer to places of residence, it does not speak of households and householders, but rather, residents of a courtyard, e.g., throughout tractate Erubin. That makes all the more interesting the usage of "householder," surveyed presently.

[93] See Ramsay MacMullen, *Roman Social Relations* (New Haven, 1966: Yale University Press), on wealth and the landowner, pp. 5ff. Absentee landownership is not within the purview of this discussion, and I find it difficult to see how the Mishnah's authorship takes account of enormous wealth in the form of absentee-holdings. Quite to the contrary, if a piece of land is held, as to usufruct, for three years, without the intervention of a putative owner, the squatter acquires ownership; that is precisely the opposite of a law meant to accommodate the absent-landowner.

[94] Lekachman, *History of Economic Ideas*, p. 3.

nomic production. The Mishnah conceives no other economic unit
of production than the household, though it recognizes that such
existed; its authorship perceived no other social unit of organization
than the household and the conglomeration of households, though
that limited vision omitted all reference to substantial parts of the
population perceived to be present, e.g., craftsmen, the unemployed,
the landless, and the like.

The social foundation of the economy of the Mishnah therefore
rested on the household,[95] which in turn formed the foundation of
the village, imagined to comprise the community of households, in
the charge of small farmers who were free and who owned their
land.[96] In fact, the entire economics of Judaism in its initial statement
addresses only the social world formed by this "household." Time
and again we shall find no economics pertaining to commercial,
professional, manufacturing, trading, let alone laboring persons and
classes. The household is a technical term, and landless workers,
teachers, physicians, merchants, shopkeepers, traders, craftsmen, and
the like cannot, by definition, constitute, or even affiliate with, a
household: an amazingly narrow economics indeed. The definition of
the market and its working, the conception of wealth, viewed within
both market- and distributive-economics, sort out affairs only as these
pertain to the household. That is to say that the economics of
Judaism omitted reference to most of the Jews, on the one side, and
the economic activities and concerns of labor and capital alike, on
the other. These formidable components of the social entity, "Israel,"
the system at hand simply treats, from an economic perspective, as
null. In the pages of the Mishnah, as we shall see, no one else but the
householder and his establishment plays a role in economic thinking—except in relationship to that householder. In passages in which
proprietary responsibilities and obligations play no role, e.g., matters
having to do with the cult, religious observance, the sacred calendar,

---

[95] The same is true of the social foundation for the metaphysics of the Mishnah.
For discussion of the role of the householder in the critical matter of classification,
and the central place of the will or intention of the householder in the working of the
system of the Mishnah, see Howard Eilberg-Schwartz, *The Human Will in Judaism.
The Mishnah's Philosophy of Intention* (Atlanta, 1986: Scholars Press for Brown Judaic
Studies, in particular, pp. 145-180. Eilberg-Schwartz quite properly treats the householder, the one assumed to own beasts that have been set aside by the owner for a
particular sacrifice, as the central figure in the issues at hand.
[96] I paraphrase Claude Mossé, *The Ancient World at Work* (N. Y., 1969: W. W.
Norton & Co.), translated from the French by Janet Lloyd, p. 49.

and the like, by contrast, the Mishnah's authorship speaks not of the householder but of "he who...," or "a man," or other neutral building blocks of society, not defined in terms of proprietary status of land-holding.

Whether, in fact, all "Israel," that is, the Jews in the land of Israel, lived in such villages or towns, made up within the neat array of householders and their dependents, we do not know. But, self-evidently, it is difficult to imagine a reality composed of such a neat arrangement of building blocks, and the Mishnah's authorship itself recognizes that the village consisted of more than households and householders, while at the same time recognizing that "household" forms an abstract entity, not a concrete and material social fact, as we shall see in a moment. Not only so, but, even without such passages, we should find it exceedingly difficult to imagine a society made up wholly of small-holders and people assembled in neat array around them, a society or community lacking such other social categories as large holders, landless workers in appreciable numbers, craftsmen laboring for a market independent of the proprietary one of householders, and numerous other categories of production and classifications of persons in relationship to means of production. That makes all the more indicative of the character of the Mishnaic system and its thought the fact that we deal with a single block, a single mold and model. In imagining a society which surely encompassed diverse kinds of person, formed in various molds and in accord with a range of models, the authorship of the Mishnah has made its statement of its vision, and that vision dictates the focus and requirements of analysis.

That "household" as the building block of village, and the two the fundamental units of Israelite society, forms an abstraction, not a concrete physical or social entity, e.g., a house separate from other houses, a family distinct from other families, is easy to demonstrate. It simply is not a concrete description of how people really lived, for instance, of the spatial arrangements of houses, or of the social units made up of distinct household-houses (or, as we shall see in a moment, families as equivalent to households). The supposition of Mishnah-tractate Erubin, for example is that households are in a village, that people live cheek by jowl in courtyards, and that they go out into the fields from the village. So the notion of the isolated farmstead is absent here. That is important in relating the household to the village, *oikos* to *polis*, and it also shows how abstract is the conception of the household, since it is conceived as a unit, even though, in fact, the households were not abstract and distinct units at all.

The singularity of the household was not in its physical let alone genealogical traits, but in its definition as a distinct unit of economic production. What made a household into a household was its economic definition as a whole and complete unit of production, and the householder was the one who controlled that unit of production; that economic fact made all the difference, and not that all of the household's members were related (that was not the fact at all), nor that all of them lived in a single building distinct from other single buildings. What made the household into a social unit was the economic fact that, among its constituents, all of them worked within the same economic unit and also worked in a setting distinct from other equivalently autonomous economic units. In the idiom of the Mishnah, they *ate* at the same table, and eating should be understood as an abstraction, not merely as a reference to the fact that people sat down and broke bread together. That seems to me an interesting point. Nor is the "household" of which courtyards are composed only Jewish. "He who dwells in the same courtyard with a gentile, or with an Israelite who does not concede the validity of the *erub*...," so Mishnah-tractate Erubin 6:1. This concession of householder-status to the gentile neighbor in a courtyard once more underlines the economic, and functional, definition of the household, rather than its genealogical and cultic meaning.[97] The premise of "the household" as an autonomous unit and building block of society contradicts the realities described by the Mishnah's framers. The social unit of "the courtyard" has numerous cultic affects but it is not an economic unit and is not recognized as such. "The householder" has no counterpart in "the shareholder of a courtyard." The one forms an economic unit, the other does not, e.g., M. Er. 6:3-4, the courtyard is a cultic unit, bearing no economic weight whatsoever. This again shows us

---

[97] By contrast, the household formed for purposes of sharing a lamb sacrificed for the Passover-offering by definition cannot include a gentile, and a convert must be circumcised before he can partake of the meat of the shared beast. Here "household" stands for cultic family, not economic unit of production. It is a social category lacking economic dimensions, hence "householder" never occurs in the context of the Passover sacrifice and who shares in it. We find instead an odd usage, *haburah* or circle of participants. Once more the precision of word-choice in the pages of the document points to the systematic conventions that governed the formulation of the document.

the precision in use of the term "household" and "householder"—the precision, but also the utter abstraction of the conception.

Two divisions, the first and the fourth, alone form the center of discourse on the householder, those on Agriculture and Civil Law, Zeraim and Neziqin, respectively. These are the divisions that take up transactions in property and the disposition of wealth. Divisions that attend to cultic considerations, the fifth, sixth, and second, e.g., the everyday conduct of the cult in Holy Things, considerations of purity and impurity at home or in the cult, Purities, rules governing special occasions in the sacred calendar, Appointed Times; as to the third division, on the conduct of family affairs, Women, the authorship tends not to refer to the householder as the subject of a great many predicates. The reason is that at issue in the specified divisions, Agriculture and Civil Law, are the disposition of wealth, which is agricultural, on the one side, and commercial transactions, real estate and farming exchanges, and the like, on the other. These form the center of discussion of issues we should today deem economic, such as marketing and prices, laws governing real estate transactions and labor law, selling and buying, disposition of wealth and conduct in the use of material goods. The other divisions do not concern the disposition of material property and, it follows, also do not find occasion to speak frequently of householders in particular. They then find a different fixed subject for diverse predicates, one that is economically neutral and applicable to persons without reference to considerations of property-holding. It follows that the householder forms a very specific classification of person, bearing particular definition, and playing a role in discourse mainly when issues of property and substance have to be sorted out.

Let me give a few examples of the foregoing generalization (omitting reference to the division on Civil Law). The householder or proprietor occurs in passages in which reference is made to the farmer, in charge of his estate and disposing of the produce of his field, as at M. Pe. 3:5 and elsewhere in that tractate, and throughout other tractates in the division of Agriculture, e.g., Terumot, Maaserot, Maaser Sheni, Orlah; in passages on business partnerships among farmers, e.g., M. Er. 7:5; rights of householders to make use of their own houses, M. Bes. 3:5; provision of support for various persons at the table of a householder, M. Git. 5:4; the intention of the householder, here meaning the owner of a beast, hence, the farmer, concerning the disposition of his beast, M. Me. 6:1; household objects, M. Kel. 15:1, and the like. By contrast, we only rarely find allusions to the householder in such tractates as Shabbat, on Sabbath law, and Erubin, on the same (and here peoples' residences are very much in evidence, but the common point of reference is to dwelling in a courtyard, made up of many houses. These results of a very rough survey of ways in which the word *baal* is used in the Mishnah suggest that most, though not all, usages bearing the sense of house-holder, that is, *baal habbayit*, occur in the divisions on Agriculture and Civil Law, with parallel usages to the ones in Agriculture occurring also in Holy Things, and for the same reason, namely, the farmer's disposition of his crop.[98]

By "household" the framers of the Mishnah meant one kind of unit of production, specifically, a landholder engaged in agriculture, essentially a subsistence farm, but one with some relationships to a sheltering market beyond. The household must be understood as an abstraction, not as a concrete and material social entity. This is in two senses. First, while the household was assumed to be a farming unit, in fact the householder was imagined to live in town. There was no distinction between country and town that affected the definition of the householder. Second, while the household was treated as an autonomous entity, in fact, the law takes for granted that houses are formed into courtyards, and none is taken to be freestanding. While, therefore, the householder formed the autonomous and formative entity of economic life, and while the household was taken to consti-tute an identifiable entity, the household did not exist in separation from other households, and hence its autonomy and distinct status were a matter of theoretical, not concrete and material reality—a systemic fact alone.

As to the actualities of social life, the fundamental premise of all social discourse in the Mishnah is that Israelites lived side by side in villages or towns, the latter different from the former only by size. For

---

[98] Cf. Chayim Yehoshua Kasovsky, *Thesaurus Mishnae.* (Jerusalem, 1956). I. *A-G*, pp. 400-401. s.v. *baal*. There are further usages, e.g., the plural, *to, with, and,* and so on. The statements given here suffice to make the point. My argument does not rest the frequency or distribution of word-usages. But the householder, as a matter of fact, is so specific and technical a category that he appears only in passages to which ownership of a domain, that is, a unit of production, is at issue. All of the Division of Purities, for one important example, manages to deal with individual Jews ("Israel-ites") without once invoking the figure of the householder in particular. The preci-sion in terminology of the authorship of the Mishnah, the selection of particular categories or classifications for particular purposes, is impressive.

cultic reasons the system could not differentiate between small and large settlements, e.g., towns and cities, or villages and towns (except for adventitious purposes), but only between Jerusalem and everywhere else. For the system formed an exercise in the study of sanctification and its affects, and therefore, for systemic reasons, Jerusalem was *the* "city," and its "city-ness" derived from its holiness.[99] "City" therefore formed a cultic, not a sociological, category. It follows that the distinction between town and village, or town and country made no difference whatsoever to the authorship of the Mishnah. That represented a distinction that made no systemic difference. What mattered is solely that people are assumed to have lived in villages, small or large, and there alone.

Within the villages any Israelite male[100] was assumed to possess the potentiality to become a householder, that is, in context, the master of a domain, a landholder. The single most important difference between the conception of the householder in the Mishnah and the conception of landholding in the Greek thinkers who in theoretical economics formed the counterpart to the Mishnah's authorship lies in that one fact, as Finley states it: "It was the Greeks who most fully preserved for citizens a monopoly of the right to own land, and who in the more oligarchic communities restricted full political rights to the landowners among their members."[101] While, as we shall see, the householder by definition always is assumed to own land and command a domain, the Mishnah knows as full citizens of the kingdom for which it legislates landless persons, and when it speaks of cultic or ritual responsibilities, all the inhabitants of a town, or other categories to which landholding bears no point of relevance whatsoever, the Mishnah speaks of "a man," or "he who...," or "all the residents of the town," and not of "the householder."

---

[99] Compare Finley, *The Ancient Economy*, p. 123. I mean to emphasize that in the pages of the Mishnah we cannot distinguish town from country.

[100] I cannot point to a passage in which it is assumed that a woman is head of a household. But women can own land and engage in the economic activities of a household, so I imagine that, in theory, the system could accommodate a woman-householder. In practice, however, a woman is always taken to relate to a man, as her father, then her husband, alive, and, when deceased, to her male sons or stepsons, who support her as a widow. It is further taken for granted that when a woman is divorced or widowed, she will remarry within a brief spell, so that the marriage-settlement is meant to tide her over until she does so. Or she reverts to her "father's house," which means that she rejoins the household of her father, alive, if dead, of her brothers.

[101] Finley, *The Ancient Economy*, p. 95.

In fact the householder is a classification serving solely economic components of the system of Judaism as a whole. It is a technical term, which occurs when we speak of either market- or distributive-economics, in the fourth and first divisions of the document, respectively. In most of the Mishnah, the differentiation between house-holder and any other Jew made no difference, and therefore the language of the document ignored that differentiation, invoking it only where for systemic reasons the distinction made a difference. Take, for instance, "And all the villagers nearby gather together there" for the reaping of the first sheaf of grain for the *omer*" (M. Men. 10:3-4), a formulation which accords no differentiation to householders, because it is not relevant. Where the identification of a person as a householder does affect the law, the authorship does specify that an actor is a householder, as in the following: "The potter who brought his pots into the courtyard of the householder without permission, and the beast of the householder broke them— the householder is exempt" (B. B.Q. 2:3A-C). Here we must know that the householder forms an actor, because the rights of ownership of a domain are involved. That point is critical to our understanding of the householder, who is not the same as any Israelite for the Mishnah's authorship, but who forms the center of interest, the prin-cipal unit of productive activity, the classification of person who forms the building block of the village. The political economy of the Mishnah is defined by the householder forming with other house-holders a village: *oikos* become *polis*.

The Mishnah's theoretical conception of its ("Israel's") political economy, that is, the village or *polis* comprising the household or *oikos*, therefore is neat and orderly, with all things in relationship and in proper order and proportion. True, the political economy encom-passed other economic entities, in particular, craftsmen and traders, both of them necessary for the conduct of the household. But each was placed into relationship with the household, the one as a neces-sary accessory to its on-going functioning, the other as a shadowy figure who received the crops in volume and parceled them out to the market. The relationships between householder and craftsman, or between householder and hired hand, are sorted out in such a way as to accord to all parties a fair share in every transaction. Responsi-bilities of the one as against the other are spelled out. The craftsman or artisan, to be sure, is culpable should he damage property of the householder, but that judgment simply states the systemic interest in preserving the present division of wealth so that no party to a trans-action emerges richer, none poorer. All that is at stake here is the preservation of wealth in its established proportions, so that one party does not emerge richer, another poorer, from any transaction or encounter. Along these same lines, laws governing relations of em-ployer to employee hold that each party must abide by its commit-ment and that the party which changes the terms of an agreement bears liability to the other. The prevailing custom must be observed in the absence of an explicit stipulation. One example of the care with which the rights of all parties are taken into account is at M. B.M. 9:12, which insures that when the worker has laid claim on his wages, the claim is paid. But the employer may pay by giving a draft on a storekeeper or money changer.

The household therefore should be understood in three aspects. First, it marked a unit of production, and the householder was the master of the means of production: it was a farming unit in particu-lar. That defines the household's indicative character and quality. Bu, second, the household also marked a unit of ownership, and the householder was the master of a piece of property. Commanding means of production meant, in particular, running a farm. Finally, third, the household also encompassed an extended family-unit. But a household—affines living together in a house,—without land sim-ply was no household. For the term bore economic, not only social, valence: a family unit by itself did not constitute a household. That is one side of the matter. The other is equally critical. Merely owning a piece of property, without using the property for farming, also did not make a man into a householder. To be a master of a household, one exercises ownership and control of real property, and real prop-erty of a particular kind, namely, a farm. Ownership is not an ab-straction; it is defined and delimited by function.

The authorship of the Mishnah cannot conceive of ownership in the absence of productive use of property and therefore calls into question the permanence of absentee ownership, e.g., the organiza-tion of properties not managed by their owners. That negative con-ception forms the underside of the positive conception of the house-holder in charge of a unit of production and in command (of course) of the means of production. We uncover the negative definition, specifically, when we consider how the authorship of the Mishnah disposes of the absentee landowner who holds property but does not work it or oversee its productive utilization. It follows that ownership is not an abstract right, divorced from all material function, but entails management and productive utilization of property, and the householder embodies that command and everyday mastery of the means of production in a way in which the absentee landowner cannot. Ownership in the present context, identified as it is with supervision and utilization and usufruct, derives from the premise of the householder as active manager and administrator of the means of production, and ownership finds its meaning in the command of the unit of production. That conception of ownership in such material terms makes its appearance only within the details of the law, to which we now turn.

To understand what follows, we have to note that one might demonstrate ownership of a property not only by presenting a valid deed but also by showing, without such a deed, that one has made use of the property for a span of uninterrupted time. Ownership is proved not only by documentary evidence, but also by testimony that a person has held, and enjoyed the usufruct of, a property for a given period of time. One therefore may lose his deed and retain the land, or, conversely, retain the deed and lose the land to a competing claim resting upon deed and usufruct. The upshot is to render impossible long-term investment in land held fallow, and, at least difficult, absentee landownership of vast and essentially unsupervised properties. For if an absentee owner, e.g., living in a distant city, held a valid deed but a claimant could show that, absent such a deed, he had full control of the usufruct of the field for a period of three years, the squatter had every possibility of gaining ownership of the land. The law at hand points toward the conception of usufruct, therefore, as a means of establishing ownership, with the concomitant notion that absentee ownership, not joined by supervision let alone usufruct, might prove parlous. That is not to suggest the notion that a person with no valid claim to land might seize a property from an absentee landlord; the claimant-squatter had the obligation to establish a prima facie claim, e.g., the deed has been lost. But the upshot is the same. Let us consider the detailed exposition of the notion of ownership established through usufruct.

3:1-2

A. [Title by] usucaption of (1) houses, (2) cisterns, (3) trenches, (4) caves, (5) dovecotes, (6) bath-houses, (7) olive-presses, (8) irrigated fields, (9) slaves,

B. and anything which continually produces a yield –

C. title by usucaption applying to them is three years,
D. from day to day [that is, three full years].
E. A field which relies on rain – [title by] usucaption for it is three years,
F. not from day to day [Danby: "And they need not be completed"].
G. R. Ishmael says, "Three months in the first year, three in the last, and twelve months in-between – lo, eighteen months [suffice]."
H. R. Aqiba says, "A month in the first year, a month in the last, and twelve months in-between – lo, fourteen months."
I. Said R. Ishmael, "Under what circumstances?
J. "In the case of a sown field.
K. "But in the case of a tree-planted field, [if] one has brought in the [grape-crop], collected the olives, and gathered the [fig] harvest,
L. "lo, these [three harvests] count as three years."
Mishnah-tractate Baba Batra 3:1

A. There are three regions so far as securing title through usucaption [is concerned]: Judea, Transjordan, and Galilee.
B. [If] one was located in Judea, and [someone else] took possession of his property in Galilee,
C. [or] was in Galilee, and someone took possession [of his property in Judea, it is not an effective act of securing title through usucaption –
D. unless [the owner] is with [the squatter] in the same province.
E. Said R. Judah, "They specified a period of three years only so that one may be located in Ispamia, and one may hold possession for a year, people will go and inform [the owner] over the period of a year, and he may return in the third year."
Mishnah-tractate Baba Batra 3:2

The basic rule is somewhat complicated, because there are some secondary issues inserted into the primary declaration of A, C. The first is the consideration at B, and the second, D/F. F bears a very heavy gloss at G-H; I-L further gloss A-C. The point is that anything which is valuable and is allowed to remain in the hands of a person for a period of three years is assumed to belong to that person. If there were a valid claim against the squatter, any other party would have made it within the specified time. This principle is implicit at A, made explicit at B, and then restated by Ishmael at I-L. The difference between D and F is explained by G-H. The only reason that E is specified is so that the stated difference may be made explicit, since otherwise E belongs perfectly happily in the opening catalogue. It follows that a good bit of editorial work has been done to produce Mishnah-tractate Baba Batra 3:1 as we have it. Mishnah-tractate Baba Batra 3:2 contains no problems, because A is neatly spelled out

by B-D. Then Judah, E, ties Mishnah-tractate Baba Batra 3:1 and
Mishnah-tractate Baba Batra 3:2 together to make sense of the specification both of the period of years of usucaption and the stipulation
on the location of the contesting owner of the property. It would be
difficult to improve upon this spelling out of a complex set of materials, particularly through the exegetical sayings of Ishmael, Mishnah-
tractate Baba Batra 3:1 I-L and Judah, Mishnah-tractate Baba Batra
3:2E. will state its principle of ownership. What is relevant is the
notion that ownership is not abstract and not unconditional but concrete and related to on-going and hands-on administration: usufruct,
not merely deed, proves a right of ownership or functional access and
use, as the case may be. And that definition of ownership draws us
once more within the orbit of the household as a unit of production,
distinct, on the one side, from the family, but different, on the other,
also from the industrial-scale agricultural unit. What makes a household a household is possession *and usufruct* of land: both. And, I repeat, it is the household that defines the building block of the village,
the oikos of the polis, and in the systemic statement of the Judaism of
the authorship of the Mishnah, the formation of households into
villages comprises "all Israel."

What we see is a system in which a principal and generative consideration derives from control of the means of production. For, as a
matter of fact, the political economy of the Mishnaic system proves
partial and highly selective, and the economic unit dictated the perception, also, of the political.[102] The householders form a social group
which also is an economic one, but, as a matter of fact, the householders comprise a group seen all in all as the basic productive unit of
society, around which other economic activities function. That is the
starting point for the politics of the system, but, more consequen-
tially, the entire frame of reference of the system as a whole finds its
definition in the issue of who controls the means of production that
the system deems important. There is, after all, production of other
than agricultural products, for example, goods and services. Production encompasses making pots and chairs, but the craftsman does not
define an economic unit, e.g., a householder, if he does not, also, own
and farm (perhaps through day-laborers) land as well. The shop-

---

[102] The implications of such a perception for "all Israel," the modes of conceiving
the nation as a whole in its land—these questions will win our attention in the next
part of my studies on the political economy of Judaism. They are not important here.

keeper or tradesman, the merchant and capitalist also command wealth and engage in productive activities of all kinds. But they too do not control those means of production that make a difference to the system of the Mishnah. But in due course, when we consider the Mishnah's version of distributive economics, we shall understand why the framers of that system consider land, and only land, to form the productive entity society, so that only the householder, who is by definition a landholder who farms, constitutes the focus of consideration and concern. And when we grasp the reason for that fact, we shall see precisely why the system delivers its message and makes its statement through economics, and why the framers of the system had no meaningful choice, given what they wished to say, but to address issues of production, in the household, as well as of market and of wealth.

To move forward, now, let me describe in general terms the householders as the framers of the Mishnah perceive them. Householders were farmers of their own land, proprietors of the smallest viable agricultural unit of production—however modest that might be. They stood at the center of a circle of a sizable corps of dependents: wives, sons and daughters-in-law, children and grandchildren, slaves, servants. Others came within their circle, though were not part of the hierarchy of the household, such as craftsmen and day-laborers. Accordingly, at the outer fringes of the Mishnah's household were such ancillary groups as craftsmen and purveyors of other specialties, wagon-drivers, providers of animals and equipment for rent, moneylenders, shopkeepers, wholesalers of grain and other produce, peddlers and tradesman, barbers, doctors, and butchers, scribes and teachers, and, of course, the ultimate dependents, the scheduled castes: priests, Levites, and the poor. This list tells us, as we shall observe presently, that, in the system of the Mishnah, the economic classes of traders and other purveyors of liquid capital ("capitalists"[103]) were essentially outside of the conceptual framework of the Mishnah's political economy.

As principal and head of so sizable a network of material relationships, the householder saw himself as pivot of the village, the irreducible building block of society, the solid and responsible center of it all. In the corporate community of the village, other components, each

---

[103] I use the word to mean those who invest wealth in on-going money-making ventures; I do not mean to innovate in any way.

with a particular perspective and program of pressing questions, surely existed, and the householder could have been only one of these. But in the perception of the Mishnah, he was the one that mattered. And the Mishnah's framers could not have erred, for the householder controlled the means of production and held the governance of the basic economic unit of the village as such. Traders and peddlers and others outside of the economy of the household also functioned outside of the framework of the village as such; they were not settled, landed, stable, and that too by definition. Their economic tasks required them to travel from place to place, for instance, to collect produce and resell it at the market. But so far as the Mishnah's picture of society in its economic relationships and productive aspects is concerned, the whole held together through the householder. This is expressed in mythic terms: one who owns something is the only one who may sanctify it, and that is, in heaven, God, and, on earth, the householder, the farmer.

The householder for his part functioned as the principal economic actor, who made the decisions for himself and his dependents. The household forms one of the two social constructs of the Mishnah's world, the other being the village, which is made up of households, thus the *oikos* and the *polis*, or, as I said just before, the foundations for the political economy envisaged by the document. By household, however, we must understand a considerably larger social unit than we do today, and as an economic unit, also, the household aimed at a self-sufficiency of production and consumption and exchange that in the world we know we cannot confuse with the contemporary family, extended or nuclear, and household unit. In personnel, the household encompassed the householder, the head of the unit, his wives and children, slaves and day-workers and other employees utilized as needed, as well as his livestock, movables, and real property. The householder's will reigned supreme, and his decisions governed.

The definition of the householder in wholly economic terms, as the one who commands the means of production—or, more accurately, those means of production of which the framers of the system propose to take note—proves critical. When we see the household as an economic unit, the social side to matters loses all importance; indeed, it hardly matters whether or not we introduce considerations of kinship, and, as noted, co-residence is not always essential in designating a person a part of a household. Propinquity means only that one is within a reasonable distance, which is to say, is part of the village, but the village takes form out of households and is (merely) a construction of households, having no other independent social forms. Accordingly, the entire system knows as its basic social unit and building block what is also its basic economic unit, defined as the component of the whole that controls the means of production, the "farm" in all that "farm" entails.

While, in recent anthropological thought,[104] the distinction between the household and the (mere) extended family has come under question, in the case of the Mishnah's world, the former is assumed to encompass the latter.[105] The framers of the Mishnah, for example, do not imagine a household headed by a woman; a divorced woman is assumed to return to her father's household. The framers make no provision for the economic activity of isolated individuals, out of synchronic relationship with a household or a village made up of householders. Accordingly, craftsmen and day laborers or other workers, skilled and otherwise, enter the world of social and economic transactions only in relationship to the householder. The upshot, therefore, is that the social world is made up of households, and, since households may be made up of many families, e.g., husbands, wives, children, all of them dependents upon the householder, households in no way are to be confused with the family.[106] The indicator of the family is kinship, that of the household, "propinquity or residence."[107] And yet, even residence is not always a criterion for membership in the household unit, since the craftsmen and day laborers are not assumed to live in the household-compound at all.

---

[104] I follow Donald R. Bender, "A Refinement of the Concept of Household: Families, Co-residence, and Domestic Functions," *American Anthropologist* 1967, 69:493-504. Bender summarizes his thesis as follows: "Families (as specific types of kinship structures), co-residence, and domestic functions are three distinct kinds of social phenomena." Families are not to be identified with households. They are to be distinguished from households, "the former having as their referent kinship, the latter having as their referent presumably propinquity or locality. In fact, this distinction left the job only half done, since the concept of the household, as formulated, included two distinct kinds of social phenomena: co-residential groups and domestic functions. While all three very frequently correspond, they also can and do vary independently."

[105] MacMullen's identification of the landholding with the family, *op. cit.*, p. 27, as "the hard shell around the peasant community," is an error. I find his account impressionistic and conceptually rather thin. It is not clear that he read any anthropological writing on the definition of the household.

[106] Bender, p. 492: "The thesis to be presented here presupposes the complete conceptual divorce of the household from the family."

[107] Bender, p. 493.

Accordingly, the household forms an economic unit, with secondary criteria deriving from that primary fact.

And the householder, then, stands for the economic unit encompassing families of a variety of relationships to the householder (or no blood-relationship at all), and he controls the means of production and also constitutes the unit of production, as we noted at the very outset. There is another side to it to be sure. If brothers eat together at their father's house(hold) but live in separate houses, they are for cultic purposes regarded as distinct and not as a single household-unit (M. Er. 6:7A-B). But that is a minor refinement. The point is clarified as follows: A father and his sons, wives, daughters-in-law, and man-servants and maid-servants, when no one else lives with them in the courtyard, do not have to prepare an *erub* (T. Er. 5:10A-C), since they are regarded for cultic purposes as a single unit. And that seems to me to be the basic conception of the family in relationship to the household.

But having defined the household as fundamentally the economic unit of Israelite society imagined by the Mishnah's authorship, we should not obscure how the economic relationship penetrates into all other human relationships within that society. Quite to the contrary, only when we understand that control of the means of production bears consequence for the shape and structure of all other relationships in society shall we fully understand what is at stake in our understanding of the householder and his systemic position. The householder's will proves paramount in all matters, not only economic decision-making; this is shown most dramatically by the systemic opposite of the householder, the slave, whose will is never effective.[108] In this regard we should not confuse the rights of the male as householder with the male's rights and power as husband. To be sure, the householder, always a male, as husband has cultic rights over his wife, e.g., in confirming or nullifying her vows. But, more to the point, as master of the household, he controls all property, so that, for the duration of the marriage, the wife's and minor children's property is his to do with as he wishes. And his disposition of real property through gift or inheritance is equally autocephalic. True, biblical rules of primogeniture may apply as to the disposition of estates. But the household may give away the property and in doing so may ignore the received rules of testamentary succession.

---

[108] Paul Flesher-McCracken, *Oxen, Women, or Citizens? Slaves in the System of the Mishnah* (Atlanta, 1987), *pass.*

That total control of real wealth, vested in the householder, then sets aside the inherited laws that dictate in some measure who gets what. In these and other ways, we see, while the householder to begin with commands the economic unit, that same control bears secondary implications for his control of other than economic matters as well. We may therefore affirm that the one who controls the means of production and who defines and constitutes the unit of production effectively is in charge of all else.

In its identification of the householder as the building block of society, to the neglect of the vast panoply of "others," "non-house-holders," the Mishnah's authorship reduced the dimensions of society to only a single component in it. But that is the sole option open to a system that, for reasons of its own, wished to identify productivity with agriculture, individuality in God's image with ownership of land, and social standing and status, consequently, with ownership and control of the land which constituted the sole systemically-conse-quential means of production. Now if we were to list all of the persons and professions who enjoy no role in the system, or who are treated as ancillary to the system, we have to encompass not only workers—the entire landless working class!—but also craftsmen and artisans, teachers and physicians, clerks and officials, traders and merchants, the whole of the commercial establishment, not to mention women as a caste. Such an economics, disengaged from so large a sector of the economy of which it claimed, even if only in theory, to speak, can hardly be called an economics at all. And yet, as we have seen and shall realize still more keenly in the coming chapters, that economics bore an enormous burden of the systemic message and statement of the Judaism set forth by the authorship of the Mishnah.

Fair and just to all parties, the authorship of the Mishnah nonetheless speaks in particular for the Israelite landholding, proprietary person. The Mishnah's problems are the problems of the householder, its perspectives are his. Its sense of what is just and fair expresses his sense of the givenness and cosmic rightness of the present condition of society. These are men of substance and of means, however modest, aching for a stable and predictable world in which to tend their crops and herds, feed their families and dependents , keep to the natural rhythms of the seasons and lunar cycles, and, in all, live out their lives within strong and secure boundaries on earth and in heaven. This is why the sense of landed place and its limits, the sharp line drawn between village and world, on the one side, Israelite and gentile, on the second, temple and world, on the third, evoke metaphysical correspondences. Householder, which is Israel, in the village, and temple, beyond, form a correspondence. Only when we understand the systemic principle concerning God in relationship to Israel in its land shall we come to the fundamental and generative conception that reaches concrete expression in the here and now of the householder as the centerpiece of society.

In this regard, therefore, the Mishnah's economics finds within its encompassing conception of who forms the *polis* and who merely occupies space within the polis its definition of the realm to which "economics" applies. In the economics of Judaism the householder is systemically the active force, and all other components of the actual economy (as distinct from the economics) prove systemically inert. As such, of course, the economics of Judaism can hardly qualify as an economics at all, since the theory ignores most of the actuality. But in the context of Aristotle's conception of economics, the Mishnah's theory of the economy qualifies full well. In this context, we do well to point to what is at stake in an economics that treats as economically beyond the realm of theory the generality of participants in the actual economy. The stakes are well defined by Finley when he observes, "All Greek states...restricted the right of land ownership to their citizens...They thereby...erected a wall between the land, from which the great majority of the population received their livelihood, and that very substantial proportion of the money available for investment which was in the hands of non-citizens." In this setting of the Judaism of the Mishnah, we find ourselves in a theory of the political economy in which anyone might own land, even though few did, and the result is no different from that to which Finley points. If only an Israelite male may own land and exercise usufruct over it (wives who own land cede to their husbands usufruct of the bulk of their estates for the duration of the marriage), then we find ourselves entirely with Finley's framework; all we need do is change "citizen" to "free, male, adult Israelite," and the Greek economic theory proves entirely a comfortable fit.

But then what of the economically active members of the polis, the one who had capital and knew how to use it? If they wished to enter that elevated "Israel" which formed the social center and substance of the Mishnah's Israel, they had to purchase land. Then matters again turn out as they did in the Greek cities described by Finley. For in both cases the upshot was that money-holding citizens turned to the land "from considerations of status, not of maximization of profits." The upshot is that "the non-citizens [kept off the land] of necessity lived by manufacture, trade and moneylending."[109] The consequence—to abbreviate Finley's interesting argument—is that "what we call the economy was properly the exclusive business of outsiders."[110] In the case of the economics of Judaism, by contrast, economic theory encompassed the market as much as the household. The same message pertained, the same statement resonated. We shall now see precisely what it was. For when we know what we now do about the household, we can describe a steady-state society, but we have not yet gained access to what the system, through its disposition of the household as the systemically active unit of economic activity, proposed to lay down as its statement concerning, and through the creation of, that steady-state, stationary world.

VII. *The Market*

How did Aristotle define the market? Finley provides the correct passage, as follows:

> Exchange by itself is natural: "shortages and surpluses...were corrected by mutual exchange...When used in this way, the art of exchange is not contrary to nature, nor in any way a species of the art of money-making. It simply served to satisfy the natural requirements of self-sufficiency."
>
> Finley, citing *Politics* 1257a 24-30

In everyday transactions as the framers of the Mishnah sorted them out, they proposed to effect the vision of a steady-state economy, engaged in always-equal exchanges of fixed wealth and intrinsic value. Essentially, the Mishnah's authorship aimed at the fair adjudication of conflict, worked out in such a way that no party gained, none lost, in any transaction. The task of Israelite society, as they saw it, is to maintain perfect stasis, to preserve the prevailing situation, to secure the stability of not only relationships but status and standing. To this end, in the interchanges of buying and selling, giving and taking, borrowing and lending, transactions of the market and exchanges with artisans and craftsmen and laborers, it is important to

---

[109] Finley, *Ancient Economy*, P. 50.
[110] Finley makes this point in *The Ancient Economy* as well.

preserve the essential equality, not merely equity, of exchange. Fairness alone does not suffice. Status quo ante forms the criterion of the true market, reflecting as it does the exchange of value for value, in perfect balance. That is the way that, in reference to the market, the systemic point of urgency, the steady-state of the polity, therefore also of the economy, is stated. The upshot of their economics is simple. No party in the end may have more than what he had at the outset, and none may emerge as the victim of a sizable shift in fortune and circumstance. All parties' rights to and in the stable and unchanging political economy are preserved. When, therefore, the condition of a person is violated, the law will secure the restoration of the antecedent status.

To understand the economics at hand, we have to recall the two distinct principles at play, market-economics as against distributive economics. We can identify two modes of carrying out the functions of the market, state or temple intervention in the organization of production and in distribution, or the working of a market. The former invokes matters of status governing people's giving and receiving, producing and consuming, the latter, a free-market-exchange.[111] The third option, an utterly self-sufficient economy, was simply not available. But the Mishnah, with its keen interest in questions of price and its active intervention in production and distribution[112] simply ignores the working of the market, even while intervening in enormous detail in the determination of prices.

To begin with we distinguish the notion of a market from the theory of market-economics, the economic theory in which the market works as a rationing device, responding to supply and demand through the mechanism of price so as to control the rational disposition of scarce resources. In antiquity, markets surely existed, much as MacMullen describes matters in the following passage: "The peasants must have not too long a journey to bring their produce to the city...They leave before dawn for the city, their donkeys laden with cereals, olives, grapes, or figs, depending on the season. Towards seven or eight o'clock the bazaar is full...Towards ten o'clock time to think of one's own purchases—the few items of luxury which the land does not yield...Towards eleven, the city is emptied and every-

---

[111] Davisson and Harper, *European Economic History* (New York, 1972: Appleton-Century-Crofts). I. *The Ancient World*, p. 115. Henceforward: Davisson & Harper.

[112] A matter we shall examine in detail in Chapter Seven.

one starts home."[113] That description of the market bears no relationship to the abstract mechanism, embodied to be sure in the market,
we mean when we speak of market-economics.

To understand the definition of the market as an economic category,
we turn, as usual, to Davisson and Harper, who state:

> A market is a series of transactions by buyer and seller where prices
> measure the scarcity of a commodity on the market. A high price indi-
> cates that the quantity of a given commodity on a market is low when
> measured against buyer demand; lower prices indicate that the quantity
> is great when measured against buyer demand...It is an essential point
> of market trading that the political authority of the society (government,
> temple, gilds) gives up control of production and distribution to this
> impersonal mechanism.[114]

The alternative to market-economics is a system of redistribution, or
distributive economics. In such a system scarce goods are collected
and allocated not by the market but by some other authority, e.g.,
political and religious.

This alternative system is described very simply as follows: "Redistribution requires central collection and allocation by a higher authority, but can be seen as satisfying the basic unit's need for services
and goods which it cannot produce alone by providing an institution-
alized channel for the pooling of resources."[115] In the case of the
Judaism of the dual Torah in the statement of the Mishnah, distributive economics is represented by the intervention, into the production
and disposition of scarce resources, of God's authority through the
priesthood. The rationality of distributive economics rests on the
conviction of God as the co-owner, with Israel, therefore with Israelite householders, of the holy land, hence all farmers or householders
are joint tenants, with God, in their fields and produce, and that
consideration introduces the justification, within the system, for distributive economics, right along side market economics. In due
course we shall further examine the workings of this alternative to
market-economics. But the present definition serves to warn us that
the representation of the market in the Mishnah will not wholly
accord with the requirement of the market, since market-decisions
are based, for the Mishnah, upon non-market considerations. In fact,

---

[113] Ramsay MacMullen, *Roman Social Relations*, p. 54.
[114] Davisson and Harper, p. 123.
[115] Sally C. Humphreys, "History, Economics, and Anthropology: The Work of
Karl Polanyi," *History & Theory* 1969., 8:165-212, p. 205.

as we have already come to suspect, and will soon find amply demonstrated, the Mishnah's framers invoked an economics of a wholly distributive character, even while legislating for a market-economy, which they fully recognized and understood in its crucial points.

Accordingly, it is a simple fact that the systemic focus and emphasis of that Judaism contradicted the fundamental function of the market and also missed the point of the market as Greco-Roman philosophy understood it, even while reiterating, in the particular and singular idiom utilized to set forth the systemic context of the Judaism at hand, precisely the conceptions of Aristotle about trade and exchange in general, and the market in particular. The market is an instrument of rationing: "The market is one of the ways in which a particular society acquires the production that it needs and allocates that production among the various groups in the society. The market is simply a rationing device. The significant difference between a market operation and the other methods of rationing is that the latter deal with real wealth, while markets deal with money wealth. Other methods of rationing deal directly with the actual things that are distributed. In market operations purchases and sales are usually made for money, not directly for other commodities or services."[116] We may describe the market by institutions or functions, e.g., private property and inheritance, money wealth and income, profit motive.[117]

To understand what is at stake we have to identify the indicators of the market and how it is defined and described. For that purpose we turn to Davisson and Harper, who state:

> A market may be described in two ways, by its institutions and by its functions. ...the market may be defined by looking at its component elements: private property and inheritance, money wealth and income, the profit motive, standardized commodities, and an exchange of price information within geographic limits.[118]

Now matters are by no means one sided. For by the stated criterion,

---

[116] Davisson and Harper, p. 123.

[117] The pertinence of "profit motive" for antiquity is not beyond question. It means not merely the desire to acquire wealth, but the propensity to make profits for the sake of profits, for the sake of making more profits: accumulation for its own sake. Such a conception, it seems to me, lies entirely outside of the frame of reference of the authorship of the Mishnah. Indeed, I cannot point to a single passage in rabbinic literature of late antiquity in which anyone even imagines the condition of accumulation for its own sake.

[118] Davisson and Harper, p. 123.

the authorship of the Mishnah did set forth the institutional requirements of the market, since it took for granted the conceptions of
private property (e.g., private domain, in real estate, as distinct from
public domain), inheritance (a conception received, of course, from
the Pentateuch, ca. 500 B.C.), wealth in the form of money,[119] consideration of the classifications of commodities, and the like. In these
important ways, the Mishnah's framers fully recognized the facts of
the market-economy with which, in reality, their country presented
them.

But in numerous ways, the framers of the system subverted the
workings of the market in favor of a distributive system, which they
imagined. For example, the authorship of the Mishnah took for
granted that price information within geographic limits was not freely
to circulate but was to be kept under control to affect market price
and supply, e.g., Mishnah-tractate Taanit 2:9: "They do not decree a
fast [in connection with the signs of a drought] for the community in
the first instance for a Thursday [which was the market day] so as
not to disturb the market-prices," since people would assume a fam-
ine was coming and hoard, consequently disrupting the stability of
prices. While sound public policy, that rule certainly indicates the
intention to intervene in the working of the market and hardly attests
to the conception of a market working in its conventional manner.
Since a controlled market is no market, and the two words "free" and
"market" are a redundancy, we find ourselves confronted by evidence that the framers of the Mishnah invoked considerations of an
other-than-economic character even when thinking, for systemic purposes, about the market. And that tells us that the market formed a
category of intense systemic concern and in no way an inert fact of
life of no conceptual or generative consequence.

In the world envisioned by the authorship of the Mishnah, markets
exist, and, the requirements of market-economics are certainly confronted. We know that fact from the simple story, told about Simeon
b. Gamaliel, noted earlier. The market-mechanism, the centerpiece of
market-economics, assuredly was understood by sages, so the Mishnah
testifies. The thrust and goal of our authorship is to overcome the—
fully-acknowledged—facts of market-economics. The tension between
the working of the market and the way in which sages proposed to
legislate for it imparts to the Mishnah's static portrait of a market a

---

[119] But this matter will await attention in Chapter Six.

dynamic tension deceptively lacking on the surface. But, in the face of clear evidence of knowledge of market-economics, in the system of Judaism in its initial statement, market-economics is set aside, so far as is possible, in favor of the principle of distributive economics, the conception of a fixed value or an intrinsic worth to an object or a commodity. For the framers of the Mishnah conceived of the economy as one of self-sufficiency, made up as it was (in their minds, at least) of mostly self-sufficient households joined in essentially self-sufficient villages. They further carry forward the odd conception of the Priestly authorship of Leviticus that the ownership of the land is supposed to be stable, so that, if a family alienates inherited property, it reverts to that family's ownership after a span of time. The conception of steady-state economy therefore dominated, so that, as a matter of fact, in utter stasis, no one would rise above his natural or inherent standing, and no one would fall either. And that is the economy they portray and claim to regulate through their legislation. In such an economy, the market did not form the medium of rationing but in fact had no role to play, except one: to insure equal exchange in all transactions, so that the market formed an arena for transactions of equal value and worth among households each possessed of a steady-state worth. Since, in such a (fictive) market, no one emerged richer or poorer than he was when he came to market, but all remained precisely as rich or as poor as they were at the commencement of a transaction, we can hardly call the Mishnah's market a market-mechanism in any sense at all.

The ideal market for the framers of the Mishnah therefore conformed to the larger principle of the system as a whole: equivalence of exchange must govern all transactions. Unlike the case of market-economics, there could be no possible risk of loss. To understand that principle, we turn first to Aristotle, as expounded by Polanyi:

> Aristotle's argument on "natural trade" in his *Politics*...rests on the premise that, like other forms of exchange, trade stems from the requirements of self-sufficiency....Natural trade is a gainless exchange....
>
> The Mishnah [Polanyi continues] is imbued with the Old Testament abhorrence of profit or advantage, derived from any transaction between members of the tribe. Its prescriptions shown an obsession with the moral peril of profiteering, even if involuntarily or inadvertently. Equivalents are here deliberately employed as a safeguard against this danger.[120]

---

[120] Polanyi, *The Lifelihood of Man*, p. 69.

The notion of equivalency also predominates in Scripture, a point to which we shall return in due course.

For the system of the Mishnah the function of the market as a price-setting mechanism, as we saw, does receive recognition—but the market-mechanism gets slight appreciation. Quite how the authorship of the Mishnah imagined that production and distribution would be worked out, if not through the mechanism of the market, we do not know, though I shall show ample evidence of the operative fantasy. But I do not imagine that that authorship asked itself such a question in an articulate way, even while answering it fully and completely. To the Mishnah's statement, the upshot of the market-mechanism made a considerable difference, since the setting of prices formed a considerable concern. The absence of a conception of the function of the market as a price-fixing mechanism that distributes goods and forces people to economize[121] is indicated in a simple way. In a world of a market-economy, the framers of the Mishnah invoked the conception of a true or inherent value, and that is an anti-market conception.

The fundamental notion operative for the Judaism of the Mishnah opposed market trading, since an authority independent of the market-mechanism intervened in the setting of prices and, hence, the rationing of scarce goods and services.

> It is an essential point of market trading that the political authority of the society (government, temple, gilds)n gives up control of production and distribution to this impersonal mechanism. The market mechanism of exchange must determine the use of resources regardless of the status of the individual participants to the transaction, regardless of the relation of the individuals to the transaction and to each other. Transactions on the market must result in price which measure only the scarcity of standardized commodities in a given market at a given time...market trading does not exist unless the elements within the society universally agree to accept the market as the method of allocating resources and commodities.[122]

By that definition, it is clear, we cannot identify in the economics of the Mishnah the working of the market, even though on the surface the system appeals to the market as its instrument of rationing and exchange.[123]

---

[121] Davisson and Harper, p. 115. I use his language.
[122] Davisson and Harper, p. 123.
[123] But the reason will become apparent only in Chapter Seven.

This brings us to the centerpiece of the Mishnah's framers' conception of the exchange of goods and services outside of the market-mechanism, which is the notion of inherent value or true worth. In line with this conception prices must accord with something akin to true value, and the market simply facilitates the reasonable exchange of goods and services by bringing people together. The market provides no price setting mechanism that operates on its own, nor is the market conceived as an economic instrument, but rather, as one of (mere) social utility in facilitating barter, encompassing, of course, barter effected through specie or money. In the following dispute, we see what is at issue:

> If one sold the wagon, he has not sold the mules. If he sold the mules, he has not sold the wagon. If he sold the yoke, he has not sold the oxen. If he sold the oxen, he has not sold the yoke.
> R. Judah says, "The price tells all."
> How so? If he said to him, "Sell me your yoke for two hundred zuz," the facts are perfectly clear, for there is no yoke worth two hundred zuz.
> And sages say, "Price proves nothing."
>
> M. B.B. 5:1

Judah's view is that there is an intrinsic value, against which the market does not operate. This notion of true value,[124] though in the minority in the case at hand, in fact dominates in Mishnaic thought about the market-mechanism. The notion that true value inheres in all transactions, so that each party remains exactly as he was prior to the engagement, comes to concrete expression in a variety of circumstances.

Not only price, e.g., in relationship to supply and demand, but also services are so negotiated that ideally no one benefits or loses. The point throughout is that one must so adjudicate disputes that no party emerges poorer or richer than he was when he entered the transaction. Here is another, extreme example of keeping the measure equal:

> He who stole something from his fellow or borrowed something from him or with whom the latter deposited something, in a settled area, may not return it to him in the wilderness. If it was on the stipulation that he was going to go forth to the wilderness, he may return it to him in the wilderness.
>
> M. B.Q. 10:6

---

[124] I cannot explain what is meant by "value," e.g., the value of the worker's work, which clearly is taken into account, as against the "true value" inherent in an object up for sale in the marketplace.

The whole notion of preserving the status quo is expressed in many other ways, but the key is the insistence that the prevailing practice be followed:

> "He who leases a field from his fellow, in a place in which they are accustomed to cut the crops, must cut them. If the custom is to uproot the crops, he must uproot them. If the custom is to plough after reaping and so to turn the soil, he must do so. All is in accord with the prevailing custom of the province"
>
> M. B. M. 9:1A-E

In this regard, Aristotle will have understood the premises of discourse concerning the market. For, we recall, the market was not perceived by Aristotle as a price-setting mechanism, but rather as the setting in which distribution took place in such a way that the principle of equivalence was enforced. In this context we review Schumpeter's judgment: "Aristotle...sought for a canon of justice in pricing, and he found it in the 'equivalence' of what a man gives and receives. Since both parties to an act of barter or sale must necessarily gain by it in the sense that they must prefer their economic situations after the act to the economic situations in which they found themselves before the act—or else they would not have any motive to perform it—there can be no equivalence between the 'subjective' or utility values of the goods exchanged or between the good and the money paid or received for it."[125]

Since the framers of the Mishnah maintain that there is a true value, as distinct from a market value, of an object, we may understand the acute interest of our authorship in questions of fraud through overcharge and not only misrepresentation. Mishnaic law therefore maintains that, if a purchaser pays more than a sixth more than true value, or if a seller receives a sixth less than that amount, in the form of an overcharge, fraud has been committed. The sale is null. The defrauded party has the choice of getting his money back or of keeping the goods and receiving only the amount of the overcharge. This point is worked out with some care at Mishnah-tractate Baba Mesia 4:3-4. There is a little prologue at Mishnah-tractate Baba Mesia 4:1-2, having to do with the right of retraction of a sale under normal circumstances, not fraudulent ones. Mishnah-tractate Baba Mesia 4:1 makes the important point that a sale is regarded as final when the buyer has drawn into his own possession the commod-

---

[125] Schumpeter, p. 61.

151 of 294

146146146146

146146146

146146146

146146146146146

G.   R. Simeon says, "Whoever has the money in is hand – his hand is
     on top."

Mishnah-tractate Baba Mesia 4:2

There are two separate matters, but the relationship is integral. The
first makes the point that the commodity of lesser value effects acquisition of the commodity of greater value. The second makes the point
that a (mere) transfer of funds does not effect transfer of ownership.
The actual receipt of the item in trade by the purchaser marks the
point at which the exchange has taken place. These two points together make a single statement. It is that barter of commodities, not
exchange of (abstract) money, is what characterizes the exchange of
things of value. Money as an abstraction. It does not merely represent something of value nor is it something itself of value. The entire
notion of trade other than as an act of barter of materials or objects
of essentially equal worth is rejected. Trade now is merely (just as
Aristotle thought) a way of working out imbalances when one party
has too much of one thing but needs the other, while the other party
has too much of the other thing but needs what the former has in
excess. Such a conception of trade ignores most trading, which took
place not because of the needs of a subsistence economy, but—by the
second century A.D.—formed an autonomous economic activity, independent of the requirements of mere survival.

The rejection of the conception of money as abstraction, a unit of
value on its own, in favor of money as a commodity, is expressed in
a simple way. What is at issue in the pericopes before us is how a
purchase is effected. The datum is that transfer of funds alone does
not complete a transaction. Only the transfer of the object—the commodity—does so. The consequences of that principle are what is
spelled out. But we should not miss the centrality of the principle that
exchanges take place only through barter. Then each party must
maintain that he has received something of equivalent value to what
he has handed over, with the further consequence that profit in trade
is simply inconceivable. In a money market, such as characterized
the world in which the framers of the Mishnah lived, establishing the
premise of barter and the priority of commodity exchange, rather
than purchase with money, demands a clear and detailed statement
in concrete facts, yielding symbolic demonstration. And since the
Judaism of the Mishnah makes its statement through symbolic demonstration, e.g., gesture and fact of behavior rather than (mere) ver-
bal explanation or exposition, the point that barter and not the

money-market operates demands ample symbolic statement in detail. This point registers in a stunning and simple way: the demonetization of money, first of all, the principle of barter instead of a money-transaction, second. The former point announces that precious metals are commodities, less precious, (mere) money. Then the more precious metal will acquire the less precious, since the commodity effects acquisition, the mere coin does not.

I cannot imagine a more stunning or subtle way of denying the working of the money-market and insisting upon barter as the "true" means of effecting trade and therefore permitting exchange and acquisition. Since money does not effect a transaction, we have to determine that sort of specie which is (functionally) deemed to constitute currency, and that which is regarded as a commodity. In general, the more precious the metal, the more likely it is to be regarded not as money or ready cash, but as a commodity, subject to purchase or sale, just as much as is grain or wine. This notion is expressed very simply: "Gold acquires silver," meaning, gold is a commodity, and when the purchaser has taken possession of the gold, the seller owns the silver paid as money for it. But if the exchange is in the reverse—someone paying in gold for silver—the transaction is effected when the seller has take possession of the gold. In an exchange of copper and silver, copper is deemed money, silver is now the commodity. All of this is neatly worked out for us at Mishnah-tractate Baba Mesia 4:1, which, in the light of these remarks, should pose no special problems.

A further mode of making the same point is to insist that, in an exchange, the transfer of money does not mark the completion of the transaction. Only when the purchaser has taken over the object of purchase is the transaction final, at which point the purchaser becomes liable to pay over funds or money-equivalents—and it does not matter which. It will follow that if the buyer has transferred the money, but the seller has not yet handed over, nor the buyer received, the object of purchase, then either party may retract. Once the buyer has taken up ("lifted up") or drawn into his own possession the object or purchase, the transaction is complete. The buyer now is liable to pay off the purchase price, if it has not already been paid; the seller may no longer retract. Mishnah-tractate Baba Mesia 4:2A-D then satisfactorily instantiate Mishnah-tractate Baba Mesia 4:1's point that the sale is complete when the buyer has made acquisition of the produce, and not when the seller has received the money.

Mishnah-tractate Baba Mesia 4:2G is important. Simeon rejects the theory that, once money has been paid, the commodity has not been fully purchased until it has been drawn into the buyer's possession. On the contrary, so soon as money changes hands, while the seller still has the power to retract, the purchaser does not. Since Simeon self-evidently rejects Mishnah-tractate Baba Mesia 4:12A-D, he must reject the theory of acquisition presented at Mishnah-tractate Baba Mesia 4:1 as well.

We continue this sequence of principles of economics, moving from the rejection of the conception of money as a unit of value to the affirmation of the principal notion, true value. The notion of true value logically belongs together with the conception of money as an item of barter or meant merely to facilitate barter, because both notions referred to the single underlying conception of the economy as a steady-state entity in which people could not increase wealth but only exchange it. Quite what true value can mean is not at all clear, since the notion is a rather murky one. But the point before us is that an object has a true or intrinsic value, which cannot be exceeded in payment or receipt by more than 18%. Fraud involves not adulteration or a product or misrepresentation of the character or quality of merchandise, such as we should grasp. We shall now see that fraud is simply charging more than something is worth. And that can only mean, than something is worth intrinsically. This profoundly Aristotelian[126] economic conception is now made explicit.

4:3

A. Fraud [overreaching] is an overcharge of four pieces of silver out of twenty four pieces of silver to the *sela* –
B. (one sixth of the purchase-price).
C. For how long is it permitted to retract [in the case of fraud]?
D. So long as it takes to show [the article] to a merchant or a relative.
E. R. Tarfon gave instructions in Lud:
F. "Fraud is an overcharge of eight pieces of silver to a *sela*—
G. "one third of the purchase price."
H. So the merchants of Lud rejoiced.
I. He said to them, "All day long it is permitted to retract."
J. They said to him, "Let R. Tarfon leave us where we were."
K. And they reverted to conduct themselves in accord with the ruling of sages.

Mishnah-tractate Baba Mesia 4:3

---

[126] I cannot suggest where, in Scripture, sages can have come upon this notion.

My earlier remarks did not exaggerate matters one bit. The definition of fraud self-evidently rests on the conception of an intrinsic or
true value. and there is no conception of fraud as mere misrepresentation of the character of merchandise. That comes later, and bears
its own considerations. Fraud here is simply charge higher than the
intrinsic worth of the object permits. That definition rejects the conception of "free" and "market," that redundancy that insists upon the
market as the instrument of the rationing of scarce resources. If an
object has a true value of twenty-four and the seller pays twenty-
eight, he has been defrauded and may retract. Tarfon gave and took,
E-K. In this connection we recall our earlier review of the counterpart views of Greek, particular Aristotle's, economics. The just price
derives from good will, *philia*, as a matter of reciprocity: "In such
exchange no gain is involved; goods have their known prices, fixed
beforehand."[127] So Haney: "An exchange is just when each gets exactly as much as he gives the other; yet this equality does not mean
equal costs, but equal wants."[128] Schumpeter's statement on the same
matter reminds us of the identity of conception between Aristotle's
and the Mishnah's authorship's ideas on true value:

> Aristotle...sought for a canon of justice in pricing, and he found it in the
> 'equivalence' of what a man gives and receives. Since both parties to an
> act of barter or sale must necessarily gain by it in the sense that they
> must prefer their economic situations after the act to the economic
> situations in which they found themselves before the act—or else they
> would not have any motive to perform it—there can be no equivalence
> between the 'subjective' or utility values of the goods exchanged or
> between the good and the money paid or received for it.[129]

Given the idiom in which they made their statement, the framers of
the Mishnah found an acutely concrete way of saying the same thing,
first, the notion of a just price, second, the emphasis upon barter; and
they said both ideas in juxtaposition, for precisely the same reason
Aristotle had to. Let me give the reason with emphasis: *the logic of the
one demanded the complementary logic of the other.* Once we impute a true
value to an object or commodity, we shall also dismiss from consideration all matters of worth extrinsic to the object or commodity;
hence money is not an abstract symbol of worthy but itself a commodity, and, further, objects bear true value. The two are really

---

[127] Polanyi, p. 80.
[128] Haney, p. 60.
[129] Schumpeter, p. 61.

different ways of saying the same thing. And what that is, from our perspective, is the negative message that the market is not the medium of rationing, because another medium is in play. But we do not, here, know what that other medium is. Only in our progress through the definition of wealth, on the one side, and the vast panoply of rules expressing the workings of the Mishnah's distributive economics, on the other, shall we grasp the entire picture.

We proceed to a still more stunning reiteration of the same, now in the notion of the perfect equivalence of both parties to a transaction. Not only must the seller not make "too much" money, the buyer also must not receive "too much" value.

4:4

> A. All the same are the buyer and the seller: both are subject to the law of fraud.

The statement is bald and unadorned. It cannot be embellished; the perfect complementarity of exchange is simply announced in the simplest possible way. Now we turn to "the merchant," who forms the counterpart to what we should call a wholesaler. It is one who collects commodities in small volume and forms a large volume for transportation and sale in distant markets.

> B. Just as fraud applies to an ordinary person, so it applies to a merchant.
> C. R. Judah says, "Fraud does not apply to a merchant."
> D. He who has been subjected [to fraud] – his hand is on top.
> E. [If] he wanted, he says to him, "Return my money."
> F. [Or, if he wanted, he says to him,] "Give me back the amount of the fraud."

Mishnah-tractate Baba Mesia 4:4

A is an important qualification. B-C in fact repeat and dispute A. D is clarified by E-F. The buyer has the power to nullify the sale or merely to collect the amount of the overcharge. In our context, fraud pertains to counterfeiting, and the same notion is introduced here. But the difference should not be missed. What is fraudulent in the counterfeit is the representation of value that is not present; that is to say, a defective coin is defective because it lacks that intrinsic value that it is supposed to contain. It is subject to fraud for the same reason that a keg of wine may be subject to fraud, that is to say, because, in a barter-exchange for a keg of wine, one may receive "too much" value, and so too, in a barter-exchange for a *sela*-coin, one also may receive "too much" value.

4:6

A. How long is it permitted to return [a defective *sela*]?
B. In large towns, for the length of time it takes to show to a money-changer.
C. And in villages, up to the even of the Sabbath.
D. [If the one who gave it] recognizes it, even after twelve months he is to accept it from him
E. But [if the one who gave the coin refuses to take it back], he has no valid claim against the other except resentment.
F. He may give it for produce in the status of second tithe, [for easy transportation to Jerusalem],
G. and need not scruple,
H. for it is only churlishness [to refuse a slightly depreciated coin].
                              Mishnah-tractate Baba Mesia 4:6
A. Defrauding involves [an overcharge of] four pieces of silver [for what one has bought for a *sela*].
                              Mishnah-tractate Baba Mesia 4:7

We go back over the issue of Mishnah-tractate Baba Mesia 4:3, now with reference to Mishnah-tractate Baba Mesia 4:5. The defective coin may be returned, within the specified time-limits, A-C. The one who handed it over has to take it back, D-E, if he recognizes the coin. But if he does not, E, the one who has been given the bad coin has no recourse. The defective coin may be exchanged for second tithe-produce and taken to Jerusalem.

This brings us to the complementary question: what sorts of things *lack* a true or intrinsic value? Given the logic that imposes upon all transactions the fiction that a barter of equal value has taken place, we should anticipate that things that are not subject to barter will lack, also, an intrinsic value. Commodities are bartered, because we can measure (so it is imagined) the intrinsic worth of things. But what has no intrinsic worth, such as a piece of paper, or what has no worth readily treated as standard for purposes of measuring equivalency, such as a person, or what is not a commodity at all, such as real estate, or what is not subject to a this-worldly evaluation as something accessible to human utilization at all, such as what has been sanctified to heaven—these will not be subject to barter and therefore also will not be given the status of commodities bearing intrinsic value for purposes of exchange. Here the really interesting item is real estate, which is removed from the scale of true value and deemed to have a value beyond all estimation. That (presently-minor) exception later on will become the touchstone and key to the system as a whole, for it reflects the definition of wealth upon which everything else depends.

4:9

A. These are matters which are not subject to a claim of fraud [on account of overcharge]:

B. (1) slaves, (2) bills of indebtedness [which are discounted and sold], (3) real estate, and (4) that which has been consecrated.

C. They are not subject to twofold restitution.

D. nor [in the case of a consecrated ox or sheep] to fourfold or five-fold restitution.

E. An unpaid bailee is not required to take an oath [on their account, that he has not inflicted damage].

F. And a paid bailee does not have to pay compensation [on their account, if they are stolen or lost].

G. R. Simeon says, "Holy Things for which one is liable for replacement [should they be lost] are subject to a claim of fraud on account of overcharge.

H. "Holy Things for which one is not liable for replacement [should they be lost] are not subject to a claim of fraud on account of overcharge" [cf. Mishnah-tractate Baba Qamma 7:4].

I. R. Judah says, "Also: He who sells a scroll of the Torah, a beast, or a pearl —

J. "they are not subject to a claim of fraud by reason of overcharge."

K. They said to him, "They have specified only these [of B]."

Mishnah-tractate Baba Mesia 4:9

The items of B are exempt from the rules governing movables which are sold, A, stolen, C-D, or subjected to negligent bailees, E-F. B2 refers to writs of indebtedness, which are sold at a discount to a bill-collector. Simeon qualifies B4. The conception of equivalency extends to transactions of a non-material character. But I see the following as essentially beside the point of the chapter in which they occur:

4:10

A. Just as a claim of fraud applies to buying and selling

B. so a claim of fraud applies to spoken words.

C. One may not say to [a storekeeper], "How much is this object?" knowing that he does not want to buy it.

The remainder of the pericope proceeds to other matters and hardly carries forward what is at stake in the foregoing. The transaction of exchange commences at the point at which the buyer and seller engage. Therefore the obligation of the buyer encompasses his or her integrity in entering into the barter. Asking about the value of an object when one does not sincerely intends to buy imposes upon the seller the courtesies of exchange that, in fact, he does not owe, and acquires for the putative purchaser the courtesies of exchange that the purchaser does not in fact deserve. That is what is at stake in preserving the integrity of the barter-transaction not only in the exchange of goods but also in the exchange of what we now call politeness-noises. The remainder proceeds to other matters entirely. But we should not miss the point of relevance. When the courtesies of exchange are not equivalent, then one party simply abuses the other, and the inappropriate examples make that simple point as to the alternatives: fair exchange, even in words, or mere abuse, in one form or another.

We recall the emphasis, for the definition of the market, upon the standardization of items of exchange. In a barter-economy, that standardization proves all the more required, since we have to make certain that each party to the exchange contributes a known and uniform value, something of entirely consistent character. If we mix diverse species, we have no exchange; but even if we mix diverse volumes of a single specie, e.g., old and new produce, we also cannot effect a fair barter. Accordingly, the provision of a transaction of barter will impose the requirement of a pure and unadulterated commodity-exchange. What is in play in the matter of pure foods is not fraud or out-and-out misrepresentation. The concern is now that we keep separate and distinct commodities that are not wholly like one another. Mixing different things together disrupts the equal exchange that is in the center of all transactions.

The economics expressed in these rules clearly is one of barter, and the transactions are exchanges of commodities of equal intrinsic worth. But the actual market, we realize full well, is made up not of householders alone, but also of traders, shop-keepers, and other holders of capital. The arena of exchange—hardly a market—conceived by the framers of our document by contrast is one in which the proprietors of the means of production exchange on a perennially equal basis the things they have produced: this for that, this worth that. It is one thing to insist that barter characterize trade in potatoes, so that the crop of one year is not to be mingled with the crop of another. But what sort of barter will permit the exchange of potatoes and, let us say, a physician's services, or a clay pot? And, more to the point, what of the role of capital? The Mishnah's economics takes a remarkably unsympathetic view of the holder of liquid capital or even of trading goods in any kind. The householder appears in the market as principal of exchange because he is in command of the goods of exchange. Moreover, as we shall see in the next chapter, the householder plays his central role in the economics of the Mishnah as borrower, not lender,. The lender is treated as outsider, watched and regulated.[130] The purpose of the market (now using the word in an inexact sense, that is, merely for the arena for exchange) is to secure for the economy precisely the opposite result of markets as occasions for the rationing of scarce goods (and services).

In all, in the Mishnah, we have a statement of a thorough-going Aristotelian economics, with the indicative conceptions of true value, money as commodity, and barter, paramount. Where we uncover a different between Plato and Aristotle, as in the matter of the definition of money, Aristotle's, and not Plato's, definition applies. And connections between topics, natural in the logic of Aristotle's system, are drawn in the Mishnah as well. But in one important way, the authorship of the Mishnah differed from Aristotle's disposition of economics. To that authorship economic questions, worked out in detail but expressive of clearly-accessible theoretical principles, played a central role in the system as a whole. In the Mishnah issues of economics take a more considerable role in sustained discourse than they do in the—on the whole paltry—role accorded to them in the writings of Aristotle, all the more so of Plato. We may judge very simply that the authorship of the Mishnah gave more sustained attention to the economic component of political economy, and invested in that matter more rigorous and far more detailed reflection, than did Aristotle, all the more so Plato, and, as we have already observed, still more than the Christian counterparts among the system-builders of antiquity.

Why so heavy an emphasis upon such matters as barter of commodities of equivalent, and true-value? And why so sustained attention to the specification of how society is to preserve stationary worth and wealth? In due course, I shall explain these facts and show that they carry us deep into the fundamental affirmations, as to this world and the supernatural as well, of the system-builders of the Mishnah. That the Mishnah forms a *Staatsroman,* a utopian statement of how things ought to be,[131] not how they actually were, as much as Plato's

---

[130] The Mishnah never represents householders as lending money to one another. It knows about factors who make a market in commodities and who provide capital to the householder, e.g., in the form of animals to be tended, raised, and then sold, with both parties sharing in the profits. The Mishnah's interest in factoring contracts is to assure that the farmer not work for nothing.

[131] But, therefore, also a recognition of widespread violation of norms in the practice of the day.

Republic and Aristotle's *Politics*, in light of conceptions of true value and "fraud" as divergence from that mystic imputed worth, no longer can be subject to doubt. The real question is why those details of distributive economics played so central a role in the economic doctrine of the system, and, still more urgent, how come this system of world-construction found so vital a concern in economics at all? But before we can answer the ultimate, and the critical issue, of why the systemic centrality accorded to economics at all, we have first of all to turn to the matter of wealth: what it was, and what it was not. The answer to that question leads us deep into the heart of matters.

VIII. *Wealth*

How, exactly, does the Mishnaic system define "wealth"? Let us begin with Aristotle's words and compare their sense to the view of the Mishnah's sages:

> There are two sorts of wealth-getting: ...one is a part of household management, the other is retail trade. The former necessary and honorable, while that which consists in exchange is justly censured; for it is unnatural, and a mode by which men gain from one another. The most hated sort, and with the greatest reason, is usury, which makes a gain out of money itself, and not from the natural object of it. For money was intended to be used in exchange, but not to increase at interest.
> Aristotle, Politics, 1258a-8b, trans. W. D. Ross[132]

The key to the importance imputed by the authorship of the Mishnah to economics lies in the definition of wealth. For economics addresses questions of value defined in material terms, the disposition of scarce resources in accord with a defined rationality concerning, as it does, things accorded palpable and concrete value. Now, as a matter of fact, I cannot find a sentence in the Mishnah and in its continuations that calls into question the worth of wealth. The contrast between that self-evident trait of the system and the recurrent leitmotif that material wealth is evil or merely irrelevant to the important matters of life characteristic of schools of Greco-Roman philosophy and Christianity alike alerts us to the generative question of description, analysis, and interpretation. It is why this system accords an important place to the disposition of wealth, the definition of right action in the market, and the delineation of the traits of the house-

---

[132] Cited by Davisson and Harper, p. 132.

holder, designated as one who controls (one of the available) means of production, in a circumstance in which other system-builders, including, after all, Plato, do not do so. And the issue having drawn us to the center of the system, we have to know first what the system understands by wealth, and, second, why the system defines wealth in that way and not in some other. The former question finds its answer in the present chapter, the latter, in the one to follow. The two answers together form the account of the economics of the Mishnah as I am able to present it.

Part of the answer to the question before us must appeal to the state of thought of the age, though, of course, that answer begs the question. Still, we do well to remember that a document so profoundly shaped by Greco-Roman conceptions and values will certainly have conformed to the simple notion stated by Finley, "The judgment of antiquity about wealth was fundamentally unequivocal and uncomplicated. Wealth was necessary and it was good."[133] Defining wealth, too, the authorship of the Mishnah fit well into the conceptions of their age. For them, as much as for Aristotle half a millennium earlier, wealth meant not money but real estate.[134] The basic wealth of the upper strata of Rome was in land, with consequent chronic shortages of cash.[135] That fact will help us to understand the prevailing bias against capital and in favor of the land-poor householder that characterizes the Mishnah's treatment of wealth, money-making, the definition and uses of money and of capital. But that bias stated, in its context, a conception integral to the Mishnaic system as a whole. Money represented something of worth, was a kind of commodity, no different in its way from land itself. Wealth was tangible and material, best embodied in real property.[136] For, as we shall see, the framers took for granted that money formed a commodity for barter, and that all forms of profit—all forms!—con-

---

[133] Finley, *The Ancient Economy*, pp. 35-6.

[134] Wealth in the system of the Mishnah also involves capital in the form of beasts, but this is not taken into account here. When beasts really do come under intense scrutiny, it has to do with the cult and its requirement. To the cult beasts are capital in a way in which, to the householder, they are not.

[135] Finley, *The Ancient Economy*, p. 56

[136] That judgment forms part of a larger theological premise of the system, which is that God is the ultimate householder and landowner of the Land of Israel, with householders only joint tenants, with God, in possession of their properties. Since all wealth was real and not movable, and since God owned everything and shared ownership with the householder, the conception of true wealth fit well into the theological datum of the system.

stituted nothing other than that "usury" that Scripture had condemned.[137] It follows that the economics of the system form a cogent
and wholly coherent chapter in the system's larger and encompassing
statement. But these familiar facts do beg the question, since they
merely repeat the simple allegation that the framers of the Mishnah
valued wealth and assigned to economics an important systemic task.
They do not tell us why, rather explaining only the context in which
the system made its choices. Others in the same setting made different choices, so we have not yet explained why this, not that.

The answer to the question of the reason for the importance of
wealth, together with consequent issues of the economic definition of
the householder, on the one side, and the correct conduct of the
market in accord with the conception of true value, on the other,
derives from one simple fact. In the system of the Mishnah, as we
shall see, wealth to the householder is (ownership of) land, and the
concerns of householders are in transactions in land. We have first
fully to appreciate the unique status, as wealth, accorded to real
property, and only then, in the chapter beyond this one, spell out the
fundamental systemic message that is borne by that fact. We begin
from the beginning, the absolute value imputed to ownership of land,
without regard to the size or productivity of that land. Any ownership
of a piece of land, however small, constitutes "wealth," and so, for
one example, is liable for the designation of God's portion in the
crop. This conception is expressed in terms of being liable to the laws
of leaving the corner of the field to the poor (*peah*), as follows:

> R. Eliezer says, "An area of land within which is planted a quarter-
> qab of seed is subject to the laws of peah."
> R. Joshua seas, "An area of land that produces at least two seahs of
> grain is subject to the laws of peah."
> R. Tarfon says, "An area of land measuring six-by-six handbreadths
> is subject to the laws of peah."
> R. Judah b. Beterah says, "An area of land that produces sufficient
> grain that the farmer must cut twice, that is, with two strokes of a cycle,
> is subject to the laws of peah.
> And the law accords with his opinion]
> R. Aqiba says, "Land of any size at all is subject to the laws of peah
> and to the laws of first fruits [Dt. 26:1]...."

> M. Peah 3:6

---

[137] The most current statement on the subject of usury is Paul E. Gottfried, "The
Western Case against Usury," *Thought* 1985, 60:89-98. See also Benjamin Nelson,
The Idea of Usury: From Tribal Brotherhood to Universal Brotherhood (Chicago, 1969: Univer-
sity of Chicago Press).

"A dying man who wrote over his property to others as a gift but left himself a piece of land of any size whatever—his gift is valid. If he did not leave himself a piece of land of any size whatever, his gift is not valid"

M. Baba Batra. 9:6A-D

The context of the opening pericope, gifts to the poor, introduces a fundamental qualification.

This brings us to the centerpiece of the system's definition of wealth. When we speak of (ownership of) "land," it is, self-evidently, land that produces a crop liable to the requirements of the sacerdotal taxes (a matter on which we shall spend ample time in the coming chapter). It follows, therefore, that ownership of "land" speaks of a very particular acreage, specifically, the territory known to the framers of the Mishnah as the land of Israel, that alone. Land not subject to the sacerdotal taxes is not land to which the legal status and traits before us are imputed.

But there is a second equally critical qualification. Land in the land of Israel that is liable to sacerdotal taxes must be owned by an Israelite. Gentiles are not expected to designate as holy portions of their crop, and if they do so, those portions of the crop that they designate as holy nonetheless are deemed secular. So we have an exceedingly specific set of conditions in hand. Wealth for the system of the Mishnah is not ownership of land in general, for example, land held by Jews in Babylonia, Egypt, Italy, or Spain. It is ownership of land located in a very particular place. And wealth for that same system is not wealth in the hands of an undifferentiated owner. It is wealth in the domain of an Israelite owner in particular. Wealth therefore is ownership of *land of Israel* in two senses, both of them contained within the italicized words. It is ownership of land located in the land *of Israel*. It is ownership of land located in the land of Israel that is *of Israel*, belonging to an Israelite. "Israel" then forms the key to the meaning of wealth, because it modifies persons and land alike: only an Israel[ite] can possess the domain that signifies wealth; only a domain within the land called by the name of "Israel" can constitute wealth. It is in the enchanted intersection of the two Israels, (ownership of) the land, (ownership by) the people, that wealth in the system of the Mishnah finds realization.

It must follow that the position of Greco-Roman economics on the ultimate value and status of real estate is vastly modified here. The distributive economics of the Mishnah is not simply an adaptation of temple-economics to the needs of the Israelite temple. The theology of the Mishnah *utilizes* the principles of distributive economics in order to make a statement of not economics but theology. In the case of the economics of Judaism, only real estate in a particular, designated area enjoys that standing as source of status (defining the householder) and value (beyond price, however, miniscule the property) that the passages at hand impute. Everything that follows derives its full meaning from that fact: ownership of land means land of Israel, that alone, and land of Israel means not land possessed by Jews wherever they are located, but land of Israel in the possession of Israelite (male householders) within the designated boundaries (whatever they were) of the Jewish part of what was then called Palestine. These, we rapidly realize, are not definitions of an economic character at all, bearing no relationship to the productivity of land or its value in producing goods and services of a material character. The system's peculiar definition of ownership of land forms the first bit of evidence toward our understanding of how the economics of Judaism adapted for the purposes of Judaism principles of distributive economics. It was in that way—through the applied principles of distributive economics as defined herein—that the system of the Mishnah was permitted to make a fundamental and acutely detailed statement of its ultimate principle in the terms and idiom in which the framers wished to speak: the humble and obscure detail of the sale of grain or beets in the marketplace. But in stating the main lines of the conclusion, I have moved ahead of my story. Let us go back to the simple question: how did the innate value of land express itself in the system of the Mishnah's definition of wealth and the exchange of wealth?

Through ownership of real estate critical, social transactions are worked out. The marriage settlement depends upon real property. Compensation for torts and damages is paid out of land of the highest quality (M. B. Q. 1:2H). The householders' measurement of value is expressed in quality of acreage, top, middle, and bottom grade.[138]

---

[138] But Ex. 22:4, which says that one must make restitution for "the excellence" of field or vineyard [JPS: he must make restitution for the impairment of that field or vineyard"] is understood to require payment of real property of the top grade in restitution for torts of the specified classification. The details of the Mishnah's system derive from a variety of sources, as I stressed in Chapter Two. But the utilization of details drawn from Scripture and the importance accorded to one scriptural fact or detail but not another one express what is particular to the system of the authorship of the Mishnah.

Civil penalties, meant to restore the social balance upset by an act of aggression against the person or property of the other, thus are exacted through restoration accomplished in payment of real property.[139] The principal transactions to be taken up are those of the householder who owns beasts which do damage or suffer it; who harvests his crops and must set aside and by his own word and deed sanctify them for use by the scheduled castes; who uses or sells his crops and feeds his household; and who, if fortunate, will acquire still more land. At Mishnah-tractate Ketubot 6:1ff., for example, the wife's dowry is assumed to be in land, or to be convertible into land, which is the only valid investment. If ready cash came to the wife in an inheritance, land is purchased with it, and the husband has the usufruct (M. Ket. 8:3). Land is the only valid investment. So too Mishnah-tractate Ketubot 10:3 treats only real property as value to be taken into account. As we saw in Chapter Four, the household exists—finds validity and definition as a unit of economic productivity—because of ownership of land, not only *upon* land, for the sharecropper is not classified as a householder,. A householder without real estate, that is, real wealth, is inconceivable. To householders that the Mishnah addresses its conception of the social order. It is the householder who is the pivot of society and its bulwark. It is the household that makes up the village; the corporate component of the society of Israel is measured in land, which, therefore, also forms the measure of wealth.

Once, moreover, we take full account of the structural components of the Mishnah's economy, the household, defined in terms of command of a ownership of landed domain, however small, composing, with other households, the village; the village constituting the market in which all things hold together in an equal exchange of a stable population in a steady-state economy, we revert to the consequent question: then what is wealth? And the answer to that question must accommodate the fact that wealth is conceived as unchanging and not subject to increase or decrease, hence, by the way, the notion of true value imputed to commodities. For if we imagine a world in which, ideally, no one rises and no one falls, and in which wealth is essentially stable, then we want to know what people understand by money, on the one hand, and how they identify riches, on the other.

---

[139] Penalties for sins or civil crimes, by contrast, are not subjected to sanctions of fines exacted in real estate. Real estate transactions are exchanges of wealth, and sins, such as are subjected to flogging, have nothing to do with wealth.

The answer is very simple. For the system of the Mishnah, wealth constitutes that which is of lasting value, and what lasts is real property (in the land of Israel), that alone. Real estate (in the land of Israel) does not increase in volume, it is not subject to the fluctuation of the market (so it was imagined), it was permanent, reliable, and, however small, always useful for something. It was perceived to form the medium of enduring value for a society made up of households engaged in agriculture. Accordingly, the definition of wealth as real and not movable, as real estate (in the land of Israel) and no where else, real estate not as other kinds of goods, conformed to the larger systemic givens. A social system composed of units of production, households, engaged in particular in agricultural production, made a decision entirely coherent with its larger conception and character in identifying real estate as the sole measure of wealth. And, as we recall, Aristotle will not have been surprised.

True enough, we find more spiritual definitions of wealth, for example, Mishnah-tractate Abot 4:2: "Who is rich? He who is happy in what he has." So too, one can become rich through keeping or studying the Torah, e.g., "He who keeps the Torah when poor will in the end keep it in wealth (M. Abot 4:9). So too we find the following, "Keep your business to a minimum and make your business Torah (M. Abot 4:10). But these sayings have no bearing upon a single passage of the Mishnah in which a concrete transaction in exchanges of material goods take place, nor does anyone invoke the notion of being satisfied with what one has when it comes to settling scores. None of them to begin with occurs in the Mishnah, but only in its later apologetic, produced about a half-century after the closure of the document. No decision in the exegetical literature generated by the Mishnah, e.g., the Tosefta, the two Talmuds, ever appealed as grounds for the practical disposition of a case of conflicting interests to the notion that, e.g., both parties should forfeit the case and go off and get rich, instead, by studying the Torah. I think we may dismiss as systemically irrelevant, indeed inconsequential, all definitions of wealth outside of the context of how actualities of conflict and exchange are sorted out, and in every such concrete and material setting, ownership of land is the medium of adjudication.

Ownership of a landed domain (by a Jew in Palestine, that is, by an Israelite in the land of Israel) therefore provides the key to much else. Transfer of land-ownership through proper deeds is subject to very careful scrutiny and detailed legislation. A piece of land, however small, was the unit of the economy deemed sufficient to support a person; if someone thought he was dying but held onto a bit of land, all his gifts in contemplation of death remained valid in the event of recovery. The small bit of property kept in reserve showed that the gifts were not on the mental stipulation that the donor die. Land served as the medium of exchange in marriage settlements and in paying compensation for torts and damages. Money bears no interest for the system of the Mishnah. As we shall see, when money comes under discussion, it is only to distinguish what functions as specie from what does not function as specie. As we fully realize, money has no intrinsic meaning; it is a commodity that, because of its universal utility and acceptability, may serve as a more convenient instrument of barter than any other commodity, that alone. Wealth is not money in volume, it is real estate, however small.

Given the range of objects, animate and inanimate, that, being valued, fall into the classification of wealth, we must find remarkable the limited definition of wealth framed by the authorship of the Mishnah. Wealth meant land, and the entire economics focused upon real property. To be rich meant to own land; to make a secure investment, along the lines of U. S. government bonds for instance, meant purchasing land, however, fragmentary, however limited the yield, by reason of size. Judicial, civil penalties were exacted by transfers of land. Women's dowries were collected in real property. Not only so, but individuals could hold and transfer wealth in the form of land. For these facts presuppose private ownership of land.[140] Otherwise, transfers from person to person cannot have formed the premise of both civil penalties, e.g., recompense for torts and damages, and dowries, and, in both instances, what was transferred, through the land, was wealth. For, as we noted, the purpose of penalties was to restore the situation prior to the commission of the tort

---

[140] The "Israel" of the Mishnah refers to both the entire people and also to the individual, and it is on that account that ownership of property in Palestine by a Jew, that is, land in the land of Israel by an Israelite, can by individual and personal, not only collective or symbolic of the collectivity. That is the theological basis for private property within the system of the Mishnah, so it would seem to me. But the problem of wealth, as I have framed it, does not require us to explain how an individual, on his (or her) own account, can own anything at all. It is clearly not on the sufferance of community ("all Israel") all the more so of government, temple, or priesthood. The right to personal, private, individual ownership is treated as inherent and intrinsic, and that seems to me joined to the definition of the individual as "Israel," as much as "all Israel" is "Israel." I should see this topic as deserving attention on its own.

(for example), so that, so far as possible, each party retained the
wealth he or she had possessed prior to the transaction that had
made one poorer, the other richer. The same conception of a steady-
state economy governed in the market. Accordingly, individuals
owned wealth. It follows that, alongside the notion of land as wealth,
the authorship understood that individuals, householders, owned and
disposed of wealth.

The Mishnah's writers, accordingly, took for granted the concept
of private property.[141] People controlled and might dispose of resources of their own, whether time, money, chattels, or land.[142] Some
public property is shared by all concerned in a village, such as a well,
bathhouse town square synagogue ark and scrolls (Mishnah-tractate.
Nedarim 5:5), but there is no passage in which a property that is
farmed is held by the village in common. Not only so, but the
Mishnah took for granted that some authority, not specified in concrete terms but assumed to be the government of the Mishnah's
"Israel," would accord to owners their legal rights, for example restoring lost or stolen goods.[143] It follows that the authorship of the
Mishnah understood by wealth not only such spiritual matters as
contentment with what one has, or vast mastery of Torah-teachings,
but also "crass," material things. In that same context of the notion
of private property, of course, the framers recognized the existence,
as well as rights of private ownership, also of chattels and movables.
But money as such bore slight permanent value and constituted no

---

[141] For the reason specified in the preceding note. But, as I said, I do not wish to
elaborate on this point now, because I think it forms part of the Mishnah's anthropology, with which I do not deal in this book. But this notion of private property in
the Mishnah requires qualification. Since God owned the land and was deemed
partner to all landowners, the conception of the absolute right of private ownership,
with which we are familiar, is not the same as was operative here. Now private
property formed a conditional and a stipulative domain.

[142] Compare Davisson and Harper, p. 124.

[143] But the Mishnah is remarkably vague about who takes responsibility for supporting rights of ownership, guarantees transfer of title, sanctions and takes charge of
the rights of private property. I cannot point in Mishnah-tractate Sanhedrin, for
example, to a single passage that places the Jewish government imagined in that
tractate in charge of the everyday economy and market. The tractates that do deal
with lost and stolen property, deeds and real estate, and other aspects of civil law and
government do not allude to the sanctions and who enforces them, only to decisions
and how they are to be reached. The silence of the Mishnah's writers on concrete
law enforcement, as distinct from their enormous obsession with penalties for sin,
e.g., in Mishnah-tractate Sanhedrin Chapters Seven through Eleven, strongly sug-
gests a problem in the conceptualization of the state. But we may postpone solution
of that problem until work on the political part of the political economy of Judaism.

measure, or form, of wealth. The operation of the market has already shown us the stipulative, indeed nearly-adventitious, status accorded to a mere transfer of coins. That fact derives from the suspicion in which transactions in money, for profit, were held.

Let us proceed to the obvious by dismissing the notion of wealth as equivalent to money. In the Greco-Roman context, MacMullen states, "Urban wealth lay chiefly in rural holdings."[144] As Schumpeter presents the matter of money as wealth, Aristotle's theory of money regards money as principally a medium of exchange. In order to serve as a medium of exchange in markets of commodities, money itself must be one of those commodities: "it must be a thing that is useful and has exchange value independently of its monetary function,...a value that can be compared with other values:"[145] None of this will have surprised the framers of the Mishnah, as we saw in the preceding chapter. Money is contingent, serves a function, bears no intrinsic worth, constitutes a mere medium of exchange, like any other commodity. It cannot form a definition of wealth. The authorship of the Mishnah of course concurred, seeing silver and gold as fundamentally commodities, subject to redefinition, under specified circumstances, also as specie—in that order.

To understand still more clearly the conception of wealth as land, we return for a brief moment to the conception of barter as natural exchange, trade as unnatural, characteristic of Aristotle's thought. Aristotle defines wealth as "a means, necessary for the maintenance of the household and the polis (with self-sufficiency a principle in the background), and, like all means, it is limited by its end."[146] Barter involves not the increase of wealth, which is contrary to nature, but only exchanges to accommodate the needs of households, which, by nature, cannot be wholly self-sufficient. Money serves as a substitute for items of barter. But money also is something people wish to accumulate on its own, and that is unnatural. Household management satisfies the needs of the household; wealth beyond those needs is meaningless, unnatural. Retail trade aims at the accumulation of coins through exchanges; there is no natural limit to the desire for money, corresponding to the natural limit to the desire for commodities. Money serves all sorts of purposes and can be hoarded. Money

---

[144] Ramsay MacMullen, *Roman Social Relations*, p. 48
[145] Schumpeter, pp. 62-3.
[146] Finley, *Ancient Economy*, p. 41.

is not the same thing as wealth. People confuse the two, however, as Davisson and Harper summarize Aristotle's view:[147]

> The cause of this confusion is that wrong-headed men believe that the purposes of household management may be served by seeking and increasing bodily pleasures. Since the enjoyment of bodily pleasures depends upon property, their aims becomes the unlimited acquisition of property, including money. When this occurs, men try to change every art into the art of getting riches, and consequently they transform the art of household management into the art of retail trade. But this is an unnatural perversion and the two should be distinguished. The profit motive attaches not to wealth but to the accumulation of riches or coin which is accomplished in a market distinct from the state and the household.

Along these same lines, as we have already noticed, the authorship of the Mishnah takes a remarkably unsympathetic view of the holder of liquid capital. The system-builders know much about factors, who provide to a householder capital in the form of animals, to be tended, raised, and sold, with both parties sharing the profits. The Mishnah's deepest interest in factoring contracts was that the farmer not work for nothing or for less than he put into the arrangement; that would smack of "usury," which, in context, stands only for making money on one's investment of liquid capital or its equivalent in livestock. The position of the householder encompassed true value not only in the now-familiar notion that a sixth of deviation from true value involved fraud, but in the conception that the value of seed and crops may vary, but capital will not. Lending money for investment is not permitted to yield a profit for the capitalist. True value (in our sense) lies in the land and produce, not in liquid capital. Seed in the ground yields a crop. Money invested in maintaining the agricultural community from season to season does not. The bias is against not only usury but interest, in favor not only of regulating fraud but restricting honest traders.

While for the Mishnah, as I said, material wealth was land, here I must introduce an important qualification. By "wealth" the framers of the Mishnah in general did not conceive of enormous land-holdings, e.g., large estates worked by sizable numbers of slaves. Theirs was not the notion that large landed estates were required for one to be held a householder, and, however, miniscule the property owned by an Israelite in the land of Israel, that property stood for wealth,

---

[147] p. 128.

that is, a domain.[148] In general, like Xenophon in his *Economics*, the framers of the Mishnah had in mind small or medium estates, in which a few slaves worked together with the householder. The notion of the *latifundia*, with gangs of slaves, makes no appearance, directly or by implication, in the world of small-holding householders conceived by the Mishnah's authorship.[149] For example, the industrial enterprise in agriculture involved housing for slaves, dormitories for men and women; it involved the housekeeper, who supervised the women slaves, and the overseer, who directed the men in the field. The authorship of the Mishnah knows nothing of dormitories; assumes the wife of the householder supervises the women-slaves; and has the householder himself working in the field alongside the slaves. When the Mishnah's authorship referred to ownership of a beast, it was assumed to be plural, hence shared; whether that is merely a linguistic convention or stands for the notion of multiple partnership in a single cow I do not know. In general, however, we form the impression, in the pages of the Mishnah, of a modest imagination, one that cannot conceive of vast estates under absentee ownership and professional management, and I doubt that in the land of Israel at that time many Jews held such estates in any event. We deal with the modest conceptions of a society of limited aspirations. Accordingly, the fundamental givens for the large estate lay beyond the imagination of our authorship. Nonetheless, that authorship recognized wealth in a single form: land, however constricted its borders.

The conception of wealth as land owned by an Israelite in the land of Israel just now outlined comes to concrete expression in Mishnah-tractate Baba Mesia Chapter Five, which defines "usury," applying and expanding the scriptural prohibition against it. The reason that discourse on usury defines the arena for thought about wealth is simple. The chapter at hand discusses the matters of interest and increase, in line with Lev. 25:35-6. And it is that prohibition that forms the arena in which the framers of the Mishnah define their conception of wealth, its identification with land and the produce of land; the exclusion, from the notion of wealth, of (mere) money; the indifference to capital and investment; and the other aspects of the

---

[148] The key is that the householder who held land (the Israelite who owned a piece of real property in the land of Israel) was like God, who owned the land of Israel. We shall return in Chapter Seven to the working out of this conception.

[149] In drawing the distinction between the small holder and the industrial estate, I follow Mossé, *Ancient World at Work*, p. 62.

profoundly Aristotelian economics characteristic of their system. For land is limited and does not increase, e.g., in volume, and hence wealth also will stand stationary and in a steady state. But matters are not quite so simple.

For before us is a long and subtle discussion. The reader may fairly ask why I point as systemically indicative of the character of the economics of the Judaism of the Mishnah, to the treatment of the prohibition of usury, a commonplace for all Judaic systems, deriving as it does from the Scripture shared among them all. There are two reasons for that view of mine, one that applies generally, the other particular to the case at hand.

What makes the chapter systemically indicative in a general way is the simple fact that the framers have chosen to expound this topic as they do—this and not some other, this one here and not elsewhere. Were we to ask for systemically active data, deriving from Scripture, in the Judaism of the Essenes of Qumran, we should look in vain for attention to the matter at hand, even though, self-evidently, the Judaism of the Essenes at Qumran rejected usury, and that by definition. To understand why I point as critical to the economics of the Judaism of the Mishnah to materials commonplace in any other Judaism, I revert to the statement of Schumpeter with which this book commences:

> In economics as elsewhere, most statements of fundamental facts acquire importance only by the superstructures they are made to bear and are commonplace in the absence of such superstructures.[150]

In the present context, the fact at hand, the prohibition of usury, scarcely prepares us for the importance accorded to that fact by the framers of the Mishnah, an importance indicated by the exegesis and development of the fact into an encompassing principle of economic transactions of exchange. Whatever the possibilities or potentialities of the scriptural prohibition of interest, the actualities at hand testify to the larger systemic bias and traits of the system-makers before us.

But there is a second consideration, particular to the case at hand. We shall now see that the words translated "usury" really refer to a variety of ordinary market procedures, and "usury" really means "profit."[151] For in the end what is prohibited is not merely interest on

[150] Joseph A. Schumpeter, *History of Economic Analysis*, p. 54

[151] By "usury" Scripture's authorship meant whatever it meant; that is of no interest to us. I do not imagine that the framers of the Mishnah were philologians, knowledgeable in comparative Semitic philology, and I take as fact that, whatever

a loan, in cash or in kind, but any transaction which leaves one party materially richer than he was when he entered the transaction, even though the other party is no poorer. So the bias is against interest per se. Not only so, but even the appearance of "usury" or profit must be avoided, as in the following:

> "He who sells a house among the houses in walled cities, lo, this person redeems the house forthwith. And he redeems it at any time in twelve months. Lo, this is a kind of usury which is not usury"
>
> (M. Arakhin 9:3A-C).

The point is that the one who redeems the house during the year does not deduct from what he repays to the purchaser the rent for the use of the house during the period between the sale and the redemption. It therefore appears that the purchaser has had the use of the house in exchange for the use of his money from the time of the sale to the time of redemption. But this is not usury, since usury applies only to a loan, not to a purchase[152]

Another, more important, case in point is the absolute prohibition of factoring. Here there is no consideration that the shopkeeper, selling goods on consignment, or the farmer, raising animals for a share in the profit, is going to be poorer than he was before he undertook the contract. Yet factoring is so organized as to prohibit the capitalist, who supplies the goods on consignment or the capital in the form of the young beasts, to make money on the (mere) labor of the trader or farmer. That is profit on investment, not "usury" in any sense in which the word is used today. Since the same prohibition is invoked for a variety of modes of the increase of capital, we have to take to heart what really is at stake for our system. And that is Aristotle's conception that profit, including, by the way, usury, is unnatural, but barter, encompassing all manner of goods (theoretically including coins, viewed as commodities), is natural. Only within

---

they understood by a word, they imputed also to Scripture's authorship. Hence the true or historical meaning of *neshekh* and *ribit* as the priestly writers of the fifth century used the words bears no particular relevance to our problem. For all we know, the authorship of the Mishnah really did receive "traditions" from the ancient priesthood, seven hundred years earlier, about the meaning of these and other words. It would not affect in any measure at all the simple fact that our authorship made *its* choices for *its* purposes, imputing to words meanings it deemed those meanings to have, in the context it defined, for the sense and system it proposed to impute and compose.

[152] See my *History of the Mishnaic Law of Holy Things* (Leiden, 1979: E. J. Brill). IV. *Arakhin. Temurah*, pp. 77-8.

that framework do we grasp the full testimony to the systemic economics that the exegesis of "usury" presents to us.

Let us turn to the exposition of the remarkable chapter on the
subject, containing, as it does, whatever theory of wealth, expressed
in concrete detail, that our authorship proposes to impose upon the
actualities of everyday trade and commerce. The chapter opens with
a distinction between interest (*neshekh*) and increase (*tarbit*). The
former is defined simply as repayment of five *denars* for a loan of a
sela, which consists of four *denars*, or repayment of three *seahs* of what
for a loan of two. The going rate of interest appears to have been 25
percent for a loan in cash, and 50 percent for a loan in kind. We do
not know the length of time of the loan. Increase is a somewhat more
subtle question. It involves payment for delivery, later on, of a commodity valued at the market-price prevailing at the time of the agreement. The one who pays the money in advance thus profits, since
prices are much lower at harvest-time than in advance. Trading in
futures occupies much attention. The prohibition of interest is expanded with great care at Mishnah-tractate Baba Mesia 5:2-6. The
concern not to trade in futures or to gain increase through commodities is at Mishnah-tractate Baba Mesia 5:7-10. The main point is to
treat as prohibited interest diverse sorts of payments in kind in consideration of a loan. Mishnah-tractate Baba Mesia 5:2 prohibits the
debtor from renting out to the creditor a courtyard at no cost or at
less than the prevailing rate. It does allow a deduction for payment of
rent in advance—a very different matter. Mishnah-tractate Baba
Mesia 5:3 takes into account the possibility of a subterfuge in which,
in exchange for what is in fact a loan, the creditor enjoys the usufruct
of a field. This matter will require close attention.

This brings us to what is an essentially unrelated matter, but one
joined to the rest because of the overriding consideration of the prohibition of "interest." For interest really stands for nothing less than
"profit," that is, getting money not through barter. Mishnah-tractate
Baba Mesia 5:4 goes on to prohibit interest in the form of what it
deems to be uncompensated labor. But what is at stake is return on
capital, and that is not interest in any sense of usury, but (merely)
profit of a different species from the profit that a farmer makes by
planting seeds and raising crops and selling them. Specifically, we
have in hand the prohibition of factoring in all forms. If a capitalist
assigns goods or capital to a storekeeper in exchange for half the
profit, the storekeeper in addition must be paid a salary for his atten-

tion to that half of the goods, the profit of which accrues to the capitalist. But, Mishnah-tractate Baba Mesia 5:5, if one hands over cattle to a rancher to raise, in exchange for half the profits, the cattle are deemed to work for their keep, so that rancher need not be paid an additional fee for his labor. One may make an advance agreement on the value of the herd, when the herd yields labor for the benefit of the rancher, Mishnah-tractate Baba Mesia 5:6, 5:7, finally, prohibits the arrangement of a farmer's tending a flock on "iron terms," that is to say, on such terms that the owner of the flock is guaranteed a return of all his capital, specified at the outset, and in addition a fixed yield, while the rancher will receive the increase of the flock over and above these two fixed items. Thus the rancher, bearing the entire risk for the upkeep of the flock, shares only part of the profits thereof. Israelites may pay or exact interest from gentiles. The notion of risk-capital as risk is rejected. In all, we must concur that Aristotle will have found himself entirely at home in the premises of these rules.

Mishnah-tractate Baba Mesia 5:7-10 go on to deal with agreements on futures and other aspects of increase. One may not agree to pay in advance a fixed sum for a certain amount of produce, if a market price is not yet available. That sort of speculation, again, has no bearing upon the conception of usury or interest, but it does form a critical component of the use of capital, further evidence that for the system at hand "usury" or "interest" are simply the same thing as profit on liquid capital. In any case, we have the opposite of market-economics, for the premise of discourse here is that the market price is administered, not set by the market itself; rather, it is announced and adhered to, as the produce of a given sort reaches the market. No one is supposed to speculate on that matter, and that is the mark of a distributive, not a market, conception of the economy. What follows from speculation? It is that something other than an agreed-upon price is determinative. All of this is translated downward into the (mere) prohibition of usury, but, we realize, now "usury" simply stands for market-economics. If the produce should prove to be more expensive, then the one who receives the money will lose out and turn out to have paid interest on the advance-money. Once there is a market price, one may pay in advance for delivery later on; enjoys an unfair advantage in exchange for his payment in advance. Mishnah-tractate Baba Mesia 5:8-9 deal with a loan to be repaid in kind. Once more barter imposes its conceptions upon the market, which means a *kor* of wheat stands for a *kor* of wheat, without regard

to market-conditions, which are inadmissible in evidence. In general
if one borrows a *kor* of wheat, he cannot pledge to repay a *kor* of
wheat. It may turn out that he will have to pay much more for the *kor*
than it cost at the time of the loan. This is interest. One may lend his
tenant-farmers a *kor* of wheat for seed, however, and receive at the
end a *kor* of wheat. That is deemed an investment by the landlord in
his own property. If one presently owns a *kor* of wheat but has not got
access to it, on the other hand, he may agree to return a *kor* later on
for one he now receives, without scruple as to violating the laws of
interest.

Mishnah-tractate Baba Mesia 5:10 has three kinds of prohibited
interest for a non-material character. If one party works for another
party in exchange for the other's equivalent labor, the equivalence
must be exact. One may not give a gift to a lender, either before or
after the loan. He also may not provide him with valuable information in consideration of the loan. Mishnah-tractate Baba Mesia 5:11,
finally, completes the ambitious and successful essay with an appropriate homily. These concluding passages lead us far beyond the
antecedent conceptions, just as we noted in our earlier encounter
with the composition of a Mishnah-chapter, and have no more to do
with "usury" in any sense than did reminding one's fellow of his
(prior) sin has to do with market-exchanges.

5:1

A. What is interest, and what is increase [which is tantamount to
taking interest]?
B. What is interest?
C. He who lends a *sela* [which is four *denars*] for [a return of] five
denars,
D. two *seahs* of wheat for [a return of] three –
E. because he bites [off too much (NW'SK)].
F. And what is increase (TRBYT)?
G. He who increase (HMRBH) [profits] [in commerce] in kind.
H. How so?
I. [If] one purchases from another wheat at a price of a golden *denar*
[25 *denars*] for a *kor,* which [was then] the prevailing price, and
[then wheat] went up to thirty] denars.
J. [If] he said to him, "Give me my wheat, for I want to sell it and
buy wine with the proceeds" –
K. [and] he said to him, "Lo, your wheat is reckoned against me for
thirty *denars,* and lo, you have [a claim of] wine on me" –
L. but he has no wine.

Mishnah-tractate Baba Mesia 5:1

The formal structure is clear, with its prologue, A, then a systematic commentary on A at B+C-E,F+G-L. M. clearly has Lev 25:35-6 in mind, since it alludes to the biblical word-choices, N'SK and TRBYT. But the remainder of the chapter is satisfied to refer solely to interest, or usury, as RBYT, which is translated "interest" or "usury" as the case requires. So Mishnah-tractate Baba Mesia 5:1 is essentially secondary to the linguistic and conceptual core of the chapter as a whole, which hardly refers to the distinction announced at the outset. The meaning of interest is clear as given. It involves a repayment of 25 percent over what is lent in cash, or 50 percent over what is lent in kind. Increase is less clear. We deal with a case of trading in futures. The purchaser agrees to pay at the current price of 25 *denars* for a *kor;* delivery is postponed until the harvest. Mishnah-tractate Baba Mesia 5:7 permits this procedure. When the purchaser calls his contract, the vendor concurs in revising the price of the contract. But he also revises the cost of wine upward to its then-prevailing price. In point of fact, the seller has no wine for sale. This would appear, in contemporary terms, to be trading in 'naked' or uncovered futures. If that is at issue, the prohibition would be based upon the highly speculative character of the vendor's trading practices. But the "increase" is that the vendor now has to pay for the wine at a higher price than is coming to the purchaser.

5:2

A.   He who lends money to his fellow should not live in his courtyard for free.

B.   Nor should he rent [a place] from him for less [than the prevailing rate],

C.   for that is [tantamount to] usury.

D.   One may effect an increase in the rent-charge [not paid in advance], but not the purchase-price [not paid in advance].

E.   How so?

F.   [If] one rented his courtyard to him and said to him, "If you pay me now [in advance], lo, it's yours for ten *selas* a year,

G.   "but if [you pay me] by the month, it's a *sela* a month" –

H.   it is permitted.

I.   [But if] he sold his field to him and said to him, "If you pay me the entire sum now, lo, it's yours for a thousand *zuz*.

J.   "But if you pay me at the time of the harvest, it's twelve *maneh* [1,200 *zuz*]," –

K.   it is forbidden.

Mishnah-tractate Baba Mesia 5:2

A-C prohibit interest in kind. D is neatly explained at F-H *vs.* I-K.

The rent falls due month by month, so there is no fee for "waiting" on the payment, while at I-K there is a 20 percent surcharge for postponing payment, tantamount to mortgage-interest. Since the rent falls due only month by month, it is not as if the tenant is gaining an undue advantage. The landlord is handing over two *selas* in exchange for the tenant's paying money which has not yet fallen due. But in the latter case, the seller of the field is owed the money as soon as the sale has been effected. By collecting 20% extra some time later, he is receiving interest on money which, in fact, already is owing to him. This is not permitted.

5:3

A. [If] one sold him a field, and [the other] paid him part of the price,
B. and [the vendor] said to him, "Whenever you want, bring me the rest of the money, and [then] take yours [the field]" –
C. it is forbidden.
D. [If] one lent him money on the security of his field and said to him, "If you do not pay me by this date three years hence, lo, it is mine"
    –
E. lo, it is his.
F. And thus did Boethus b. Zonin do, on instruction of sages.

Mishnah-tractate Baba Mesia 5:3

At issue here, in the contrast of A-C,D-E, is a subterfuge for the payment of interest. A-C indicate the possibility, for, as we shall see, either the vendor or the purchaser may prove to be the lender at interest, involving usufruct of the field. All depends upon whether the sale is actually consummated through the payment of the whole of the stipulated price. The case of A-C involves partial payment for a field. Transfer of ownership is postponed until full payment is made. The transfer is dated from the time of the sale. What of the usufruct? The vendor, by the terms of B, will enjoy the usufruct of the field in the meantime. If, then, the sale *is* completed, the vendor will retrospectively have made use of what in fact turns out to belong to the purchaser from the date of sale. That usufruct is a form of interest on the outstanding balance of the debt. But what if we assign the usufruct of the field to the purchaser? Then, if the sale is *not* completed, the purchaser will turn out to have enjoyed the usufruct of a field from the time of the deposit. The deposit will be returned to him. The usufruct thus will appear to be interest on it. So the terms hide a usurious loan, whether of purchaser-lender to owner-borrower or *vice versa*.

The second, and contrasting case, simply permits a loan on security, with the proviso that the security or pledge is transferred to the lender only in the event of default at the end. That is not conceived to be interest. The case at D differs from that at B because the status of the field is not left in doubt. It remains the property of the borrower, who is not represented as a purchaser, just as the lender is not a vendor. So there is no unclarity as to the status of the usufruct, which remains fully in the domain of the borrower. That is why the stated precedent, F, is acceptable.

5:4

A. They do not set up a storekeeper for half the profit,
B. nor may one give him money to purchase merchandise [for sale] at [the return of the capital plus] half the profit,
C. unless one [in addition] pay him a wage as a worker.
D. They do not set the hens [of another person to hatch one's own eggs] in exchange for half the profit.
E. and they do not assess [and commission another person to rear calves or foals] for half the profit,
F. unless one pay him a salary for his labor and his upkeep.
G. But [without fixed assessment] they accept calves or foals [for rearing] for half the profits,
H. and they raise them until they are a third grown –
I. and as to an ass, until it can carry [a burden] [at which point profits are shared].

Mishnah-tractate Baba Mesia 5:4

The conception before us involves interest in the form of personal service, which also is prohibited. The case has a man commission a tradesman to sell goods in his shop and take half of the profits. But the condition is that, if the goods are lost or destroyed, the tradesman has to bear responsibility for half of the loss. Even if the stock depreciates, the tradesman makes it up at full value. Half of the commission, therefore, is in fact nothing but a loan in kind, for which the tradesman bears full responsibility. It follows that his personal service in selling the owner's half of the stock, if not compensated, in fact is a kind of interest in labor on that loan.

D, E, and G, restate this matter in the context of a factor, who commissions a farmer to raise his cattle. At D the man gives eggs to a fowl-keeper, who is to have them hatched. The keeper receives half the profits. He also bears full responsibility for half the loss. It follows that he must be paid a salary. At E, we make an assessment of the value of the calves or foals. Half of this sum becomes the fixed responsibility of the cattle-rancher. If the calves or foals die or depreciate, the rancher has to pay back that sum. So it is a loan in kind. If

in addition he is not compensated for time spent taking care of the
cattle-factor's share of the herd, once more his work will constitute
interest. If, G-H, there is no assessment in advance of the fixed value
for which the rancher bears full responsibility, however, then there is
a genuine partnership. The rancher receives half the value of the
profit. He acknowledges no responsibility for their loss, so there is no
loan here. The conditions of the contract are such that the man's
labor is amply compensated by his participation in the potential profits on half the herd.

5:5

A. They assess and put out for reading] a cow, an ass, or anything
    which works for its keep,
B. for half the profits.
C. In a locale in which they are accustomed to divide up the offspring
    forthwith, they divide it forthwith.
D. In a place in which they are accustomed to raise the offspring, they
    raise it.
E. Rabban Simeon b. Gamaliel says, "They assess [and put out] a
    calf with its dam, a foal with its dam."
F. (And) one may pay increased rent [in exchange for a loan for the
    improvement of] one's field,
G. and one need not scruple by reason of interest.

Mishnah-tractate Baba Mesia 5:5

The one who supplies the capital, in the form of the cow or ass,
benefits from the work of the rancher in raising the animal. But,
unlike the case of Mishnah-tractate Baba Mesia 5:4D-F, since the
animal works for its keep, the rancher gains the usufruct of the animal and so cannot be thought to pay "interest" to the capitalist in
exchange for his share in the capital, namely, in the profits on the
animals when they are sold. The rancher gets the work of the beast in
return both for what he feeds it and his own work with it, so that the
considerations of Mishnah-tractate Baba Mesia 5:4 are not invoked.
C-D provide a minor qualification. Simeon even goes so far, E, as to
permit the offspring of a dam to be assessed and raised, even though
it is only the dam which will work. F-G, which are separate, complete
the list of permissible investments. The point of F-G is that the increased capital investment in the land may yield an increased fee to
the landowner for use of the land, without scruple as to usury.

5:6

A. They do not accept from an Israelite a flock on 'iron terms' [that
    the one who tends the flock shares the proceeds of the flock but

restores the full value of the flock as it was when it was handed over to him],

B. because this is interest.
C. But they do accept a flock on 'iron terms' from gentiles.
D. And they borrow from them and lend to them on terms of interest.
E. And so is the rule for the resident alien.
F. An Israelite may lend out the capital of a gentile on the say-so of the gentile,
G. but not on the say-so of an Israelite. [If the gentile had borrowed money from an Israelite, one may not lend it out on interest with the Israelite's knowledge and consent.]

Mishnah-tractate Baba Mesia 5:6

We continue the interest of the foregoing. Terms of "iron flock" are such as to guarantee to the investor both full restitution of capital and a fixed return on the capital. Unlike the conditions at Mishnah-tractate Baba Mesia 5:4-5, the rancher undertakes to share in the profit but to bear the full burden of loss. This arrangement involves "interest" in the form of unequal risk. There must be a full participation in both profit and loss in any shared undertaking involving the investment of capital – the animals – on one party's part and of labor and grazing land on the other party's part. (It goes without saying that the perspective of M. is that of the rancher.)

C-D are linked to the foregoing in detail only, but in theme they proceed to conclude the entire discussion of interest. Their point is that the stated prohibition of Mishnah-tractate Baba Mesia 5:1-5 applies solely to transactions among Israelites. Gentiles may receive or pay interest. Israelites may work for gentiles in this context. G's language is obscure. It may mean that gentiles may not borrow funds from Israelites and then, through the medium of an Israelite factor, lend them to other Israelites. Or G may wish to say that on his own initiative an Israelite may not lend on interest money belonging to a gentile. The main point is clear.

5:7

A. They do not strike a bargain for the price of produce before the market-price is announced.
B. [Once] the market-price is announced, they strike a bargain,
C. for even though this one does not have [the produce for delivery], another one will have it.
D. [If] one was the first among the reapers [of the given crop], he may strike a bargain with him
E. for (1) grain [already] stacked [on the threshing-floor],
F. or for (2) a basket of grapes,
G. or for (3) a vat of olives,

H. or for (4) the clay-balls of a potter,

I. or for (5) lime as soon as the limestone has sunk in the kiln.

J. And one strikes a bargain for the price of manure every day of the year.

K. R. Yosé says, "They do not strike a bargain for manure before the manure is on the dung-heap."

L. And sages permit.

M. And one may strike a price at the height [of the market, the cheapest rate prevailing at the time of delivery].

N. R. Judah says, "Even though one has not made a bargain at the cheapest rate [prevailing at the time of delivery], one may say to him, 'Give it to me at such-and-such a rate, or give me back my money.'"

Mishnah-tractate Baba Mesia 5:7

We take up the second general theme of Mishnah-tractate Baba Mesia 5:1, "increase." The case before us involves a prepayment for merchandise, e.g., produce. If the merchandise or produce is not yet on the market, one may not strike a price for delivery and accept prepayment on the contract. For this smacks of "increase," in line with M.5:1 – trading in naked contracts for futures. When a market-price is available, then prepayment may be accepted for later delivery, B-C. As we shall see, Judah, N, maintains that that price must be assumed to be the lowest available, that is to say, either the price at the time of the agreement or the price at the time of the delivery, whichever is lower. M. will spell this matter out in a principal generalization, A-C, a secondary and gray area, D-I, a special problem, J-L, and then a concluding qualification, M-N, the whole a most interesting exposition.

The main objection to trading in futures in the form of "naked calls" is that it smacks of usury. Why? First, The seller of the contract has the use of the money without clear knowledge of what his ultimate costs will be. Second, the buyer of the contract has no protection from the seller's default, should the produce not be available to the seller of the call, all in line with M.5:1. That is why one cannot undertake to deliver a quantity of produce at a given price, unless there is some indication of the prevailing market price for the produce. B-C complete the thought of A. Even though a given farmer has not harvested his crop, he may sell what he is going to harvest, since now there is clear evidence as to what he will receive and what the purchaser should have to pay. In the case of crop-failure, the farmer can make it up, C.

D-I present a secondary qualification of foregoing rule. The prohibition of A pertains to crops which both have not been harvested, and also have not been subjected to a prevailing market price. If crops have been harvested, even though there is no prevailing market, one may strike a bargain. Why? Because the crops are now in hand and nearly ready for delivery. There is no possibility of trading in futures as naked calls. D bears five illustrations. The items are not fully manufactured. So there is an agreement to make delivery later on. The market price may go up. The prepayment, however, is not deemed to fall into the category of interest, in line with Mishnah-tractate Baba Mesia 5:1's conception, because it is lower. So what D-I treat is a gray area between crops which are still in the field (Mishnah-tractate Baba Mesia 5:1) and those which are fully harvested and ready for delivery (Mishnah-tractate Baba Mesia 5:7M-N). There is no market for the former. The market-price is set for the latter. There will be a lower price, when prepayment is involved, for partially completed produce, and, as we see, this is all right.

J-K go on to deal with what is always in production. J's view is that the market-price is perpetual. Yosé regards the manure as subject to a process of preparation, and L repeats the theory of J. M-N are important. M allows striking a price at the height of the market, when the produce is cheap. The vendor then agrees to supply the produce through the year at the lowest prevailing price for each delivery. This is an important qualification of A, since the market-price is now set as a maximum, not a minimum – the theory of D-I all over again. Judah fundamentally concurs and carries the conception still further. Even though we have assumed that we speak of an advance payment at a fixed rate, Judah holds that that fact is always implied, even when it is not stipulated. The purchaser has the right to retract the sale if the lowest prevailing price is not allowed.

5:8-9

A. A man may lend his tenant-farmers wheat [to be repaid in] wheat, [if] it is for seed,

B. but not [if it is] for food.

C. For Rabban Gamaliel would lend his tenant farmers wheat [to be repaid in] wheat [when it was used] for seed.

D. [If one lent the wheat when the price was] high and [wheat] became cheap,

E. [or if he lent the wheat when the price was] cheap and [wheat] became expensive,

F. he collects from them at the cheapest price,

G. not because that is what the law requires,

H. but because he wished to impose a strict rule upon himself.

Mishnah-tractate Baba Mesia 5:8

A. A man should not say to his fellow, "Lend me a *kor* of wheat, and I'll pay you back at [a *kor* of wheat] at threshing-time."

B. But he says to him, "Lend it to me until my son comes [bringing me wheat],"

C. or, "... until I find the key."

D. Hillel prohibits [even this procedure].

E. And so does Hillel say, "A woman should not lend a loaf of bread to her girlfriend unless she states its value in money.

F. "For the price of wheat may go up, and the two women will turn out to be involved in a transaction of usury."

Mishnah-tractate Baba Mesia 5:9

Once more our concern is to avoid setting a price so long in advance that there is the possibility of usurious profit. If someone lends a *kor* of wheat and is to be repaid a *kor* of wheat six months later, then there is the variable that the *kor* of wheat may now be much less or ore, expensive than the *kor* of wheat later on. Consequently we have to make provision for what is, and is not, permissible, in line with the basic theory of Mishnah-tractate Baba Mesia 5:1, 5:7, 5:8 and 5:9 go over this ground. Mishnah-tractate Baba Mesia 5:8A-B make a fundamental distinction between a *kor* of wheat which is invested in the land owned by the lender, be lent with the proviso that it will be returned, in like kind and quantity, at the harvest. Even though it may increase in value, the lender is deemed not to lend but to invest in his own property (= Mishnah-tractate Baba Mesia 5:3F-G), since, after all, he recovers a share in the profit. But if the loan of the wheat is solely for the benefit of the tenant, then it cannot be repaid in kind, for the stated reason. C-H then provide an illustration of this matter. Gamaliel's procedure, C, is worked out at D-F and glossed at G-H. F means to speak separately to D and to E. If wheat was high when he lent it to his tenants for seed, at the harvest, when it is cheaper, he simply collects the same volume of wheat as he had lent. This then is to their advantage. So it is volume for volume. If wheat was cheap when he lent it for see, and then, in consequence of a poor harvest, the price went up, he collects in return not the same volume of wheat, but the same value as he had lent, thus collecting less wheat than he had lent but wheat worth the same amount of money as he had handed over. This benign procedure must be in mind, even though F is rather succinct and hardly explicit, for otherwise G-H would be meaningless.

Mishnah-tractate Baba Mesia 5:9A-C provide for a mode by which the loan may be effected. In line with Mishnah-tractate Baba Mesia 5:8A-B, one cannot promise to give back the same volume of wheat. But if he owns that amount of wheat at this time, but e.g., his son is bringing it, or he does not have the key to the granary, he may effect a loan to be repaid in the exact volume, without reference to the variation in price which may take place in the meantime. Hillel prohibits even this procedure, for the reasons stated at F. We now revert to a still more encompassing definition of "usury" or "interest," a definition so lacking in concrete action, let alone potential sanction, as to indicate the end of actualities and the entry of mere morality.

5:10

A. A man [may] say to his fellow, "Weed with me, and I'll weed with you,"

B. "Hoe with me, and I'll hoe with you."

C. But he [may] not say to him, "Weed with me, and I'll hoe with you,"

D. "Hoe with me, and I'll weed with you."

E. All the days of the dry season are deemed equivalent to one another.

F. All the days of the rainy season are deemed equivalent to one another.

G. One should not say to him, "Plough with me in the dry season, and I'll plough with you in the rainy season."

H. Rabban Gamaliel says, "There is usury paid in advance, and there is usury paid at the end.

I. "How so?"

J. "[If] one wanted to take a loan from someone and so sent him [a present] and said, 'This is so that you'll make a loan to me,' –

K. "this is a usury paid in advance.

L. "[If] one took a loan from someone and paid him back the money and [then] sent [a gift] to him and said, 'This for your money, which was useless [to you] when it was in my hands,' –

M. "this is usury paid afterward."

N. R. Simeon says, "There is usury paid in words."

O. "One may not say to him, 'You should know that so-and-so from such-and-such a place is on his way.'"

Mishnah-tractate Baba Mesia 5:10

The passage covers three final matters, usury exacted through labor in excess of what one has coming, A-G, usury paid through a voluntary gift, H-M, and usury paid through inside information, N-O. The point of the first group is that an exchange of labor must be abso-

lutely equal in all details. That of the second is that gifts either prior
to the making of a loan or after the repayment of the loan are
prohibited. Finally, as is clear, one must not provide inside information in exchange for a loan.

5:11

A.   These [who participate in a loan on interest] violate a negative
     commandment:
B.   (1) the lender, (2) borrower, (3) guarantor, and (4) witnesses.
C.   Sages say, "Also (5) the scribe."
D.   (1) They violate the negative commandment, *You will not give [him]
     your money upon usury (Lev. 25:37).*
E.   (2) And [they violate the negative command], *You will not take usury
     from him (Lev. 25:36).*
F.   (3) And [they violate the negative command], *You shall not be a
     creditor to him (Ex. 22:25).*
G.   (4) And [they violate the negative command], *Nor shall you lay upon
     him usury (Ex. 22:25).*
H.   (5) And they violate the negative command, *You shall not put a
     stumbling block before the blind, but you shall fear your God. I am the Lord
     (Lev. 19:14).*

Mishnah-tractate Baba Mesia 5:11

M. concludes with a striking homily, with the apodosis laid out in
accord with sages' enumeration.

To this point we have concentrated on Aristotle's conception of
economics and in the (somewhat uneven) workings of the market-
economy within that conception.[153] But distributive economics, that

---

[153] I have not dwelt upon the conservative character of Aristotle's thought, his
incapacity to come to grips with a market-economics and his introduction of the
considerations of "natural and unnatural" activity and transaction. For him the
market is an intrusive factor, to be kept in check. Any representation of Aristotle's as
a market economics would be as much a distortion as identifying the Mishnah's as a
market economics. Quite to the contrary, both economic theories, the one stated in
general terms, the other spelled out only in its details, share the trait of somehow
holding together two contradictory theories of economics. But each party has chosen
to preserve the received distributive economics, the one of status and intervention of
non-market forces into the market's working, and both look backward, to thousands
of years of distributive economics. In Aristotle's case, economic historians concur,
market-economics was a new development. But in the instance of the authorship of
the Mishnah, that was not the case. Indeed, that temple that formed the centerpiece
of the Mishnah's distributive economics was then not standing, and the priesthood
that was to make the system work had no real tasks or authority. The appeal to
archaic times (in the Mishnah's case, the days of Moses at Sinai) formed part of the
cultural baggage of the Second Sophistic, in which the Mishnah, temporally at least,
finds its place, but that matter is to be investigated in the setting of the Second
Sophistic, not of the matter of economics.

historically-prior, and independent, source of economic theory, worked out only in detail and not made explicit in general terms, predominated and vastly contributed to the economics of Judaism, yielding a mixed theory, partly a market-, partly a distributive-economics. For our survey of Judaism's economics of the householder, the market, and wealth has repeatedly shown us a puzzling fact. As we shall now see, market-economics persistently has appeared not to compete with but to be subordinated to a theory of distributive economics, in which a political authority, in the present case, the temple, intervenes in the control of production and distribution. Distributive economics in the Mishnah's theory in fact sets aside the market mechanism by according consideration to the status of individual participants to the transaction of distributing goods and services. The priests got goods and services for which they did not have to work or compete in the market place; the rules of the temple imposed taboos on the processes of production; the definition and evaluation of wealth bore no close relationship to market-realities.

In these principal components of its economics, concerning the definition of ownership of the means of production, the market, and wealth, the Judaism of the Mishnah restated, in its odd and particular idiom, the distributive economics of the paramount, three-thousand year old system of the Near East, going back to Sumerian times, to the details of which, for the Mishnah's theoretical economics of the householder, market, and wealth, we now turn. For when we understand the details of the Mishnah's theory of distributive economics, we can explain with little difficulty the reason that the authorship of the Mishnah has appealed to economics for the exposition of its systemic message. But, predictably, God lives in the details, a statement peculiarly congruent to the facts we shall now survey. At the heart of matters is who owns what, when, why, for what purpose and with what outcome. And these are questions essentially beside the point of market-economics, which deal, after all, with other forces than those that (adventitiously) define ownership, and which care little for the character and definition of what is traded in the market.

IX. *The Mishnah's Distributive Economics: Householder, Market, Wealth*

The economic data with which the Mishnah's framers made their statement came to them from the Priestly Code. On the face of matters, therefore, the authorship of the document appealed to an economic theory that derived from an ancient age (we would say it was seven hundred years old, back to ca. 500 B.C., but they would say it was fourteen hundred years old, back to Sinai, which would bear a date of ca. 1200 B.C.). The truly anachronistic character of the Mishnah's distributive economics[154] becomes clear, however, when we realize that by the fourth century B.C., the Middle East received and used the legacy of Greece, brought by Alexander, in which a type of private property, prerequisite to the development of the market and available for the free use of the holder of that property independent of the priesthood or other government intervention, had developed.[155] For the theory of the Mishnah both the market and the distributive systems form one system and represent two components of one system. So we deal with a single theory, holding together two distinct economics. What we shall now see is how the distributive component of the Mishnah's economic theory reshapes the three principal categories that have occupied our attention, the household, the market, and wealth. But we ask, first of all, why the system of the Mishnah appealed to economics to begin with, and the answer to that question comes to us from theology, not economics. What the Mishnah's authorship wished to say, we shall now see, they could express only by utilizing the principal categories of economics under study here.

At the center of the Mishnah's economics is the disposition of resources with unremitting regard to the status of recipients in the transaction. In no way does the economics of Judaism in its initial statement conform to the definition of market-economics just now cited. Our task therefore is now to understand in detail the foundation of the principles of distribution that define the theory of economics within the larger system of the Mishnah. In this way we grasp how profoundly the economics of the system has been shaped by the

---

[154] For an account of archaizing tendency of the Second Sophistic in general, that is to say, the age of philosophy in which the Mishnah's authors did their work, see E. L. Bowie, "Greeks and their Past in the Second Sophistic," in M. I. Finley, ed., *Studies in Ancient Society* (London and Boston, 1974: Routledge & Kegan Paul), pp. 166-209. Bowie shows that "the archaism of language and style known as Atticism is only part of a wider tendency, a tendency that prevails in literature not only in style but also in choice of theme and treatment, and that equally affects other areas of cultural activity." I shall address this matter more systematically in my coming study of the Mishnah in the context of the philosophy of the Second Sophistic, *The Philosophy of Judaism: The Mishnah in its Intellectual Context.*

[155] Davisson and Harper, p. 125.

larger systemic statement and message. The Mishnah's distributive economics derives from the theory that the temple and its scheduled castes on earth exercise God's claim to the ownership of the holy land. It is, in fact, a theology that comes to expression in the details of material transactions. The theology derives from the conviction expressed in the Psalm, "The earth is the Lord's." That conviction is a statement of ownership in a literal sense. God owns the earth. But the particular earth that God owns is the land of Israel, and, within that land, the particular earth is land in the land of Israel that is owned by an Israelite. With that Israelite, a land-owner in the land of Israel, God is co-owner.[156]

From that theological principle, spun out of the notion that when Israelites occupy the land that God has given to the Israelites, namely, the land of Israel, that land is transformed, and so too are the principles of ownership and distribution of the land, all else flows. The economics of the Judaism rests upon the theory of the ownership of a designated piece of real estate, ownership that is shared between God and partners of a certain genus of humanity whose occupancy of that designated piece of real estate, but no other, affects the character of the dirt in question. The theology consists in an account of what happens what ground of a certain locale is subject to the residency and ownership of persons of a certain genus of humanity. The generative conception of the theology involves a theory of the affect—the enchantment and transformation—that results from the intersection of "being Israel:" land, people, individual person alike. But let us turn directly to the economics of it all.

Since God owns the land of Israel, God—represented by, or embodied through, the temple and priesthood and other scheduled castes—joins each householder who also owns land in the land of Israel as an active partner, indeed, as senior partner, in possession of the landed domain. God not only demands a share of the crop, hence comprises a householder. God also dictates rules and conditions concerning production, therefore controls the householder's utilization of the means of production. Furthermore, it goes without

---

[156] How about "and the fullness thereof, the world and they that dwell therein"? The same reasoning leads to the view that God owns all the produce of the world and that everyone is God's slave. But in the system as it unfolded, Israel is described as God's slaves, and the system is consistent in its reading of both the bondage of Israel to God and the status of the land, that is, the land of Israel in particular, as God's particular land.

saying, God additionally has provided as a lasting inheritance to Israel, the people, the enduring wealth of the country, which is to remain stable and stationary and not to change hands in such wise that one grows richer, the other poorer. Every detail of the distributive economics therefore restates that single point: *the earth is the Lord's.* That explains why the householder is partner of the Lord in ownership of the land, so that the Lord takes his share of the crop at the exact moment at which the householder asserts his ownership of his portion.

But the on-going partnership between God and Israel in the sanctification and possession of the land is not a narrowly secular arrangement. Both parties share in the process of the sanctification of the land, which accounts for, and justifies, Israel's very possession of the land. The Israelite landowner has a particular role in effecting the sanctification of the land, in that, land is holy and subject to the rules of God only when the Israelite landowner owns land in the land of Israel. Once more, land located elsewhere owned by Israelites, and land located in the land of Israel but not owned by Israelites, has no material relationship to the processes of sanctification, in utilization and in the disposition of the products of the land, that are at the heart of the distributive economics at hand. That fact is demonstrated by the conception about the character of the land, and of God's relationship to it, that the longer Israel has lived in the land of Israel, the holier that part of the land. Israel's dwelling in the land makes it holy. "Areas in which Israelites have lived for longer periods of time are holier and are subject to more rigorous restrictions,"[157] than those in which Israel has lived for a shorter period. The laws of the sabbatical year apply more strictly to the territories in which Israel lived before and after 586. Areas occupied only before but not after, or vice versa, are subject to fewer restrictions. This has an important implication for the nature of God's ownership of the land. Newman comments, "In Leviticus the land is sanctified by God alone, who dwells in it and who has given it to Israel, his people. The Mishnah's framers by contrast, claim that Israelites also play an active part in sanctifying the land."[158] Accordingly, in the Mishnah's system, the partnership of Israel, represented by the householder, with God in ownership of the land affects the very character of the

---

[157] Louis E. Newman, *The Sanctity of the Seventh Year: A Study of Mishnah-Tractate Shebi'it* (Chico, 1983: Scholars Press for Brown Judaic Studies), p. 19..

[158] Newman, p. 19.

land itself, making it different from other land, imparting to it the status of sanctification through the presence of the two sources of sanctification, God and the Israelite, the Israelite householder in particular, as we shall presently see.

To understand the full impact of that one conception, we must recall that the Mishnah's utopian vision is realized in the exquisite detail of rules. Hence before proceeding to the secondary exposition of the implications for the distributive theory of economics of God's ownership of the land, we turn to a particular statement of the rules to see what it means, in rich exegesis, to conceive that God and the householder have formed a partnership in joint tenancy of the land that the householder owns. The tractate on tithing, Maaserot, gives expression to the definition of the householder's relationship to his partner and joint-tenant in possession of the land, God, meaning, the priesthood.[159] The basic point is that produce may be tithed as soon as it ripens, for, as Jaffee says, "at this point the crop becomes valuable as property." But one is required to pay the tithes only when the householder "actually claims his harvested produce as personal property."[160] That moment arrives when the householder brings untithed produce from the field to the house, or when he prepares untithed produce for sale in the market.[161] The reason is that that is the point at which the householder claims the produce for his own benefit and gain, at which point the partner, God, is to receive the portions that belong to him. The authorship of the tractate, for its part, develops a quite subordinate issue, as Jaffee defines it:

> The framers of the tractate, however, are troubled by their own notion that produce need be tithed only after it has been claimed as property. What disturbs them is that now there normally will be a lengthy period of time—beginning with the ripening of the crop and extending until well after the harvest—during which the produce will remain untithed. It is precisely during this indeterminate period prior to tithing, however, that some of the produce is likely to be eaten by those who harvest it or who are otherwise involved in its processing or transport. This is what concerns Tractate Maaserot, for untithed produce presents a taxonomical problem. On the one hand, such produce is not sacred food, restricted for the use of priests, for the dues have not yet been designated within the produce and set aside from it for their meals. On the other

---

[159] Martin S. Jaffee, *Mishnah's Theology of Tithing: A Study of Tractate Maaserot* (Chico, 1981: Scholars Press for Brown Judaic Studies), p. 1.
[160] Jaffee, p. 1.
[161] Jaffee, p. 1.

hand, the produce cannot be used as profane or common food, for it is capable of yielding offerings which stand under the claim of God. Untithed produce, it follows, is subject to a special set of rules which take account of its ambiguous character...produce which is neither sacred nor profane, neither wholly God's nor wholly man's.[162]

The upshot is that that produce may not be eaten in meals, but it may be used for a snack or in some other informal way. Again Jaffee: "The point is that the anomalous character of untithed food prevent it from serving the normal purpose of food which is sanctified to priests or of tithed food which is available for the use of commoners." A variety or rules then govern the use of untithed produce from the time of its ripening in the field, through the harvest field, until the point at which it is taken into the courtyard of the householder or sold in the market, at which the produce must be tithed.

At that moment before the householder exercises his property rights, he must give the partner's share to Him. The process is precipitated by the householder's evaluation of the state of the crop. Priests have a claim, as God's surrogates, not whenever they wish, but only when the householder determines that the crop is of value to him, so Jaffee: "God's claims against the Land's produce...are only reflexes of those very claims on the part of Israelite farmers. God's interest in his share of the harvest is first provoked by the desire of the farmer for the ripened fruit of his labor...God acts and wills in response to human intentions."[163] The centrality of the householder to the entire system of the Mishnah cannot be stated with greater force than this.

In the conception of the authorship of the Mishnah therefore all land was held in joint tenancy, with the householder as one partner, God as the other. That mixed ownership then placed side by side two economic systems, one distributive, resting on control of property by the temple acting in behalf of the owner of the land, who was god, the other the market-system in which private persons owned property and with legal sanction could use it and transfer title without intervention from any other power. As Davisson and Harper state, "For an economic system to be a market system, exchanges of private property must be accompanied by simultaneous exchanges of legally recognizes rights in property and its use."[164] To the degree that the

---

[162] Jaffee, p. 2.
[163] Jaffee, p. 5.
[164] Davisson and Harper, p. 124.

private person, the householder in our system's instance, shared those rights with another and functioned within limits imposed by that other, the consequent economy was not wholly a market-economy at all. That is the case, particularly, when other-than-market considerations affected the use of land or other good and when the other defined limits bearing no congruence to the policies and plans of the (secular) partner, the householder.

In the case of the conception of ownership of wealth set forth by the authorship of the Mishnah, a conception informed by the rules of Leviticus, God's joint ownership and tenancy with the farmer imposed a dual economics, the one, a distributive economic order, the other, a market system. The one partner, God, had no strong interest in the market-system; the other partner, the householder, was assumed to have only such an interest in the rational utilization and increase of scarce resources, land and crops, herds and chattels. God's share was to be distributed in accord with God's rules, the farmer keeping the rest. That is what I mean by a mixed system, one partner framing policy in line with a system of distributive economics, the other in market economics. The authorship of the Mishnah thus effected and realized in a systematic way rules governing land-use, placement of diverse types of crops, rights of ownership, alongside provision of part of the crop to those whom God had designated as recipients of his share of the produce. That explains why that authorship could not imagine a market-economy at all, and why the administered market (which, as we noted, is no market at all) in which government—priests' government—supposedly distributed status and sustained economic relationships of barter took the place of the market.

We have now to ask, precisely how does God assert his claim to his portion of the crop? The way in which we know God's portion of the crop is through some sort of accident that separates grain from the normal crop. This is taken to represent God's intervention in matters, in line with the casting of lots, e.g., with the Urim and Thummim, or in the story of Esther, constitutes the way of finding out God's preference. Designating God's portion by the workings of chance is illustrated by the category of the forgotten sheaf, an offering separated when the farmer has completed reaping the field and binds the grain into sheaves. A sheaf forgotten by all involved in the processing then becomes the forgotten sheaf that is the property of the poor (M. Pe. 5:7). Single grapes that fall due to no identifiable cause during the harvest fall into the category of the separated grape. Clusters that

grow without shoulders or pendants are defective and go to the poor
(M. Pe. 7:4). When the farmer thins the vineyard, the law of the
defective cluster begins to apply; that is the point at which the householder asserts his right of ownership (M. Pe. 7:5).

Produce that is designated without any intention of the householder and not by identifiable cause has been chosen by God. That
portion of the crop is what goes to the poor, or, under other circumstances, to the priest (hence: offering that is raised up for priestly
rations). As Brooks explains, "Whether it is the grain that happens to
grow in the rear corner of the field (and that the farmer himself will
later designate as *peah*) or the stalks that by chance fall aside from the
edge of the farmer's sickle (gleanings), all this food apportioned seem-
ingly by accident must be left for the poor. So the framers of the
Mishnah believe that God alone determines what produce falls into
the category of poor-offerings."[165] The same consideration affects the
designation of produce for the priests' rations. The procedure for
designating those rations at the threshing floor is for the priest to
declare that the priestly ration ("heave offering") is isolated in one
part of the pile of grain. Whatever the householder then grabs from
the pile falls into the status of sanctified grain, and there can be no
measuring nor designing specific grain. Again Brooks: "It is through
chance alone that God determines which particular grain in which
quantity will fall into the category of priestly rations." The householder's partner can be relied upon, therefore, to make his selection
of the shared crop.

Disposition of the crop also involves presenting to the temple
priesthood the first fruits of the crops. But only householders are
liable to present first fruits of their produce. Others are exempt. This
negative rule bears in its way the same message as the positive one.
Those who do not own the land are not liable to bring first fruits,
even though they own them as sharecroppers. Those who own land
but are proselytes, or who do not fully own the land, may not make
the recitation. Only full ownership of the land permits one to carry
out the rite. God's claim is limited to what God has made and distributed, the land. This is a mark that the householder occupies a
distinctive place in the scheme of things.[166] First fruits are thereby

---

[165] Brooks, p. 18.
[166] See Margaret Wenig Rubenstein, "A Commentary on Mishnah-Tosefta
Bikkurim, Chapters One and Two," in W. S. Green, ed. *Approaches to Ancient Judaism*
(Chico, 1981: Scholars Press for Brown Judaic Studies) 3:47-87.

distinguished from other agricultural gifts, obligation to provide which apply to all.

No wonder then that the householder stands alone in sharing with God ownership of the land, and, it follows, it is the householder alone, among all Israelites, who can effect an act of intention and designation that transforms the status of produce from secular or neutral to sacred. That power of consecration matches the control over Israel's history that is assigned, through the law of firstfruits, to the householder. How so? The householder's produce becomes consecrated as heave-offering only through the intention or thought and the deed of the Israelite householder. The householder is the one—the only one—who has the power to cause produce to be deemed holy. This he does by (in Avery-Peck's words) "formulating the intention to consecrate produce as the priestly gift. Then he pronounces a formula by which he orally designates a portion of his produce to be heave-offering. Finally, he effects his intention by physically separating that portion from the rest of the batch. Through these thoughts and actions the householder determines what produce, and how much of it, is to be deemed holy."[167] While human intention in general plays a central role, because of the arena defined by the law, namely, the disposition of the crop by its mortal owner, it is the intention of the householder in particular that is determinative. That intention is what changes the substance at hand from secular to holy, for holiness does not inhere but only is imputed by the householder.[168]

The householder, for the system of the Mishnah, therefore occupies an exalted position as God's partner. Consequently, the opinions, attitudes, plans, and intentions of the householder form the centerpiece of the system. Indeed, the will and intention of the householder, in matters of the disposition of scarce resources in particular, are what make the system work. For one example among many, at M. Kil. 7:6, we find that the action and attitude of the householder set aside the violation of the taboo which, had the householder deliberately done the deed, would have rendered forfeit the entire vineyard. If a usurper who sow a vineyard with mixed seeds and the vineyard left his possession, the rightful owner must cut down the sown crop immediately. If he does so, however, there is no conse-

---

[167] Alan J. [Avery-]Peck, *The Priestly Gift in Mishnah. A Study of Tractate Terumot* (Chico, 1981: Scholars Press for Brown Judaic Studies), p. 3.

[168] Alan J. [Avery-]Peck, p. 3.

quence to the prior presence of what should have been prohibited. The decision and action of the landowner make all the difference, e.g., if a wind hurled vines on top of grain, the householder cuts the vines at once and there is no further penalty, since the householder bears no responsibility for the violation.

The Mishnah's economics of the householder confirms to the theory of the market. As we now realize, the Mishnah's economics knows the market, but it is not a market-economics. Distributive economics, that is, the distribution of scarce goods and services not through the market-mechanism, involves designation of recipients who do not form normal participants or undifferentiated constituents of the market. These scheduled castes[169] lay an enormous claim, therefore, upon the resources of the economy, that is, the harvest of the household, for reasons other than their providing a quid pro quo.

One such designated group is the poor, who do not own a share of the Land. They are comparable to the priests and Levites, likewise not given a share of the Land (Dt. 18:1-5), and, like the sacerdotal castes, the poor therefore receive a share of the crop.[170] The rationale always is the same: God is the partner, in ownership of the land, with the householder. Consequently, God's share of the crop is apportioned to the castes or classes who form the surrogate for God in the division of the crops among the rightful owners. The rules governing the poor's share occur in tractate Peah, that is, "the corner-offering for the poor," which asserts that the poor have a claim on the produce of the land.[171] In point of fact there are several such portions of the crop reserved for the caste of the poor. The first is the rear corner of the field, peah, Lev. 19:9, 23:22; then come gleanings, Lev. 19:9, 23:22; the forgotten sheaf (Dt. 24:19; the separated grape, Lev.

---

[169] Since at stake here is hierarchization, I am justified in invoking the notion of caste, in line with Louis Dumont, *Homo Hierarchicus* (Chicago, 198?: University of Chicago Press). I refer to "scheduled" ones in particular, because there are other castes—groups of persons bearing the same indicative traits, e.g., women, slaves, minors—that are hierarchized in the Mishnah's vast hierarchization of all social reality, but that are not accorded a special share in, or claim upon, the distribution of scarce resources, as are the priests, Levites, and poor. The ones on the schedule within the larger hierarchical structure then fall into the classification I have invoked here.

[170] The poor do not have to separate from food they receive as a scheduled caste the share that the priesthood would otherwise claim (M. Pe. 8:2-4). Since God cannot lay claim on the same share twice, produce designated as *peah* is exempt from separation of tithes (M. Pe. 1:6).

[171] Roger Brooks, p. 1.

19:10;m the defective cluster (Lev. 19:10, Dt. 24:21, and poorman's tithe, Dt. 26:12, a tenth of the crop separated in the third and sixth years of the sabbatical cycle and handed over to the poor. Some of these offerings therefore involve leftovers or rejected portions of the crop, others quite marketable produce.

To understand the true character of this support for the poor, we must take account of the simple fact that it is not support accorded out of sympathy or social concern. The system of the Mishnah knows a quite distinct source of eleemosynary support for the poor, in addition to the provision of God's share of the crop to them. It was a system of soup kitchens. Through them transient poor are supported (M. Pe. 8:7), and the community maintains a soup kitchen as well. We should not therefore confuse the holy, Godly rights of the scheduled castes, on the one side, with the social benefits of supporting the poor, on the other. The former constitute a chapter in distributive economics, the latter do not. The difference is in the rights of ownership. In the case of the scheduled castes, the poor stand in for the "other Householder," who is God, and the disposition of the crop follows rules of distribution decreed by God, that is to say, by the priesthood that forms the authorship of parts of the Pentateuch, and the editorship of the whole of the Pentateuch, as the framers of the Mishnah among all Israel possessed the document.

The rationale for poor relief, in its several forms, differs in Scripture. The priestly authorship of Leviticus identifies God as the cause: "You shall leave them for the poor and for the sojourner: I am the Lord your God" (Lev. 19:9-10), 23:22). The Deuteronomist promises that God will reward those who do the same, but does not invoke God's name and ownership. Rather, he gives an essentially eleemosynary reason: "When you reap your harvest in your field and have forgotten a sheaf in the field, you shall not go back to get it. It shall be for the sojourner, the fatherless and the widow, that the Lord your God may bless you in all the work of your hands...You shall remember that you were a slave in the land of Egypt, therefore I command you to do this" (Dt. 24:19-022). The reason then has nothing to do with God's ownership of the whole land. It is, rather, that the Israelites too were once members of the scheduled caste of slaves, and that is why they must now act generously. Here too we discern two distinct forms of poor-relief, the one an expression of the land-theology of the priestly writings, the other of the social concern of the

Deuteronomic code. These produce the same kind of action, to be sure, but appeal to different motives.

We have now to identify that component of the goods and services of the market that is subjected to distributive, rather than market, economics, within the mixed economics at hand. It is, in particular, food that is subjected to the distributive system at hand—food and, in point of fact, nothing else, certainly not capital, or even money. Manufactured goods and services, that is, shoes on the last, medical and educational services, the services of clerks and scribes, goods in trade, commercial ventures of all kinds—none of these is subjected to the tithes and other sacerdotal offerings. The possibility of the mixed economics, market- and distributive- alike, rests upon the upshot of the claim that God owns the holy land. It is the land that God owns, and not the factory or shop, stall and store, ship and wagon, and other instruments and means of production. Indeed, the sole unit of production for which the Mishnah legislates in rich and profound exegetical detail is the agricultural one. The distributive component of the economy, therefore, is the one responsible for the production of food, inclusive of the raising of sheep, goats, and cattle. Again, the centerpiece is ownership of land. What does not derive from the earth owned jointly by God and the Israelite householder falls outside the economics of Judaism in its initial statement.

The agricultural produce of which God owns a share is explicitly what is marketable: it is that which is edible, tended, grown in the Land of Israel, harvested as a crop, and can be stored (M. Pe. 1:4-5). These traits, of course, characterize the produce that a householder will cultivate. Edibility guarantees use; tending defines an indicative trait of the household and further guarantees that the produce is valued by the householder, indicating by his cultivating it; the land of Israel is God's land; harvesting involves the taking of possession; and storage, like edibility, is a mark of valuing the crop. But produce that is not owned, e.g., what grows wild, what is used for feed for beasts, and seed, all are exempt; God's claim extends only to what the householder will use for his own needs and his family's and dependents'. There is no divine share in what is not owned to begin with, and that accounts also for the suspension of the designation of God's share of crops in the seventh year in the Sabbatical cycle, when the householder, for his part, exercises no rights of cultivation or ownership of in the land.

The definition of wealth forms a component of the rationale for the system as a whole. As we now recognize full well, the object of concern, in connection with tithing, is land and its produce. That conception is expressed in the following statement:

> A general principle they stated concerning tithes:
> Anything that is food, cultivated, and which grows from the earth, is subject to the law of tithes.
> And yet another general principle:
> Anything which at its first stage of development is food and which at its ultimate stage of development is food, even though the farmer maintains its growth in order to increase the food it will yield, is subject to the law of tithes, whether it is small or large, that is, at all points in its development.
> But anything which at its first stage of development is not food, yet which at its ultimate stage of development is food, is not subject to the laws of tithes until it becomes edible.
>
> M. Maaserot 1:1[172]

The point is that all plants cultivated by man as food are subject to the law of tithes. When the householder harvests the crop, he must designate a fixed per centage of it as heave-offering or tithes; these are sanctified and set aside from the rest of the harvested crop and handed over to the priests and other scheduled castes. Only then is the rest of the produce available to the owner. What therefore falls into the system of sanctification is what grows from the land through the householder's own labor ("cultivated"), is useful to the householder for sustaining life ("food"). God owns the land, the householder is the sharecropper, and the wealth of the householder therefore is the land that God allows for the householder's share and use.

At the end we have to listen not only to what the authorship of the Mishnah says, but also to what it does not treat. In fact, the economics of the system expresses in tacit omissions a judgment concerning the dimensions of the economy that to begin with falls subject to the enchantment of sanctification expressed in glorious triviality by our authorship. For matching the explicit rules are the authorship's ominous silences. Its land-centeredness permits its economics to have no bearing not only upon the economy comprising Jews who were not householders, but also Jews who lived overseas. The Mishnah's distributive economics is for the "Israel" of "the land of Israel" to which the Mishnah speaks. There is no address to the economics of "Israel" outside of the land. For distributive economics governs only agricul-

---

[172] Jaffee, p. 28.

tural produce of the land of Israel, and, it follows, market-economics, is tacitly assigned as the mode of distribution for everything else, and operative everywhere else.[173] No wonder, then, that the framers of the Talmud of Babylonia, addressing, as they did, Jews who did not live on holy or sanctified dirt, took no interest whatsoever in the Mishnah-tractates upon which we have focused here, the ones that state in rich detail the theory of a distributive economics of God as owner, scheduled caste as surrogate, temple as focus, and enlandisement as rationale, for an utterly fictive system.

X. *Conclusion*

I said earlier that the Mishnah's economics is *economics* only in the classic and not in the modern sense of the word. For economics from the eighteenth century became a distinct science on its own, treating economics not as a chapter in politics ("political economy") but as a disembedded corpus of knowledge and distinct component of social reality. On economics as the science has evolved from its eighteenth century origins, of course, the Judaism studied here has nothing whatsoever to say. My analysis therefore treats not the issues of economics broadly construed, e.g., how the framers of the Mishnah understood the difference between a commodity and specie, or how they defined the fundamental unit of production. Nor does the Mishnah's authorship tell us anything at all about the economy of the Jews in the time of the Mishnah even reveal economic attitudes that demand attention.

What that authorship tells us, in grand scope and acute detail, is the answer to a different question. It is, specifically, what we learn about the Judaism of the dual Torah in its initial statement when we ask those questions that economics instructs us to ask. So the issue is systemic analysis: economics as an indicator of the character of a system in context. From economics as conceived in antiquity, we gain perspective on the Mishnah. What we shall learn is that the Mishnah is a document of political economy, in which the two critical classifications are the village, *polis*, and the household, *oikos*. Since, however, the Mishnah's framers conceived of the world as God's possession

---

[173] And that conception is consistent with the temple-centeredness of the holiness-system worked out by the Mishnah.

and handiwork, theirs was the design of a university in which the God's and humanity's realms flowed together. In their statement bears comparison, therefore, to Plato's *Republic* and Aristotle's *Politics* as a utopian program of a society as a political entity, encompassing, also, its economics; but pertinent to the comparison also is Augustine's conception of a city of God and a city of man. In the Mishnah we find thinkers attempting, in acute detail, to think through how God and humanity form a single *polis* and a single *oikos*, a shared political economy, one village and one household on earth as it is in heaven.[174]

---

[174] That is why I conceive the more profound inquiry to address the politics of Judaism, as the Mishnah presents that politics: the city of God which is the city of humanity, unlike the distinct cities conceived by Augustine. The matter is neatly expressed in numerous specific rules. See for example Roger Brooks, *Support for the Poor in the Mishnaic Law of Agriculture: Tractate Peah* (Chico, 1983: Scholars Press for Brown Judaic Studies), p. 49 to Mishnah-tractate Peah 1:4-5: "...The Mishnah's framers regard the Land as the exclusive property of God. When Israelite farmers claim it as their own and grow food on it, they must pay for using God's earth. Householders thus must leave a portion of the yield unharvested as *peah* and give this food over to God's chosen representatives, the poor. The underlying theory is that householders are tenant farmers who pay taxes to their landlord, God." In this concrete way the interpenetration of the realms of God and humanity is expressed. That conception of the household and the village made up of households, the *oikos* and the *polis*, yields not only an economics but also a politics. And the politics is the foundation for the economics, as we shall repeatedly observe.

CHAPTER THREE

THE MISHNAH AND ARISTOTLE'S POLITICS

I. *Politics*

Judaism falls into the classification of a political religion because its foundation-document, the Mishnah, sets forth a view of power and of the disposition of power in society that is fundamentally political: a theory of legitimate exercise of violence. What makes this view political is that the system treats violence as legitimate when exercised by proper authority. Indeed, it specifies who may impose his will through coercion. That is, the initial system of Judaism defines within the framework of the faith a political structure and system that are integral to its religious plan for the social order. In the first systemic statement beyond Scripture itself, this Judaism secured for the institutions of the social order the power to exercise legitimate violence for the social entity. The institutions of this particular Judaism permanently ration and rationalize the uses of that power.

It is certainly not a typical situation. Consider: not all prior Judaisms appealed to political categories. In fact, after the Pentateuch few of them even set forth a politics. Moreover, from the writing down of the highly political fantasies of the Pentateuchal compilers to the formation of the Judaism that began with the Mishnah, no Judaism in the Land of Israel systematically incorporated politics within its system or framed any part of its statement in political categories. But this one did. In consequence, we classify it as a political religion and undertake to study the genus, political religion, through the species of a particular and appropriate Judaism.

To the sages of Judaism represented by the Mishnah, the separation of power in the form of legitimate violence from power in other forms, supernatural ones, for instance, proves implausible. To them, as to the Greco-Roman philosophical tradition in political theory, politics forms a component of the social order. Power is not to be separated from other critical elements of that same order. Politics and power cannot be treated as an independent topic of inquiry; for in antiquity, what we say about politics forms a chapter in a larger statement within our theory of the social order. Politics then is subordinated, contingent, instrumental. Treating politics as limited to the use of violence to achieve one's will proves a distinctively modern reading of matters; politics disembedded from economics and philosophy formed a point of analysis only with Hobbes' *Leviathan*, economics was disembedded from politics only a century later.

But it is precisely because we cannot take for granted the severing of the relationship between religion and political power that the Judaism analyzed here provides us with such an interesting case. Here I set forth a politics that is thoroughly integrated into a larger systemic structure and that bears a principal part of the systemic message. Rabbinic political theory, beginning with the Mishnah, integrated politics with economics and philosophy and provided a first-rate example of a political religion and a religious politics—both, equally. Here, of course, we focus only on the description, analysis, and interpretation of a political religion. Others will want to consider the same writings that I treat here within the framework of the representation of a religious politics.

For many religions, political power has no relevance; by contrast, this Judaism set forth as part of a large philosophical structure and system a political religion—a religious and also, therefore, a theological politics. Indeed, the power posited by the Judaism of the dual Torah in its initial document, and, as a matter of fact, by all Judaisms deriving from this formulation exactly matches that described by Finley.

Of course, all religions speak of power, and thus of legitimate violence. In their view, power is exercised by or in behalf of God and his divine agencies. But religions talk politics in another manner, too. A religion's intellectuals claim to explain the workings of power. That is, they try to explain why things are the way they are. And in accounting for why legitimate power works, why things are as they are, they commonly propound a causative theory of how things began. Further, the assertion of how things began serves as an apologia for the religion's legitimate violence, for when we say how things originated, we implicitly claim that that is how things were when they were right, and therefore how they should be even now. This combination of circumstances explains why in this book we address the politics of a religion, that is to say, we analyze a political religion. It further explains why we cannot limit our analysis to data that directly concern coercion and violence, legitimate or otherwise, but must extend our interest to the considerations of all aspects of the social order that the Mishnah means to describe. We cannot treat politics as disembedded from myth and philosophy and economics.

In fact, in imagination and intellect the system-builders of the Judaism in the Mishnah invented a political theory to bear a principal part of their systemic statement. That theory precipitated a system comprising, in correct position, proportion, and composition, the components of the social order. Its Judaism therefore comprises an ethos (an account of a world-view, in secular terms, a philosophy), an ethics (a prescription of a corresponding way of life, in secular terms, an economics), and an ethnos (a definition of the social entity that finds definition in the one and description in the other). These three components sustain one another in explaining the whole of this Judaism's social order, in constituting the theoretical account of its system. In Judaism's foundation-document (after Scripture) they combine to define in the context of a Judaism what is meant by "Israel."

Since the Mishnah, unlike Plato's *Republic* or Aristotle's *Politics* is not broadly received as a treatise in politics, it remains to explain precisely what kind of data I claim do provide information on the politics of Judaism. My criteria for selecting the data I examine derive from the theory of politics just now adumbrated. So far as politics is the theory of the exercise of legitimate power, dictating who may do what to whom and upon which basis, sanctions embody politics— imposing sanctions marks an extreme exercise of that power that works best when left tacit and implicit. The politics of Judaism invokes in vast detail the naked exercise of legitimate coercion. Coercion takes the form of judicial acts of killing, judicial infliction of injury, confiscation of valued property and services, ostracism and exclusion.[1] These penalties are specific to particular actions. Over and over again, we shall find in the details of the system's picture of sanctions the facts we require for the composition of the theory of politics we seek. Its myth accounts for what political institution imposes which sanction.

What kind of politics, exactly, do we now describe? It is not a practical politics, one that describes how things actually happened,

---

[1] True, sanctions are abnormal, obedience normal. The indication of political success is when the politics works, day in, day out, year in year out. The measure of success derives in the case before us from this Judaism's achieving its goals not through coercion but through collective effort and assent.

but only a utopian politics, a structure and system of a fictive and a fabricated kind. It is an intellectual's conception of a politics. In making up a politics, religious intellectuals' pictures of how things are supposed to be appeal to archaic systems. Politics then emerges as invention by Heaven or in the model of Heaven, not as a secular revision and reform of an existing system. To see religion—exemplified here by a Judaism in particular—in this way is to take religion seriously as a way of realizing, in classic documents, a large conception of the world. That is why we appropriately turn to a Judaism as an example of a religion that composes for itself a cogent account of the social order.

An analysis of the politics of a religious system therefore yields insight not into politics, but into the nature of that religious system. It reveals how that system delivers its message through the topics it selects for detailed analysis, what its message is, and why it chooses (in this case) politics as the appropriate medium for stating its message. But political culture in the politics of Judaism, though prominent , is essentially peripheral to the systemic problematic. That is why, in this context, the questions at hand fall entirely outside the frame of reference of the politics we shall examine.

To begin with, we ask about the context of the text before us. The facts of history show us why we find a politics thus congruent with our experiment's requirements in the Judaism of the Mishnah, why we find a made-up politics for a utopian society. In the middle second century, Rome incorporated the Land of Israel, as Palestine, into its imperial system. Further, Rome denied Jews access to their capital, Jerusalem. That is, the Romans permanently closed the Jews' cult-center, their Temple. Yet at the same time, the Mishnah's authorship, Judaism's religious intellectuals, its philosophers, made up a politics. Despite their circumstances, which undermined their entire pursuit, they described a government comprising a king, a high priest and an administration fully empowered to carry out the law through legitimate violence. It follows that if we want to know what a politics made up whole cloth looks like, we do well to describe, analyze, and interpret in theoretical context the politics of Mishnaic Judaism.

To identify those data of the Mishnah that contribute to a picture of the politics of the document, we take up the considerations of the disposition and rationalization of the uses of power—who can tell whom what to do and why. This question rapidly is redefined in terms of sanctions. For the system describes a variety of political institutions and persons, and what the system selects as its principal point of exegesis is the differentiation between and among those who legitimately impose sanctions. If the question, who does what to whom, finds its answer in the theory of differentiation among those who impose sanctions, that theory transcends questions of power and addresses, rather, theological issues of God's relationship to humanity. Once we ask about legitimate power, therefore, we move past a restricted definition of politics altogether and find our way outward toward the systemic center, which is not political in its basic classification at all, but theological, and, in context, mythical.

The case of finding myth within sanctions provides the rule. At each point, we seek in the Mishnah for evidences of the concrete working of power, in particular cases. When we know how power is legitimately exercised, we may work our way back from cases involving sanctions, the naked edge of power, to the theoretical system that sorts out the issues of politics. What we do, therefore, in the case of myth, is to seek guidance in the conception of how power works as we uncover the conception of what validates power's working as it does. That is to say, to identify relevant evidence of the working of a myth is to return to our simple definition of politics. When we have surveyed what a given type of authority may legitimately do to secure conformity to the system and its rules, we may ask why authority may act in such a way, why it may use physical force to enforce the law and sustain the system. From the end-product, the sanctions that are legitimately invoked, we may describe the myth of the politics of Judaism. And that is the rule throughout: from power in the form of sanctions we may derive a description of the political structure and system that accounts for those sanctions and organizes power for the purposes of the social order.

But the study of politics also requires the comparison of one politics with some other—for if we know only one thing, as I have suggested, we understand nothing. So once we have identified the case for description, we face the task of defining the categorical basis for description, analysis, and interpretation. There can be no analysis without comparison and contrast, and no interpretation out of context. But with what politics shall I compare and contrast the politics of Judaism, and how shall I define the context for interpretation? We gain the perspective required for the analysis and interpretation of that same structure and system in the politics of Aristotle. The choice of Aristotle's politics is far from random; it is rather pointed and particular.

We choose Aristotle because, for him, as for the philosophers of the Mishnah, politics formed a medium of choice for making an important part of a coherent systemic statement. Aristotle sees politics as a fundamental component of his system. He says: "political science...legislates as to what we are to do and what we are to abstain from." As to the institutionalization of power, I cannot imagine a more ample definition of politics than that.[2] And the Mishnah's sages stand well within the philosophical mode of political thought that begins with Aristotle, Furthermore, each politics—the Mishnah's and Aristotle's—originates in intellectuals' theoretical and imaginative life. And within that life, they each form an instance, of the concrete realization of a larger theory of matters.[3]

II. *Politics within the Judaic Myth*

The principal structural components of Judaism's politics are easily defined. Just as a systemic myth expresses the teleology of a worldview, telling people why things are the way they are, a political myth expresses that element of a social entity's worldview that instructs people why coercive power is legitimate in forcing people to do what they are supposed to do. It presents the narrative equivalent of legitimate violence, because it means through the force of its teleological apologia to coerce conformity with the social order and its norms. As we shall see, the political institutions envisaged by a politics convey details of the way of life of the same entity that, in theory at least, exercises the coercive power to secure compliance with the rules. Finally, the management of politics delineates, within the social entity's on-going affairs, how the institutions secure suitable and capable staff to carry out their public tasks. Politics defines the concrete and material component of the conception of a social system, and the theory of politics, defining both how things should be and also how they should be done, forms the critical element in a religious system.

The task undertaken by the political myth of Judaism is not only to make power specific and particular to cases. It is especially a labor of differentiation of power, indicating what agency or person has the

---

[2] Cited by R. G. Mulgan, *Aristotle's Political Theory* (Oxford: Clarendon Press, 1977), p. 3.
[3] That may be said of most political theories—and most of those evolve less subject to intervention by practitioners of statecraft.

power to precipitate the working of politics as legitimate violence at all.[4] When, therefore, we understand the differentiating force of myth that imparts to politics its activity and dynamism, we shall grasp what everywhere animates the structures of the politics and propels the system. In the case of the politics of Judaism, we shall work our way downward, into the depths of the system, toward a myth of taxonomy of power. Appealing to a myth of taxonomy, the system accomplishes its tasks by explaining why this, not that, by telling as its foundation story a myth of classification for the application of legitimate violence. The myth appeals in the end to the critical bases for the taxonomy, among institutions, of a generalized power to coerce. Let me make these somewhat abstract remarks more concrete.

Specifically, we analyze the mythic foundations of sanctions. And when we move from sanctions to the myth expressed and implicit in the application and legitimation of those sanctions, we see a complex but cogent politics sustained by a simple myth. This somewhat protracted survey of sanctions and their implications had best commence with a clear statement of what we shall now uncover.

The encompassing framework of rules, institutions and sanctions is explained and validated by appeal to the myth of God's shared rule. That dominion, exercised by God and his surrogates on earth, is focused partly in the royal palace, partly in the Temple, and partly in the court. For us, the issue here is the differentiation of power, which is to say, which part falls where and why? Helpfully, the political myth of Judaism explains who exercises legitimate violence and under what conditions, and furthermore specifies the source for differentiation. The myth consequently serves a particular purpose—which is to answer that particular question. Indeed, the Judaic political myth comes to expression in its details of differentiation, which permit us to identify, and of course to answer, the generative question of politics.

Moving from the application of power to the explanation thereof, we find that the system focuses upon finding answers to the question of who imposes which sanction, and why. And those answers contain the myth, nowhere expressed, everywhere in full operation. So we begin with cases and end with cases, only in the mid-stages of analysis uncovering the narrative premises for our diverse cases that, when

---

[4] A fundamental premise of my mode of systemic analysis is that where a system differentiates, there it lays its heaviest emphasis and stress. That is how we may identify what particular questions elicit urgent concern, and what other questions are treated as null.

seen together, form the myth of politics in the initial structure of post-Temple Judaism. Through the examination of sanctions, we identify the foci of power. At that point we ask how power is differentiated.

Let me explain. Institutions of political persuasion and coercion dominate not only through physical but also through mental force, through psychological coercion or appeal to good will. So my inquiry's premise is not far to seek. I take as a given that a political myth animates the structure of a politics. But the authorship of the Mishnah has chosen other media for thought and expression than narrative and teleological ones. It is a philosophical, not a historical (fictive) account; it is conveyed through masses of detailed rules about small things. While the Mishnah through its cases amply informs us on the institutions of politics, the mythic framework within which persuasion and inner compliance are supposed to bring about submission to legitimate power scarcely emerges, remaining only implicit throughout.[5] But it is readily discerned when we ask the right questions. If we were to bring to the authorship of the Mishnah such questions as "who tells whom what to do?" they would point to the politics' imaginary king and its equally fictive high priest, with associated authorities. Here, they would tell us, are the institutions of politics—represented in personal rather than abstract form, to be sure. But if we were to say to them, "And tell us the story (in our language: the myth) that explains on what basis you persuade people to conform," they would find considerable difficulty in bringing to the fore the explicit mythic statements made by their writing.

How then are we to identify, on the basis of what the Mishnah does tell us, the generative myths to which the system is supposed to appeal? The answer derives from the definition of politics that governs this entire study. A myth, we recall, explains the exercise of legitimate power. Now, we know, power comes to brutal expression when the state kills or maims someone or deprives a person of property through the imposition of legal sanctions for crime or sin.[6] In the

---

[5] Given the authority of Scripture and the character of the Pentateuch as a design of a holy state, on holy land, made up of holy people, living a holy life, we should not be surprised by silence, on the surface at least, about the reason why. People everywhere acknowledge and confess God's rule and the politics of the Torah, in its written form as the Pentateuch, claiming legitimacy attained through conformity to the law and politics. But we cannot take for granted that Scripture has supplied a myth. That is something to be shown in context, as we shall see in just a moment.

[6] I do not distinguish crime from sin, since I do not think the system does. At the same time our own world does make such a distinction, and it would be confusing not to preserve it. That accounts for the usage throughout.

absence of a myth of power, we therefore begin with power itself. We shall work our way back from the facts of power to the intimations, within the record of legitimately violent sanctions, of the intellectual and even mythic sources of legitimation for the exercise and use of that legitimate violence. For it is at the point of imposing sanctions, of killing, injuring, denying property, excluding from society, that power operates in its naked form. Then how these legitimate exercises of violence are validated will set before us such concrete evidence of the myth. And, so far as there is such evidence, that will identify the political myth of Judaism.

Since the analysis of sources will prove somewhat abstruse, let me signal in advance the main line of argument. Analyzing myth by explaining sanctions draws our attention to the modes of legitimate violence that the system identifies. There we find four types of sanctions, each deriving from a distinct institution of political power, each bearing its own mythic explanation. The first comprises what God and the Heavenly court can do to people. The second comprises what the earthly court can do to people. That type of sanction embodies the legitimate application of the worldly and physical kinds of violence of which political theory ordinarily speaks. The third comprises what the cult can do to the people. The cult through its requirements can deprive people of their property as legitimately as can a court. The fourth comprises conformity with consensus—self-imposed sanctions. Here the issue is, whose consensus, and defined by whom? Across these four types of sanction, four types of coercion are in play. They depend on violence of various kinds—psychological and social as much as physical. Clearly, then, the sanctions that are exercised by other than judicial-political agencies prove violent and legitimately coercive, even though the violence and coercion are not the same as those carried out by courts.

On this basis we can differentiate among types of sanctions—and hence trace evidences of how the differentiation is explained. Since our data focus upon who does what to whom, the myth of politics must explain why various types of sanctions are put into effect by diverse political agencies or institutions. As we shall see, the exercise of power, invariably and undifferentiatedly in the name and by the authority of God in Heaven to be sure, is kept distinct. And the distinctions in this case signal important differences which, then, require explanation. Concrete application of legitimate violence by [1] Heaven covers different matters from parts of the political and social world governed by the policy and coercion of [2] the this-worldly political classes. And both sorts of violence have to be kept distinct from the sanction effected by [3] the community through the weight of attitude and public opinion. Here, again, we find a distinct set of penalties applied to a particular range of actions. When we have seen the several separate kinds of sanction and where they apply, we shall have a full account of the workings of politics as the application of power, and from that concrete picture we may, I think, identify the range of power and the mythic framework that has to have accommodated and legitimated diverse kinds of power.

Our task therefore is to figure out on the basis of sanctions' distinct realms, Heaven, earth, and the mediating range of the Temple and sacrifice, which party imposes sanctions for (in modern parlance) what crimes or sins. Where Heaven intervenes, do other authorities participate, and if so, what tells me which party takes charge and imposes its sanction? Is the system differentiated so that where earth is in charge, there is no pretense of appeal to Heaven? Or do we find cooperation in coextensive jurisdiction, such that one party penalizes an act under one circumstance, the other the same act under a different circumstance? A survey of the sanctions enables us to differentiate the components of the power-structure before us. So we wonder whether each of these three estates that enjoy power and inflict sanctions of one kind or another—Heaven, earth, Temple in-between— governs its own affairs, without the intervention of the others, or whether, working together, each takes charge in collaboration with the other, so that power is parceled out and institutions simultaneously differentiate themselves from one another and also intersect. The survey of sanctions will allow us to answer these questions and so identify the myth of politics and the exercise of power that Judaism promulgated through the Mishnah.

What has been said about the relationship of the Mishnah to Scripture—the system makes its own choices within the available revelation—imposes the first task. We must address this obvious question: can we not simply open the Hebrew Scriptures and choose, therein, the operative political myth? No, we cannot. Why? First, the system-builders choose what they find useful and ignore what they do not. Second, Scripture presents for a political myth pretty much everything and its opposite; it allows for government by the prophet (Moses), the king (David), the priest (Ezra). So if we are to appeal to Scripture in our search for myth, we can do so only by showing that,

in the very context of the concrete exercise of power, the framers of
the Mishnah turn to Scripture. They then will tell us where to look
and why. In fact, our authorship does represent the entire system as
the realization of God's dominion over Israel. And this representation is specific and detailed. It thus justifies an inquiry, once we have
identified the questions the myth must answer, into how, in Scripture, we find responses to just those questions.

Here, then, is one instance of the way in which Scripture provides
a detail of a myth accompanying a detail of legitimate coercion. The
following lists the number of law-violations that one commits by
making a profit, which is to say, collecting interest:

> Those who participate in a loan on interest violate a negative com-
> mandment: these are the lender, borrower, guarantor, and witnesses.
> Sages say, "Also the scribe."
> They violate the negative commandment, "You will not give him
> your money upon usury" (Lev. 25:37); "You will not take usury from
> him" (Lev. 25:36); "You shall not be a creditor to him" (Ex. 22:25);
> "Nor shall you lay upon him usury" (Ex. 22:25); and they violate the
> negative command, "You shall not put a stumbling block before the
> blind, but you shall fear your God. I am the Lord" (Lev. 19:14)
>
> M. Baba Mesia. 5:11

We appeal to the Torah to justify law-obedience and to impose sanction for disobedience. But where is the myth that sustains obedience?
Let me explain this question, which is critical to all that follows. On
the basis of the passage just cited, we do not know what actually
happens to me if I do participate in a loan on interest and so violate
various rules of the Torah. More to the point, we do not know who
that penalty or effects it. That is to say, the generalized appeal to the
law of the Torah and the assumed premise that one should obey that
law and not violate it hardly tell me the morphology of the political
myth at hand. They assume a myth that is not set forth, and they
conceal those details in which the myth gains its sustaining vitality
and power.

Clearly, simply knowing that everything is in accord with the Torah and that God wants Israel to keep the laws of the Torah does not
reveal the systemically active component of the political myth. On
the one hand, the propositions are too general; on the other hand,
they do not address the critical question. The sequence of self-evident
premises that runs [1] God revealed the Torah, [2] the political
institutions and rules carry out the Torah, and therefore [3] people
should conform, hardly sustains a concrete theory of *just* where and

how God's authority serves the systemic construction at hand. The appeal to Scripture, therefore, reveals no incisive information about the Mishnah's validating myth.

This conclusion is reinforced by the references we find here and there to "the kingdom of Heaven"[7] that appeal to God's rule in an everyday framework. These form a mere allegation that, in general, what the political authorities tell people to do is what God wants them to do illuminates not at all. For example, at M. Ber. 2:5, to Gamaliel is attributed the statement, "I cannot heed you to suspend from myself the kingdom of Heaven even for one hour." Now as a matter of fact that is not a political context[8]—there is no threat of legitimate violence, for instance—for the saying has to do with reciting the *Shema*. No political conclusions are drawn from that allegation. Quite to the contrary, Gamaliel, head of the collegium of sages, is not thereby represented as relinquishing power to Heaven, only as expressing his obedience to divine rule even when he does not have to. Indeed, "the kingdom of Heaven" does not form a political category, even though, as we shall see, in the politics of Judaism, all power flows from God's will and law, expressed in the Torah. In this Judaism the manipulation and application of power, allowing the impositions of drastic sanctions in support of the law for instance, invariably flow through institutions, on earth and in Heaven, of a quite concrete and material character. "The kingdom of Heaven" may be within, but violate the law deliberately and wantonly and God will kill you sooner than you should otherwise have had to die. And, as a matter of fact, the Mishnah's framers rarely appeal in the

[7] In line with the Mishnah's usage, I refer to God and God's heavenly court with the euphemism of "Heaven," and the capital H expresses the simple fact that "Heaven" always refers to God and God's court on high. The Mishnah is not clear on whether its authorship thinks God personally intervenes throughout, but there is a well-established belief in divine agents, e.g., angels or messengers, so in speaking of Heaven or Heaven's intervention, we take account of the possibility that God's agents are meant.

[8] I am puzzled by the fact that in the Mishnah "kingdom of Heaven" never occurs in what we should call a political context, rather, it occurs in the context of personal piety. My sense is that this usage should help illuminate the Gospels' presentation of sayings assigned to Jesus concerning "the kingdom," "my kingdom," "the kingdom of God," and the like. Since the Mishnah presents a highly specific politics, the selection of vocabulary bears systemic weight and meaning (something I have shown in virtually every analytical study I have carried on); these are in context technical usages. But their meaning in their own context awaits the kind of systemic analysis conducted here on the political vocabulary of Judaism, treated systemically and contextually and not just lexicographically.

context of politics and the legitimate exercise of violence to "the kingdom of Heaven," which, in this setting, does not form a political institution at all.

Indeed, from the Pentateuchal writings, we can hardly construct the *particular* politics, including the mythic component thereof, that operates in the Mishnah's (or any other) Judaism. First of all, the Pentateuch does not prepare us to make sense of the institutions that the politics of Judaism for its part designs—government by king and high priest, rather than, as in the Pentateuch, prophet. Second, and concomitantly, the Pentateuchal myth that legitimates coercion— rule by God's prophet, governance through explicitly revealed laws that God has dictated—plays no active and systemic role whatsoever in the formulation and presentation of the Mishnah's politics of Judaism. Rather, of the types of political authority contained within the scriptural repertoire, the Mishnah's philosophers reject prophetic and charismatic authority and deem critical authority exercised by the sage's disciple who has been carefully nurtured in rules, not in gifts of the spirit. The authority of sages in the politics of Judaism does not derive from charisma, (revelation by God to the sage who makes a ruling in a given case, or even from general access to God for the sage). The myth we shall presently explore in no way falls into the classification of a charismatic myth of politics.

True, everybody knows and believes that God has dictated the Torah to Moses. But the Mishnah's framers do not then satisfy themselves with a paraphrase of what God has said to Moses in the Torah. How might they have done so? The answer to that question provides perspective on what our authorship has done. The following allows us to see how matters might have been phrased—but never were:

M. Rosh Hashshanah 3:8

A. *Now it happened that when Moses held up his hand, Israel prevailed, and when he let his hand fall, Amalek prevailed* (Ex. 17:11).
B. Now do Moses's hands make war or stop it?
C. But the purpose is to say this to you:
D. So long as the Israelites would set their eyes upward and submit their hearts to their Father in Heaven, they would grow stronger. And if not, they fell.
E. In like wise, you may say the following:
F. *Make yourself a fiery serpent and set it on a standard, and it shall come to pass that every one who is bitten, when he sees it, shall live* (Num. 21:8).
G. Now does that serpent [on the standard] kill or give life? [Obviously not.]

H.   But: So long as the Israelites would set their eyes upward and
     submit to their Father in Heaven, they would be healed. And if
     not, they would pine away.

M. Rosh Hashshanah 3:8

The silence now becomes eloquent. We look in vain in the pages of
our systemic writing for a *single* example in which authorities ask
people to raise their eyes on high and so to obey what said authorities
command. Such a political myth may, however, be implicit. But
when made explicit and systemically active, not left in its inert condition, the myth we seek by definition precipitates not obedience in
general, but rather concrete decision-making processes, to be sure
inclusive of obedience to those decisions once made. And we shall
know the reason why.

More to the point, is God's direct intervention (e.g., as portrayed
in Scripture) represented as a preferred or even available sanction?
Yes and no, but mostly no. For in our system what is important is
that the myth of God's intervention on an *ad hoc* and episodic basis in
the life of the community hardly serves to explain obedience to the
law in the here and now. What sort of evidence would indicate that
God intervenes in such wise as to explain the obedience to the law on
an everyday basis? Invoking God's immediate presence, a word said,
a miracle performed, would suffice. But in the entirety of the more
than five hundred chapters of the Mishnah, no one ever prays to
have God supply a decision in a particular case.[9] More to the point,
no judge appeals to God to put to death a convicted felon. If the
judge wants the felon killed, he kills him. When God intervenes, it is
on the jurisdiction assigned to God, not the court. And then the
penalty is a different one from execution.

It follows that an undifferentiated myth explaining the working of
undifferentiated power by appeal to God's will, while relevant, is not
exact and does not explain this system in its rich detail. How the
available mythic materials explain the principles of differentiation
now requires attention. The explanation must be both general and
specific. That is to say, while the court orders and carries out the
execution, the politics works in such a way that all three political
institutions, God, the court and the Temple, the three agencies with
the power to bestow or take away life and property and to inflict
physical pain and suffering, work together in a single continuum and
in important ways cooperate to deal with the same crimes or sins.

---

[9] The ordeal inflicted on the wife accused of infidelity is not germane here.

The data to which we now turn will tell us who does what to whom and why, and, in the reason why, we shall uncover the political myth we seek.

Predictably, when we work our way through sanctions to recover the mythic premises thereof, we begin with God's place in the institutionalization and execution of legitimate violence. Of course, the repertoire of sanctions does encompass God's direct intervention, but that is hardly a preferred alternative or a common one. Still, God does commonly intervene when oaths are violated, for oaths are held to involve the person who invokes God's name and God. Further, whereas when faced with an insufficiency of valid evidence under strict rules of testimony, the earthly court cannot penalize serious crime, the Heavenly court can and does impose a penalty. Clearly, then, God serves to justify the politics and account for its origin. Although God is never asked to join in making specific decisions and effecting policy in the everyday politics of the state, deliberate violation of certain rules provokes God's or the Heavenly court's direct intervention. Thus obedience to the law clearly represents submission to God in Heaven. Further, forms of Heavenly coercion such as we shall presently survey suggest a complex mythic situation, with more subtle nuance than the claim that, overall, God rules, would indicate. A politics of rules and regulations cannot admit God's *ad hoc* participation, and this system did not do so. God joined in the system in a regular and routine way, and the rules took for granted God's part in the politics of Judaism.

Precisely how does the intervention of God into the system come to concrete expression? By appeal to the rules handed down at Sinai as an ultimate reference in legal questions, for instance. This is the case in the story about R. Simeon of Mispah, who sowed his field with two types of wheat. Simeon's problem is that he may have violated the law against sowing mixed seeds in a single patch. When the matter came before Rabban Gamaliel, the passage states:

> C. They went up to the Chamber of Hewn Stone and asked [about the law regarding sowing two types of wheat in one field].
> D. Said Nahum the Scribe, "I have received [the following ruling] from R. Miasha, who received it from his father, *who received [it] from the pairs, who received [it] from the prophets, [ho received] the law [given] to Moses on Sinai*, regarding one who sows his field with two types of wheat...."

> M. Peah. 2:6 (my emphases)

Here, the law's legitimacy clearly depends on its descent by tradition from Sinai. But that general principle of descent from Sinai was invoked only rarely. Indeed, R. Simeon's case undermines the Mishnah's relation to God's intervention. R. Simeon's problem is minor. Nothing important requires so drastic a claim to be made explicit. That is to say, it is a mere commonplace that the system appeals to Sinai.

But this is not a politics of revelation, for a politics of revelation consistently and immediately appeals to the myth that God works in the here and now, all the time, in concrete cases. That appeal is not common in the Mishnah's statement of its system, and, consequently, that appeal to the myth of revelation does not bear important political tasks and is not implicit here. Indeed I do not think it was present at all, except where Scripture made it so (e.g., with the ordeal inflicted on the wife accused of adultery). Why the persistent interest in legitimation other than through the revelation of the Torah for the immediate case? The answer to that question draws upon the traits of philosophers, who are interested in the prevailing rule governing all cases and the explanation for the exceptions, rather than upon those of historian-prophets, who are engaged by the exceptional case which is then represented as paradigmatic.[10] Our philosophers appeal to a myth to explain what is routine and orderly, and what they wish to explain is what is ordinary and everyday: institutions and rules, not cases and *ad hoc* decisions yielding no rule at all.

The traits of the politics of Judaism then emerge in the silences as much as in the acts of speech, in the characteristics of the myth as much as in its contents. The politics of Judaism appeals not to a charismatic but to a routine myth, in which is explained the orderly life of institutions and an administration, and by which are validated the rules and the workings of a political structure and system. True, as I have repeatedly emphasized, all of them are deemed to have been founded on revelation. But what kind of revelation? The answer derives from the fact that none of the political institutions appeal in the here and the now to God's irregular ("miraculous") intervention. Treatment of the rebellious elder and the false prophet as we shall see tells us quite the opposite. The political institutions not only did not invoke miraculous intervention to account for the imposition of sanc-

---

[10] A fine distinction, perhaps, but a critical one, and the distinction between charisma and routine is not a fine one at all.

tions, they would not and did not tolerate the claim that such could take place.

It is the regularity and order of God's participation in the politics that the character of the myth of the politics of Judaism maintains we have to understand and account for. Mere allegations in general that the law originates with God's revelation to Moses at Sinai do not serve to identify that middle-range myth that accounts for the structure and the system. If God is not sitting at the shoulder of the judge and telling the judge what to do (as the writers of Exodus 21ff. seem to suppose), then what legitimacy attaches to the judge's decision to give Mr. Smith's field over, or back, to Mr. Jones? And why (within the imaginary state at hand) should people support, sustain, and submit to authority? Sages' abstract language contains no answers to these questions. And yet sages' system presupposes routine and everyday obedience to power, not merely the utilization of legitimate violence to secure conformity. That is partly because the systemic statement to begin with tells very few stories. Matters that the Pentateuchal writers expressed through narrating a very specific story about how God said thus and so to Moses in this particular case, rewarding the ones who obeyed and punishing those who did not, in the Mishnah come to expression in language of an allusive and philosophical, generalizing character.

Here, too, we discern the character of the myth even before we determine its contents. While we scarcely expect that this sort of writing is apt to spell out a myth, even though a myth infuses the system, we certainly can identify the components of the philosophical and theological explanation of the state that have taken mythic form.

Even here, to be sure, the evidence proves sparse. First, of course, in the mythic structure comes God, who commands and creates, laying out what humanity is to do, exercising the power to form the social world in which humanity is to obey. God then takes care of God's[11] particular concerns, and these focus upon *deliberate* violation of God's wishes. If a sin or crime is inadvertent, the penalties are of one order, if deliberate, of a different order. The most serious infraction of the law of the Torah is identified not by what is done but by

---

[11] I cannot refer to "God" as "he" or as "she," hence the recurrent circumlocution, which is, admittedly, not ideal. The Judaic system before us of course took for granted the male-ness of God, with little to say about the explicit statement to the contrary at Gen. 2:27.

the attitude of the sinner or criminal.[12] If one has deliberately violated God's rule, then God intervenes. If the violation is inadvertent,
then the Temple imposes the sanction. And the difference is considerable. In the former case, God through the Heavenly court ends the
felon's or sinner's life. Then a person who defies the laws—as these
concern one's sexual conduct, attitude toward God, relationships
within the family—will be penalized either (if necessary) by God or (if
possible) by the earthly court. This means that the earthly court
exercises God's power, and the myth of the system as a whole, so far
as the earthly court forms the principal institutional form of the
system, emerges not merely in a generality but in all its specificity.
These particular judges, here and now, stand for God and exercise
the power of God. In the latter case, the Temple takes over jurisdiction; a particular offering is called for, as the book of Leviticus specifies. But there is no need for God or the earthly court in God's name
to take a position.

Now come the data of real power, the sanctions. We may divide
sanctions just as the authorship of the Mishnah did, by simply re-
viewing the range of penalties for law-infraction as they occur. These
penalties, as we mentioned above, fall into four classifications: what
Heaven does, what political institutions do, what religious institutions
do, and what is left to the coercion of public opinion, that is, consensus, with special attention to the definition of that "public" that has
effective opinion to begin with. The final realm of power, conferring
or withholding approval, proves constricted and, in this context, not
very consequential.

Let us begin with the familiar, with sanctions exercised by the
earthly court as they are fully described in Mishnah-tractates Sanhedrin and Makkot. We will review at length the imposition of sanctions as it is represented by the earthly court, the Temple, the heavenly court, the sages. This review allows us to identify the actors in
the system of politics—those with power to impose sanctions, and the
sanctions they can inflict. Only from this perspective will the initial
statement of Judaism, in its own odd idiom, be able to make its points
in the way its authorship has chosen. When we take up the myth to
which that statement implicitly appeals, we shall have a clear notion

---

[12] The distinction between secular felony and religious sin obviously bears no
meaning in the system, useful as it is to us. I generally will speak of "felon or sinner,"
so as not to take a position on a matter unimportant in my inquiry.

of the character of the evidence, in rich detail, on which our judgment of the mythic substrate of the system has been composed.

The most impressive mode of legitimate violence is killing; it certainly focuses our attention. The earthly court may justly kill a sinner or felon. This death-dealing priority accorded to the earthly court derives from the character of the power entrusted to that court. The earthly court enjoys full power to dispose of the property and life of all subject to its authority—in the context imagined by Judaism, of all residing in territory that comes under the state's control.

Imposing the death penalty is described in the following way:

Mishnah-tractate Sanhedrin 7:1-3
A. Four modes of execution were given over to the court [in order of severity]:
B. (1) stoning, (2) burning, (3) decapitation, and (4) strangulation.
C. R Simeon says, "(2) Burning, (1) stoning, (4) strangulation, and (3) decapitation."

M. San. 7:1

The passage leaves no doubt that the court could put people to death. Only the severity of suffering imposed by each mode of execution is in question. Thus, Simeon's hierarchy of punishments (C) differs from that of B in the degradation and suffering inflicted on the felon, not in the end result. The passage details four modes of execution, that is, four forms of legitimate violence. In the account, the following is of special interest. I have emphasized the key-words.

A. The religious requirement of decapitation [is carried out as follows]:
B. They would cut off his head with a sword,
C. just as the government does.
D. R Judah says, "This is disgusting.
E. "But they put the head on a block and chop it off with an ax."
F. They said to him, "There is no form of death more disgusting than this one."
G. The religious requirement of strangulation [is carried out as follows:]
H. They would bury him in manure up to his armpits, and put a towel of hard material inside one of soft material, and wrap it around his neck.
I. This [witness] pulls it to him from one side, and that witness pulls it to him at the other side, until he perishes.

M. San. 7:3

In among all the practical detail, Judah's intervention stands out. It leaves no doubt that carrying out the law ("way of life") realizes a particular world view. Specifically, his language implies that the felon remains a human being, in God's image. Clearly, then, at stake in the theoretical discussions at hand is how to execute someone in a manner appropriate to his or her standing after the likeness of God. This problem obviously presupposes that in imposing the penalty in the first place and in carrying it out, the court acts wholly in conformity with God's will. This being the case, a political myth of a dominion belonging to God and carrying out God's plan and program certainly stands behind the materials at hand.

But that observation still leaves us struggling with a mere commonplace. On the strength of our knowledge that God stands behind the politics and that the consideration that human beings are in God's image and after God's likeness applies even in inflicting the death penalty, we still cannot identify the diverse media by which power is carried out. More to the point, we can hardly distinguish one medium of power from another, which we must do if we are to gain access to the myth that sustains what we shall soon see is the fully-differentiated political structure before us. We do well at this turning point to remember the theoretical basis for this entire inquiry: a politics is a theory of the on-going exercise of the power of coercion, including legitimate violence. Sanctions form the naked exercise of raw power—hence will require the protection and disguise of a heavy cloak of myth.

How to proceed? By close attention to the facts of power and by sorting out the implications of those facts. A protracted journey through details of the law of sanctions leads us to classify the sanctions and the sins or crimes to which they apply. What precisely do I think requires classification? Our project to see who does what to whom and, on the basis of the consequent perception, to propose an explanation for that composition. For from these sanctions of state, that is, the legitimate exercise of coercion, including violence, we may work our way back to the reasons adduced for the legitimacy of the exercise of coercion, which is to say, the political myth. The reason is that such a classification will permit us to see how in detail the foci of power are supposed to intersect or to relate: autonomous powers, connected and related ones, or utterly continuous ones, joining Heaven to earth, for instance, in the person of this institutional representative or that one. What we shall see is a system that treats Heaven, earth, and the mediating institution, the Temple, as interrelated, thus, connected, but that insists, in vast detail, upon the distinct

responsibilities and jurisdiction accorded to each. Once we have perceived that fundamental fact, we may compose for ourselves the
myth, or, at least the point and propositions of the myth, that accounted for the political structures of Judaism and persuaded people
to obey or conform even when there was no immediate threat of
penalty.

A survey of [1] types of sanctions, [2] the classifications of crimes
or sins to which they apply, and [3] who imposes them, now yields
these results. First come the death-penalty on earth and its counterpart, which is extirpation (death before one's allotted time) imposed
by Heaven:

HEAVEN	EARTH	TEMPLE	COMMUNITY
EXTIRPATION *for deliberate actions*	*DEATH-PENALTY*	*DEATH-PENALTY*	
sexual crimes – incest – violating sex taboos (bestiality, homosexuality)	*sexual crimes:* in improper relationships: – incest		
religious crimes against God – blasphemy – idolatry – magic – sorcery – profaning Sabbath	*religious crimes against God:* – blasphemy – idolatry – magic – sorcery – profaning Sabbath		
	religious sins against family: – cursing parents		
	social crimes: – murder – communal apostasy – kidnapping		

HEAVEN	EARTH	TEMPLE	COMMUNITY
	social sins:		
	– public defiance of the court		
	– false prophecy		
religious sins, deliberately committed, against God			
– unclean person who ate a Holy Thing			
– uncleanness in sanctuary			
– violating food taboos			
– making offering outside of Temple			
– violating taboos of holy seasons			
– replicating Temple incense or oil outside			

Next we deal with court-inflicted sanctions carried out against property or person (e.g., fines against property, flogging or other social or physical violence short of death for the felon or sinner):

HEAVEN	EARTH	TEMPLE	COMMUNITY
	flogging	*obligatory*	*shunning*
	exile	*offering and/or flogging for inadvertent action*	*or approbation*
	– manslaughter	– uncleanness	– repay moral obligation (debt
	– incest	– eating Temple	cancelled by
	– violation of menstrual taboo	food in violation of the law	sabbatical year)
	– marriage in violation of caste rules	– replicating Temple oil, incense outside	– stubbornly rejecting majority view
		– violating Temple food taboos	– opposing majority will

HEAVEN	EARTH	TEMPLE	COMMUNITY
			– opposing
		– violating taboos	patriarch
		of holy days	
		(Passover,	– obedience to
		atonement	majority
			or patriarch
		– uncleanness	
		(Zab, mesora, etc.)	
		– Nazirite	
	– violating food	sex with bondwoman	
	taboos	– unclean Nazirite	
		– false oath of testimony	
	– removing dam	– false oath of deposit	
	with offspring		
	– violating negative		
	commandments		

The operative distinction between inflicting a flogging and requiring a sacrifice (Temple sanctions against person or property), and the sanction of extirpation (Heavenly death-penalty), is made explicit as follows: "For those [transgressions] are people liable, for deliberately doing them, to the punishment of extirpation, and for accidentally doing them, to the bringing of a sin-offering, and for not being certain of whether or not one has done them, to a suspensive guilt-offering." (That distinction is suspended in a few instances, as indicated at M. Ker. 2:1-2.)

This summary yields a simple and clear fact, and on the basis of that simple fact we may now reconstruct the entire political myth on which the politics of Judaism rested. Let me emphasize: *some of the same crimes or sins for which the Heavenly court imposes the penalty of extirpation are those that, under appropriate circumstances (e. g., sufficient evidence admissible in court) the earthly court imposes the death-penalty.* That is, the Heavenly court and the earthly court impose precisely the same sanctions for the same crimes or sins. The earthly court therefore forms down here the exact replica and counterpart, within a single system of power, of the Heavenly court up there. This no longer looms as an empty generalization; it is a concrete and systemically active and indicative detail, and the system speaks through its details.

But this is not the entire story. There is a second fact, equally indicative for our recovery of the substrate of myth. We note that there are crimes for which the earthly court imposes penalties, but for which the Heavenly court does not, as well vice versa. The earthly and Heavenly courts share jurisdiction over sexual crimes and over what I classify as serious religious crimes against God. The Heavenly court penalizes with its form of the death-penalty religious sins against God, in which instances a person deliberately violates the taboos of sanctification.

And that fact calls our attention to a third partner in the distribution and application of power, the Temple with its system of sanctions that cover precisely the same acts subject to the jurisdiction of the Heavenly and earthly courts. The counterpart on earth is now not the earthly court but the Temple. This is the institution that, in theory, automatically receives the appropriate offering from the person who inadvertently violates these same taboos of sanctification. But this is an odd choice for the Mishnah, since there is now no Temple on earth. The juxtaposition appears then to involve courts and Temple, and the upshot is that both are equally matters of theory. In the theory at hand, then, the earthly court, for its part, penalizes social crimes against the community that the Heavenly court, on the one side, and the Temple rites, on the other, do not take into account at all. These are murder, apostasy, kidnapping, public defiance of the court, and false prophecy. The earthly court further imposes sanctions on matters of particular concern to the Heavenly court, with special reference to taboos of sanctification (e.g., negative commandments). These three institutions, therefore, exercise concrete and material power, utilizing legitimate violence to kill someone, exacting penalties against property, and inflicting pain. The sages' modes of power, by contrast, stand quite apart, apply mainly to their own circle, and work through the intangible though no less effective means of inflicting shame or paying honor.

The facts we have in hand draw us back to the analysis of our differentiation of applied and practical power. In the nature of the facts before us, that differentiation tells us precisely for what the systemic myth will have to give its account. Power flows through three distinct but intersecting dominions, each with its own concern, all sharing some interests in common. The Heavenly court attends to deliberate defiance of Heaven, the Temple to inadvertent defiance of Heaven. The earthly court attends to matters subject to its jurisdiction by reason of sufficient evidence, proper witnesses, and the like, and these same matters will come under Heavenly jurisdiction when the earthly court finds itself unable to act. Accordingly, we have a tripartite system of sanctions—Heaven cooperating with the Temple

in some matters, with the court in others, and, as noted, each bearing
its own distinct media of enforcing the law as well. What then can we
say concerning the systemic myth of politics? The forms of power
and the modes of mediating legitimate violence draw our attention to
a single political myth, one that we first confronted, if merely as a
generality and commonplace to be sure, at the very outset. The unity
of that myth is underlined by the simple fact that the earthly court
enters into the process right along side the Heavenly court and the
Temple; as to blasphemy, idolatry, and magic, its jurisdiction prevails. So, as I have stressed, a single myth must serve all three correlated institutions.

It is the myth of God's authority infusing the institutions of
Heaven and earth alike, an authority diffused among three principle
foci or circles of power, Heaven's court, the earthly court, and the
Temple in-between. Each focus of power has its own jurisdiction and
responsibility, Heaven above, earth beneath, the Temple in the position of mediation—transmitting as it does from earth to Heaven the
penalties handed over as required. And all media of power in the
matter of sanctions intersect at some points as well: a tripartite politics, a single myth drawing each component into relationship with a
single source and origin of power, God's law set forth in the Torah.
But the myth has not performed its task until it answers not only the
question of why, but also the question of how. Specifically, the details
of myth must address questions of the details of power. Who then
tells whom to do what? And how are the relationships of dominion
and dominance to compliance and obedience made permanent
through myth?

We did not require this sustained survey to ascertain that God
through the Torah has set forth laws and concerns. That generality
now may be made quite specific, for it is where power is differentiated and parceled out that we see the workings of the political myth.
So we ask, how do we know who tells whom to do, or suffer, what
sanction or penalty? It is the power of myth to differentiate that
defines the generative question. The key lies in the criterion by which
each mode of power, earthly, mediating, and Heavenly, identifies the
cases over which it exercises jurisdiction. The criterion lies in the
attitude of the human being who has done what he or she should not:
did he act deliberately or unintentionally?

I state the upshot with heavy emphasis: *the point of differentiation
within the political structures, supernatural and natural alike, lies in the attitude*

and intention of a human being. We differentiate among the application of power by reference to the attitude of the person who comes into relationship with that power. A person who comes into conflict with the system, rejecting the authority claimed by the powers that be, does so deliberately or inadvertently. The myth accounts in the end for the following hierarchization of action and penalty, infraction and sanction: [1] If the deed is deliberate, then one set of institutions exercises jurisdiction and utilizes supernatural power. [2] If the deed is inadvertent, another institution exercises jurisdiction and utilizes the power made available by that same supernatural being.

A sinner or criminal who has deliberately violated the law has by his or her action challenged the politics of Judaism. Consequently, God or God's surrogate imposes sanctions—extirpation (by the court on high), or death or other appropriate penalty (by the court on earth). A sinner or criminal who has inadvertently violated the law is penalized by the imposition of Temple sanctions, losing valued goods. People obey because God wants them to and has told them what to do, and when they do not obey, a differentiated political structure appeals to that single hierarchizing myth. The components of the myth are two: first, God's will, expressed in the law of the Torah, second, the human being's will, carried out in obedience to the law of the Torah or in defiance of that law.

Have we come so far and not yet told the story that the myth contains? I have now to explain and spell out the story that conveys the myth of politics in Judaism. It is not in the Mishnah at all. Do I find the mythic foundation in Scripture, which accounts for the uses and differentiation of power that the Mishnah's system portrays? Indeed I do, for, as we realize, the political myth of Judaism has to explain the differentiation of sins or crimes, with their associated penalties or punishments, and so sanctions of power. And in Scripture there is a very precise answer to the question of how to differentiate among sins or crimes and why to do so. Given the position of the system of the Mishnah, the point of differentiation must rest with one's attitude or intentionality And, indeed, I do have two stories of how the power of God conflicts with the power of humanity in such wise as to invoke the penalties and sanctions in precisely the differentiated modes we have before us. Where do I find such stories of the conflict of wills, God's and humanity's?

The first such story of power differentiated by the will of the human being in communion or conflict with the word of the commanding God comes to us from the Garden of Eden.[13] We cannot too often reread the following astonishing words:

> The Lord God took the man and placed him in the garden of Eden... and the Lord God commanded the man, saying, "Of every tree of the garden you are free to eat; but as for the tree of knowledge of good and bad, you must not eat of it; for as soon as you eat of it, you shall die."
>
> ...When the woman saw that the tree was good for eating and a delight to the eyes, and that the tree was desirable as a source of wisdom, she took of its fruit and ate; she also gave some to her husband, and he ate...
>
> The Lord God called out to the man and said to him, "Where are you?"
>
> He replied, "I heard the sound of You in the garden, and I was afraid, because I was naked, so I hid."
>
> Then He asked, "Who told you that you were naked? Did you eat of the tree from which I had forbidden you to eat?"
>
> ...And the Lord God said to the woman, "What is this you have done!"
>
> So the Lord God banished him from the garden of Eden...

Now a reprise of the exchange between God, Adam, and Eve, tells us that at stake was responsibility: who has violated the law, but who bears responsibility for deliberately violating the law:

> "The woman You put at my side—she gave me of the tree, and I ate."
>
> "The serpent duped me, and I ate."
>
> Then the Lord God said to the serpent, "because you did this...."

The ultimate responsibility lies with the one who acted deliberately, not under constraint or on account of deception or misinformation, as did Adam and Eve Then the sanction applies most severely to the one who by intention and an act of will has violated God's intention and will.

Adducing this story by itself poses several problems. First, the story-teller does not allege that Adam intended to violate the commandment; he followed his wife. Second, the penalty is not extirpa-

---

[13] This is not to suggest that the distinction behind the system's differentiation is important only in the myth of Eden. Quite to the contrary, the authorship of the laws of Leviticus and Deuteronomy repeatedly appeals to that same distinction. But our interest is in myth, and I find in the myth of Eden the explanation for the point of differentiation that the political myth of Judaism invokes at every point. So, as I have said, the sanctions lead to the systemic question that requires mythic response, and once we know the question, we can turn to Scripture for the myth (as much as we can find in Scripture ample expansion, in law, of that same myth).

tion but banishment. That is why to establish what I conceive to be the generative myth, I turn to a second story of disobedience and its consequences, the tale of Moses's hitting the rock:

> The community was without water, and they joined against Moses and Aaron...Moses and Aaron came away from the congregation to the entrance of the Tent of Meeting and fell on their faces. The Presence of the Lord appeared to them, and the Lord spoke to Moses, saying, "You and your brother Aaron take the rod and assemble the community, and before their very eyes order the rock to yield its water. Thus you shall produce water for them from the rock and provide drink for the congregation and their beasts."
>
> Moses took the rod from before the Lord as He had commanded him. Moses and Aaron assembled the congregation in front of the rock; and he said to them, "Listen, you rebels, shall we get water for you out of this rock?" And Moses raised his hand and struck the rock twice with his rod. Out came copious water, and the community and their beasts drank.
>
> But the Lord said to Moses and Aaron, "Because you did not trust me enough to affirm My sanctity in the sight of the Israelite people, therefore you shall not lead this congregation into the land that I have given them."
>
> Those are the waters of Meribah, meaning that the Israelites quarreled with the Lord—through which He affirmed His sanctity.
>
> Numbers 20:1-13

Here we have not only intentional disobedience, but also the penalty of extirpation. Both this myth and the myth of the fall make the same point. They direct attention to the generative conception that at stake in power is the will of God over against the will of the human being, and in particular, the Israelite human being.

The political myth of Judaism now emerges in the Mishnah in all of its tedious detail as a reprise—in now-consequential and necessary, stunning detail—of the story of God's commandment, humanity's disobedience, God's sanction for the sin or crime, and humanity's atonement and reconciliation. The Mishnah omits all explicit reference to myths that explain power and sanctions, but invokes in its rich corpus of details the absolute given of the story of the distinction between what is deliberate and what is mitigated by an attitude that is not culpable, a distinction set forth in the tragedy of Adam and Eve, in the failure of Moses and Aaron, and in countless other passages in the Pentateuch, Prophetic Books, and Writings. Then the Mishnah's is a politics of life after Eden and outside of Eden. The upshot of the matter is that the political myth of Judaism sets forth the constraints of freedom, the human will brought to full and unfettered expression, imposed by the constraints of revelation, God's will made known.

Since it is the freedom of humanity to make decisions and frame intentions that forms the point of differentiation among the political media of power, we are required, in my view, to return to the paradigmatic exercise of that same freedom, that is, to Eden, to the moment when Adam and Eve exercise their own will and defy God. Since the operative criterion in the differentiation of sanction—that is, the exercise of legitimate violence by Heaven or by earth or by the Temple—is the human attitude and intention in carrying out a culpable action, we must recognize the politics before us rehearses the myth of Adam and Eve in Eden—it finds its dynamic in the correspondence between God's will and humanity's freedom to act however it chooses, thus freely incurring the risk of penalty or sanction for the wrong exercise of freedom.

At stake is what Adam and Eve, Moses and Aaron, and numerous others intend, propose, plan, for that is the point at which the politics intervenes, making its points of differentiation between and among its sanctions and the authorities that impose those penalties. For that power to explain difference, which is to say, the capacity to represent and account for hierarchy, we are required, in my opinion, to turn to the story of the fall of Adam and Eve from Eden and to counterpart stories. The reason is that the political myth derives from that same myth of origins its points of differentiation and explains by reference to the principal components of that myth—God's and humanity's will and power— the dynamics of the political system at hand. God commands, but humanity does what it then chooses, and in the interplay of those two protean forces, each power in its own right, the sanctions and penalties of the system apply.

Power comes from two conflicting forces, the commanding will of God and the free will of the human being. Power expressed in immediate sanctions is also mediated through these same forces, Heaven above, human beings below, with the Temple mediating between the two. Power works its way in the interplay between what God has set forth in the law of the Torah and what human beings do, whether intentionally, whether inadvertently, whether obediently, whether defiantly. That is why the politics of Judaism is a politics of Eden. True, as we shall now see, we listen in vain in the creation-myth of Genesis for echoes resounding in the shape of the institutions such as those the politics of Judaism actually invents. But the points of differentiation of one political institution from another will serve constantly to remind us of what, in the end, serves to distinguish this from that, to set forth not a generalized claim that God rules through whoever is around with a sword (or the right, that is, Roman sponsorship).

The careful descriptions of, and distinctions among, institutions, through a vastly and richly nuanced account of concrete and enduring institutions, will once more emphasize the main point. It is how people know that power lies here, not there, is exercised by this bureau, not that, that we find our way back to the myth of differentiation and hierarchization. In what is to follow, we shall see how effectively the politics of Judaism distinguishes one institution from another, just as, in our survey of sanctions, we recognize the points of intersection and of separation. At every point we shall therefore be reminded of the most formidable source of power, short of God, in all. That always is the will of the human being. And he and she are never mentioned as paramount actors, even though, in this politics, humanity is what is at issue. Only at the end, in Chapter Twelve, shall we fully grasp what is at stake.

III. *Why Aristotle in Particular?*

The comparison of Judaism's politics goes forward solely in the encounter with Aristotle's.[14] Why? Three considerations make Aristotle's system uniquely valid for comparison with the Mishnah's.

> "It is natural to begin with Aristotle, who was in a class by himself among the political theorists and sociologists of antiquity: he studied the politics and sociology of the Greek city more closely than anyone else; he thought more profoundly about these subjects and he wrote more about them than anyone"
>
> G. E. M. de Ste. Croix[15]

---

[14] But—I repeat—I do not claim to contribute to the study of Aristotle's politics, except in the context of the history in antiquity of political thought, on the one side, and of comparative politics, on the other. I do not claim to tell specialists on Aristotle anything they did not know about Aristotle.

[15] G. E. M. de Ste. Croix, *The Class Struggle in the Ancient Greek World. From the Archaic Age to the Arab Conquests* (London: Gerald Duckworth & Co. Ltd., 1981) p. 69. My colleague Professor Martha Nussbaum kindly called my attention to that book. In connection with Aristotle's politics, note also Ernest Barker, *The Political Thought of Plato and Aristotle* (N.Y.: Russell & Russell, Inc., 1959); Donald Kagan, *The Great Dialogue. History of Greek Political Thought from Homer to Polybius* (N.Y.: The Free Press, 1965; and London: Collier-Macmillan Ltd., 1965). Kagan, p. 205, has a good de-

First, the Mishnah's generative mode of inquiry is the same as that pursued by Aristotle in his natural philosophy. It depends on the formation of genera made up of species.

Second, if we wish to compare a politics with another politics, we have also to compare an economics with an economics, for since a politics tells who may do what to whom, it consequently dictates who gets to keep what. That constitutes a judgment extending to the disposition of scarce resources. In antiquity, the only economics of importance is that of Aristotle. Since, in my judgment political theory forms a chapter in a larger assessment of the material relations of the social order, and Aristotle's politics is integrated with his economics as we shall see, Aristotle's politics is our prime and, I think, our only candidate for comparison and contrast with the Mishnah's.

Third, in addition to these two rather general considerations, there is a particular one that makes the comparison ineluctable. For both accounts of the social order in its structure and system, the building block of the social entity is identified as the irreducible unit of production, and the formative component in the social entity is the person who controls the means of production. In both cases this is the householder. Aristotle's economics, embedded in his system for the social order, and the Mishnah's framers' economics, likewise integral to their system of the social order, in method and in fact identify the householder as the building block of the social system. So the two systems are methodologically congruent; they both treat politics as part of an account of the larger social order; and they concur upon the building block of politics. With these fundamental points in common, we shall undertake a comparison yielding an important contrast. The building block of Aristotle's politics and economics is one and the same, the householder.[16] But that is not the case for the

---

scription of the teleological view of Aristotle's defense of the polis, he traces its development, e.g. village, association of households, and polis, association of villages. See also G. E. M. de Ste. Croix, pp. 69-81: Aristotle's sociology of Greek politics; and M. I Finley, *Politics in the Ancient World* (Cambridge: Cambridge University Press, 1983). Bernard Lewis, *The Political Language of Islam* (Chicago and London: University of Chicago Press, 1988). I found Lewis's lexicographic definition of politics less helpful than the more analytical readings of Aristotle's politics produced by the philosophers just now cited.

[16] That is not to suggest that only a householder could be a citizen in a Greek city. That is not the case. But to be a citizen, one had to have the wealth to enjoy the leisure to engage in politics, and the principal form of investment was in real estate and hence farming. So while one did not have to own land and supervise a farmer in order to qualify as a citizen, in point of fact citizens ordinarily were also householders.

politics of this Judaism. This fact produces the analytical question that allows us to enter deep into the heart of the politics of this Judaism. And that, of course, is our goal.

As a matter of fact, in their method the Mishnah's framers analyzed problems in the manner of Aristotle. In the philosophy of Judaism, the fundamental purpose of all intellectual inquiry is to discover the way things are and therefore are supposed to be. It aims, then, to secure for each thing its correct place in the natural order. If we know the category to which what appears to be an apparent singleton belongs, then we define the rule that governs that item too. We secure for what appears abnormal a normal status, and for what seems odd a routine position with other things of its class. In so doing, we accomplish rational explanation; we find a genus for what appears to be *sui generis*, beyond rationality. Classification therefore represents the medium by which we explain. By definition, therefore, that mode of thought applies in a single way to all domains of being—he natural and the social in the natural world and the supernatural realm as well. A single rationality pertains to the givens of all being, here and above too. The power of intellect, obeying the laws of correct classification or organization of things, holds the whole together in perfect balance, sense, and consequence. At stake in identifying the principles of classification therefore is the correct understanding of the dynamic of the philosophy of Judaism.

In philosophical method I see three basic principles that the Judaic system represented by the Mishnah repeatedly invokes. The first is to identify the correct definition or character of something and to preserve that essence. So we begin with the thing itself. Our premise is that we can identify the intrinsic or true or inherent traits of a thing, the thing seen by itself.[17] But we then ask in what way something is like something else, and in what way it differs. Our premise is that in some ways things are like other things; traits may be shared. So we proceed to the comparison of things. That requires us to identify the important traits that impart the definitive character or classification to a variety of distinct things. So we proceed to a labor of comparison and contrast. The third principle is that like things fall into a single classification, with its rule, and unlike things into a different classification, with the opposite rule. That conception, simple on the surface, defines the prevailing logic throughout the entire philosophy. At no

---

[17] A subset of this principle, of course, is the conception of true value, inherent in a thing, shared between the philosophers of the Mishnah and Aristotle.

point do we find any other logic in play. The problems develop, as we shall see in the next chapter, when we turn to concrete problems of classification.

The system of ordering all things in their proper place and under the proper rule maintains that like belongs with like and conforms to the rule governing like—the unlike goes over to the opposite and conforms to the opposite rule. When we make lists of the like, we also know the rule governing all the items on those lists. We know that and one other thing, namely, the opposite rule, governing all items sufficiently like to belong on those lists, but sufficiently unlike to be placed on other lists. That rigorously philosophical logic of analysis, comparison and contrast, serves because it is the only logic that can serve a system that proposes to make a statement concerning order and right array.

The mode of thought, of course, comes from natural philosophy, out of which natural science has evolved. But while the speciation of genera is not Aristotle's alone, it is Aristotle who set matters forth with the greatest clarity and power. The method is simply stated. Faced with a mass of facts, we are able [1] to bring order—that is to say, to determine the nature of things—by finding out which items resemble others and, [2] determining the taxic indicator that forms of the lot a single classification, and then [3] determining the single rule to which all cases conform. That method of bringing structure and order out of the chaos of indeterminate facts pertains, on the very surface, to persons, places, things; to actions and attitudes; to the natural world of animals, minerals, vegetables; to the social world of castes and peoples, actions and functions, and to the supernatural world of the holy and the unclean, the possession of Heaven and the possession of earth, the sanctified and the common.

Enough has been said to justify using a shared method when comparing Aristotle's and Judaism's philosophies, but I have yet to specify what I conceive to be the generative point of comparison. It lies in three matters. The paramount consideration is the shared principles of formal logic, described in Chapter One of this book. This I find blatant in the Mishnah, and all presentations of Aristotle's philosophy identify it as emblematic. The second consideration is obviously the taxonomic method, viewed from afar. We come now to the last of the three considerations that lead to the comparison of the Mishnah's politics with Aristotle's, the simple fact that the two systems share convictions about the centrality of the householder in the economic system. Having something fundamental in common, they may well be contrasted, also, in other aspects of their larger visions of society. And both conceive, as a matter of method, that the social order rests upon the means of production, and social relationships spin out issues of disposition of scarce resources. That fundamental fact validates the claim that the two systems are fundamentally alike and permits comparing them. That fact also explains why, it must follow, the differences between the two systems matter and so provide perspective on the character of the Mishnah's politics.[18]

Not only as a matter of method do both Aristotle's and the Mishnah's modes of formulating the social order begin with economic considerations. As a matter of fact, both systems identify the same component of the social entity in particular, in the same language, as the principal figure in the economics of their respective accounts of political economy. That is the one who is held by both system-builders to control the means of production.[19] In the mythic and symbolic language shared by Aristotle and the Mishnah's authorship, that party, in command of the irreducible minimum of productive capacity, is called the householder. And since for the philosophy of the sages of the Mishnah and for the system of Aristotle, it is the householder that defines the starting point for social thought, we are on firm ground indeed in comparing the system of the one to that of the other.

Aristotle presents us with a political economy, in which economics is embedded in a larger theory of the social order. That cogency of political economy is seen in his joining of economic to political issues

---

[18] Whether or not Aristotle's framing his political economy around the figure of the classification of person who controls the means of production, and whether or not the Mishnah's philosophers' identification of that same figure as the starting point (and ending point) of their economics makes either system Marxist is not a question taken up here. It is critical to the argument of de Ste. Croix. In this connection I call attention to Martha C. Nussbaum, "Nature, Function, and Capability: Aristotle on Political Distribution," *Oxford Studies in Ancient Philosophy*, 1988, and *Proceedings of the Eleventh Symposium Aristotelicum*, ed. G. Patzig.

[19] Whether such a one actually did control the means of production is not at issue. The economics of the Mishnah simply ignores most of the participants in the economy. Craftsmen, professionals, capitalists or entrepreneurs in capital, manufacturing, trading—these considerable participants in, and sectors of, the economy are treated only in relationship to the unit of production comprising the household. Entire classifications of persons in the economy, women and slaves and foreigners, for instance, play no role. The issues of economics are framed not only from the viewpoint of the householder but also within the frame of reference of the householder; the other issues, and they are many, are simply ignored.

when he refers to the household. We cannot overstress the fact that for *both* politics and economics, the irreducible, minimal unit of production, deemed to be the household, formed the building block and foundation for all higher structures. For one probative example, wealth is measured by the household and the town or *polis*, that is, the political unit of the social order, so that Aristotle defines wealth as "a means, necessary for the maintenance of the household and the polis (with self-sufficiency a principle in the background), and, like all means, it is limited by its end."[20] The basic thrust of the economics bears a political message, a lesson for the maintenance of the self-sustaining political unit or *polis*. Indeed, the aim of economics is to sustain the politics. And the goal of politics is to maintain the balance and order of the household and *polis*. Consider the following. In a system that appeals for validation to the teleology of nature, exchange by itself is natural: "shortages and surpluses...were corrected by mutual exchange...When used in this way, the art of exchange is not contrary to nature, nor in any way a species of the art of money-making. It simply served to satisfy the natural requirements of self-sufficiency."[21] Clearly, money makes possible the correct exchange of value. Quite logically, then, he regards the usurer (e.g., the one who offers consumer-loans) as practicing the art of money-making in an unnatural way: "interest makes [money] increase," and that violates the purpose of money, which is merely for the sake of exchange. But Aristotle also states that profit is made not according to nature, but at the expense of others. Indeed, Aristotle in general insists on the "unnaturalness of commercial gain." Therefore he does not consider the rules or mechanics of commercial exchange. Finley notes: "Of economic analysis there is not a trace."[22]

The Mishnah's system focuses upon the society organized in relationship to the control of the means of production, that is, it focuses on the farm, for the household is always—as a matter of fact—the agricultural unit. The Mishnah's authorship set forth the same fantastic conception as Aristotle, one of a simple economy. Each system invented a neat world of little blocks formed into big ones, households into villages, villages, for Aristotle, into the *polis*. There were then no empty spaces, but also no vast cities (for a reason characteristic of the system as a whole, as I shall specify presently). As the

---

[20] Finley, p. 41.
[21] Finley, citing *Politics* 1257a24-30.
[22] Finley, p. 44.

Mishnah's authorship saw matters, community or village (which is not the same as the *polis*) is made up of households, and the household (*bayit/oikos*) constitutes the building block of both society or community, and also of economy. It follows that the household forms the fundamental, irreducible, and of course, representative unit of the economy, the means of production, the locus and the unit of production. The household constituted "the center of the productive economic activities we now handle through the market."[23] Within the household all local, as distinct from cultic, economic, therefore social activities and functions, were held together. For the unit of production comprised also the unit of social organization, and, of greater import still, the building block of all larger social, now also political, units with special reference to the village.[24]

In the conception at hand, which sees Israel as made up, on earth, of households and villages, the economic unit also framed the social one, and the two together composed, in conglomerates, the political one, hence a *political economy (polis, oikos)*, one that is initiated within an economic definition formed out of the elements of production. The Mishnah makes a single cogent statement that the initial unit of society and politics finds its definition in the irreducible unit of economic production. It conceives no other economic unit of production than the household, though it recognizes that such existed; its authorship perceived no other social unit of organization than the household and the conglomeration of households, though that limited vision omitted all reference to substantial parts of the population perceived to be present (the craftsmen, the unemployed, the landless, and the like). Had Aristotle been shown a copy of the Mishnah and taught how to make sense of its mode of discourse—expressing large abstractions in small and concrete cases—he would have found its economics entirely familiar.[25]

---

[23] Lekachman, *History of Economic Ideas*, p. 3.

[24] But in classical Greece, while only citizens could own land, it is not the case that one had to own land in order to be a citizen. I owe to the reader the following clarification: "For Aristotle, citizenship is a matter of having the right to participate in judicial or legislative decision-making, and in many Greek states it was not necessary to be a landowner to have this right. Furthermore, Aristotle thinks of the ideal citizen as someone who has sufficient leisure to engage in farming as a regular activity, since that would take time away from the more important business of politics. For this reason it might mislead the reader to suggest that Aristotle's ideal citizen is a farmer."

[25] I qualify that statement in line with the comment given in the adjacent note, above.

IV. *Aristotle's Politics and the Politics of the Mishnah*

> It follows that the *polis* belongs to a class of objects which exist in nature and that man is by nature a political animal...Nature...does nothing without some purpose, and for the purpose of making man a political animal, she has endowed him alone among the animals with the power of reasoned speech. Speech is something different from voice...speech serves to indicate what is useful and what is harmful, and so also what is just and what is unjust.
>
> *Aristotle*[26]

Aristotle's politics forms an important chapter in his larger inquiry into the properties of things and into how, by nature, things are meant to be. His system's teleological focus, its concentration on the realization of what, in their nature, things may become, illuminates politics too.[27] That is why, when Aristotle reaches his stunning generalization about the nature of the human being, he forthwith adduces in evidence the traits of humanity. How otherwise explain the odd juxtaposition of politics and anthropology or account, in the setting of the *polis* as the political entity, for appeal to politics as the natural outcome of humanity's power of speech! Psychology, politics, economics, anthropology—all deliver the same message about the priority of how things are by nature.

But politics bears a particular burden of the larger systemic message. For Aristotle, according to Martha Nussbaum, politics and economics bear the same task, namely, the proper distribution of scarce resources to the correct recipients (for economics), and the appropriate distribution of capacities or opportunities for the realization of capabilities (for politics).[28] Nussbaum expresses the union between economics and politics in affording the correct and natural distribution of scarce resources and the effects of power as follows:

> "The aim of political planning is the distribution to the city's individual people of the conditions in which a good human life can be chosen and lived. This distributive task aims at producing capabilities. That is, it aims not simply at the allotment of commodities, but at making people able to function in certain human ways. A necessary basis for being a

---

[26] *Politics*, cited by Mulgan, p. 23

[27] I rely on Nussbaum, cited in the next note.

[28] Martha C. Nussbaum, "Nature, Function, and Capability: Aristotle on Political Distribution," *Oxford Studies in Ancient Philosophy*, 1988, and *Proceedings of the Eleventh Symposium Aristotelicum*, ed. G. Patzig. What makes this paper of special importance is Nussbaum's demonstration that there is a counterpart to distributive economics in Aristotle's politics.

recipient of this distribution is that one should already possess some less developed capability to perform the function in question. The task of the city is...to effect the transition from one level of capability to another. This means that the task of the city cannot be understood apart from a rather substantial account of the human good and what it is to function humanly."[29]

It follows that we understand Aristotle's politics in the correct context only when we identify the ubiquitous systemic message carried in particular by the politics—and can explain why the subject of politics forms the particularly suitable medium for that message. The same, we shall see, is true for the politics of this Judaism. In identifying and accounting for the generative difference between the Aristotle's political systems and that of the Mishnah, we better understand not only the politics but also—and especially—the respective systems for which each politics forms an indicative component.

To begin with, let us survey Aristotle's idea that the householder as the generative component not only of economics but also of politics, that he operates in structure and system alike. Taking R. G. Mulgan's description of Aristotle's politics as our model, we look first not at the household, but at the *polis*, which is to say, at the political community.[30] Mulgan quotes Aristotle:

> "...every *polis* is a community of persons formed with a view to some good purpose. I say 'good' because in their actions all men do in fact aim at what they think good. Clearly then, as all communities aim at some good, that one which is supreme and embraces all others will have also as its aim the supreme good. That is the community which we call the *polis*, and that type of community we call political."[31]

But what constitutes that "community of persons"? This seems to me the critical question here. Mulgan notes that of the two lesser communities that comprise the *polis*, the household and the village (which are parts of the polis and precede it in time), the household is much more important in Aristotle's ethical and political theory. Though the village provides a necessary link between the household and the polis in the chain of historical development, Aristotle ignores it as an integral part of the fully developed *polis*. The household, on the other hand, continues to have important functions for him. It operates as

---

[29] Nussbaum, op. cit., pp. 1-2.

[30] R. G. Mulgan, *Aristotle's Political Theory. An Introduction for Students of Political Theory* (Oxford: Clarendon Press, 1977), pp. 13ff. for the *polis* and the household, as indicated in the following notes.

[31] Cited by Mulgan, p. 13.

an educational institution. Indeed, it manifests the center of life for
over half the population of the city, that is, for women, children, and
slaves. Consequently, for Aristotle the head of the household is the
pivotal figure. He acts as a link between the political community and
the smaller community of the household.[32]

Mulgan identifies the political community as supreme, most powerful; the *polis* comprises the institutions that control the rest of society. Mulgan notes, "This conception of the political community is
similar to the modern notion of the state, which is usually defined in
terms of the monopoly of legitimate coercion."[33] The *polis* controls
other communities, which are included in it and form parts of it: "All
forms of community are like parts of the political community."[34]
Accordingly, the political community is coextensive with the society
of the city-state.[35]

Aristotle's principal political polemic forms part of a larger systemic program, the investigation of what accords with nature or exists by nature. This investigation pursues that which derives from
basic human motives and promotes the human "good." True, Aristotle argues that the polis is an institution, and came into being at some
point in history. But he holds that the political community or *polis* is
natural in the sense that it derives from basic human motives and
promotes the human good.[36] Mulgan explains the matter, giving its
crux as follows:

> Aristotle begins his argument that the *polis* is natural with a sketch of
> the development of the *polis* from the household and the village. He
> considers the polis as if it were a biological organism and tries to dis-
> cover its nature by examining the pattern of its growth and develop-
> ment. The first stage is the household which is based on two fundamen-
> tal distinctions in human nature. One is the difference between male
> and female which enables the human race to reproduce itself. The other
> is the difference between ruler and ruled, in particular between the man

---

[32] Mulgan p. 38-39
[33] Mulgan, p. 16.
[34] Mulgan, p. 17, from the Ethics.
[35] The Mishnah's political community in no way corresponds to the society of the
city-state. Its political community is its Israel. That leads us to anticipate no role for
the city at all, and, as we shall presently see, there is none. And that same fact also
explains the utopian, anti-locative quality of the politics of Judaism, even of a
Judaism that has at its center the one city that counts, which is Jerusalem. But we are
getting ahead of our story.
[36] That is not to say that the *polis* came into existence on its own, like a wild
flower, without the intervention of human thought and ingenuity. Aristotle does not
maintain that no institutions are man-made.

who has the intellectual capacity for ruling as a master and the man who can do no more than carry out his master's orders. These two instinctive relationships, male and female and master and slave, together with that of parent and child, ... form the household.

The household provides only the simplest necessities and so a number of households unite into a village which can supply more than men's daily needs. But the village is still too small, and so several villages unite in a further community, the *polis*, which alone is large enough to be self-sufficient. The original impetus for this larger community comes from the need for the necessities of life, but it continues to exist for the sake of the good life. That is, men first form the *polis* for relatively modest reasons, but, once created, it makes possible the realization of more elevated aims which men then come to see as the main reason for its existence. Being self-sufficient, the *polis* marks the final stage in a process of natural growth and development; indeed, as it is the final stage, it is itself the 'nature' of human development, the 'essence' which is realized at the end of natural growth.[37]

In Aristotle's words, "the *polis* is a perfectly natural form of community."[38]

The important point from our perspective is the role of the household in this judgment concerning the *polis*. Mulgan cites Aristotle as follows:

Therefore the *polis* is a perfectly natural form of community, as the earlier communities from which it sprang were natural. This community is the end of those others and its nature is itself an end; for whatever each thing is when fully grown, that we call its nature, that which man, house household, or anything else aims at being.[39]

In other words, the *polis* is natural because it is the natural outcome of the full maturing of the household, and because the household itself is natural, being founded (in Mulgan's words) on "innate biological differences." Evidently, it is therefore quite *natural*, in Aristotle's clearly defined sense, for the household to serve as the fundamental building block in the political structure that comes to full realization in the *polis*. This is not to assign priority in time or importance to the household over the *polis*. Indeed, as we shall see in a moment, Aristotle assigns the polis priority over the household and over any individual in it, "for the whole must be prior to the parts." But it does mean that there cannot be a *polis* without a household, and vice versa. Accordingly, the household must be seen to constitute

---

[37] Mulgan, pp. 20-21.
[38] Cited by Mulgan, p. 21.
[39] Cited by Mulgan, p. 21.

an essential component in the political community. For my comparison, the critical point is very simple and, I think, self-evident: for
Aristotle, the household constitutes a principal category in the political structure.

That fact cannot be taken for granted, for other social classifications were available for inclusion within the political structure. To
take a blatant example, Aristotle knew about the ethnos, or nation
state, a political entity that would exceed the *polis* in size.[40] But he
regarded such states as too large for good government, since not
every citizen of the polis can participate. This recalls Mulgan's statement, "Aristotle's argument that the *polis* is natural because it is self-
sufficient and therefore the culmination of a natural process of social
evolution thus rests ultimately not on biological or historical fact but
on his conception of the good life." Mulgan details the politics' systemic quality with great clarity. He writes:

> "Aristotle's preference for the *polis* is not due to ignorance of the exist-
> ence of other types of state; he is aware of possible alternatives, espe-
> cially the ethnos or nation-state which was often larger than the *polis*.
> But such states, though large enough to provide the right level of mate-
> rial prosperity, will not be able to offer the good life. Once a community
> has grown beyond a certain size it cannot be well governed and cannot
> provide the political participation which every citizen of the ideal *polis*
> will expect...The whole life of ethical virtue, as described in the Ethics,
> assumes the community of the *polis*...Aristotle's argument that the *polis* is
> natural because it is self-sufficient and therefore the culmination of a
> natural process of social evolution thus rests ultimately not on biological
> or historical fact but on his conception of the good life.[41]

The upshot is very simple. For Aristotle, politics like economics begins with the household, and political structures and the systems that
make them work form conglomerates of households. Innate or natural traits of households and householders form the justification for the
claim that "man is a political animal," which is to say, "an animal
that lives in a *polis*, or *polis*-animal."[42] And that is not only a fact that
derives from innate properties. It also forms a judgment of how
things should be: it comprises a teleological justification for the *polis*,
made up of households, as how things are meant to be:

---

[40] Mulgan, p. 22. Note Mulgan p 141 n. 22 on "the ethnos," which means a
political community larger than the *polis*, e.g., nation or people or race, e.g., Greeks
or Persians.
[41] Mulgan, p. 22.
[42] Mulgan, p. 23.

> Man is therefore a *polis*-animal also in the sense that, if he is to realize his moral potential, he needs the order and control which are provided by the government of the *polis*; the moral perfection of the members of the *polis* can be achieved only by means of publicly administered law.[43]

And this brings us to Aristotle's conception of the household as a political entity, the smallest irreducible whole political unit.

The representation of the household in this way should not be misunderstood. Aristotle does not maintain that the *polis*, being secondary, is therefore subordinate to the household in the political structure:

> The *polis* has priority over the household and over any individual among us. For the whole must be prior to the parts. Separate hand or foot from the whole body and they will no longer be hand or foot...It is clear then that the polis is both natural and prior to the individual....[44]

"Prior" in this sense constitutes a teleological, not a temporal, judgment. But the *polis* is prior in another sense: "A third is said to be prior to other things when, if it does not exist, the others will not exist, whereas it can exist without the others."[45] So when we say that the *polis* develops from the household and the village, it means that "the *polis* is posterior in the order of becoming, but prior in the order of nature, because it is the end towards which man's social development is directed." The *polis* can exist without a particular household, but it cannot come into existence without the corpus of households of which it is composed. In Mulgan's judgment, what we have is a restatement of the conviction that the *polis* is natural.

The household, joined to the *polis* through the formation of the villages and the agglomeration of the villages into the *polis*, retains fundamental importance in Aristotle's politics.[46] It existed by nature, allowing for the expression of the natural instincts of reproduction and self-preservation, and providing the basic necessities of life. These natural tasks accommodating innate traits, then, defined the household, which "provides for the procreation and rearing of children and which produces much of the economic wealth of the *polis*."[47] Within the *polis* too, the household undertakes fundamental political tasks within the larger life of the community. These are

---

[43] Mulgan, p. 25.
[44] Mulgan, pp. 30-31.
[45] Mulgan, p. 31.
[46] Mulgan, p. 38.
[47] Mulgan, p. 38.

educational, on the one side, and socially controlling (over women, children, and slaves), on the other. So Aristotle relates the household to the political entity:

> Every household is part of a *polis*; and the virtue of the part ought to be examined in relation to the virtue of the whole. This means that children and women too must be educated with an eye to the whole constitution of the *polis*—at least if it is true to say that it makes a difference to the goodness of a state that its children should be good and its women good. And it must make a difference; for women make up half the adult free population and from children come those who will participate in the constitution.[48]

The householder, then, forms the critical link between the political community and the household, that is to say, the smaller political community that, in conglomeration with other such units, makes up the political community or the *polis*. Hence we see the embeddedness of the economics in a political economy.

Not only so, but the economic tasks of the household form a principal part in the political role of that same social entity. As we have already noted, the second of the two innate traits of the household is the possession and acquisition of wealth.[49] Aristotle's politics in no way can be distinguished from his economics, as we have already observed. But why should that be so? The reason is that integral to his system as a whole is this claim that the innate traits of humanity are what account for the development of the household, then of the village, then of the town or *polis*. That uniformity in social classification, using the same building block throughout, derives from the method of classifying things by their traits and then appealing from the traits of things to their purpose. Accordingly, it is teleology that accounts for the natural condition of things. That quality by nature that makes the household the simplest whole unit of society also applies to the *polis* or political community as the complex composition of such simple whole units of society.

It now suffices to repeat that for both systems—the Mishnah's and Aristotle's—the one who controls the means of production, the householder, also defines the basic unit of economic activity. And, we now recognize in full nuance, that same persona, the householder, also defines for Aristotle the basic unit of political activity.

---

[48] Mulgan, p. 39.
[49] Mulgan, p. 47.

THE MISHNAH AND ARISTOTLE'S POLITICS

For the Mishnah's politics, the household plays no role whatsoever. It is not an indicative category. Nor does the householder serve
as the subject of a single statement of a political character. Rather,
the subjects of all the sentences are supplied by figures within the
monarchy, cult, or bureaucracy (king, priest, scribe). That separation
of the economic actor from the political one is especially astonishing
since all economic thought prior to the eighteenth century treats
economics as part of the science of political economy, that is, as an
aspect of public policy (i.e. a mode of distribution of wealth by appeal
to considerations extrinsic to wealth). Mulgan states matters for Aristotle, by extension revealing for us the truly exceptional character of
Judaism's separation of politics from economics:

> Wealth and production are aspects of the general life of the *polis*, like
> education, warfare, or drama, and so are equally subject to ethical
> evaluation and political control. The question of 'economics' in Aristo-
> tle illustrates a more general difficulty which we face when we try to
> understand Greek political thought. We tend to divide our thoughts and
> activities into different, autonomous categories, such as the economic,
> the religious, the moral, the legal, the political, and the educational. For
> the Greeks some of these distinctions did not exist and those that did
> were much more blurred than they are for us. Greek society...was more
> 'integrated,' less' differentiated,' than our own. Though we cannot
> avoid using words like 'economics' when we discuss Aristotle's political
> theory, we must not let them distort his meaning. At the same time, the
> absence of such sharp distinctions in his view of society may help us to
> a better understanding of our own society. Though more differentiated
> than Greek society, it is not so sharply divided as our categories some-
> times suggest. Aristotle's approach to politics reminds us that the
> spheres of economics, law, morality, and education are not isolated but
> closely interdependent.[50]

What Mulgan says of Aristotle's economics and politics applies with
no important variation to economics and politics, embedded within
the social system and its purpose, of all modes of political and economic theory prior to the Enlightenment. Then, and only then, economics was disembedded and developed into an autonomous intellectual construction on its own.

Since, in the case of the initial system of post-Temple Judaism, the
basic building block of the economy is not the fundamental and irreducible social unit of which the politics is composed, we find in this
Judaism no system of thought that we may call a political economy,

---

[50] Mulgan, p. 52.

and that we might link to the politics of this Judaism. The economics is not embedded in the social system and structure but defines a categorical entity—an imperative—on its own. How it is that Judaism could produce a politics distinct from economics in its fundamental structure and system? How could it comprise a disembodied economics.

From this point, two tasks lie before us. The first is to show as fact the negative proposition that the household in the politics of this Judaism does not play the role that it does in the economics of Judaism; the second is to explain why, and characterize through comparison and contrast the Mishnah's system in particular.

What evidence sustains the claim that the householder in the politics of this Judaism does not constitute a political category, a topic of political discourse? The answer is not merely the silence of the Mishnah's politics on the householder as a political entity. It is that the social unit of the village, made up of households, does not form a political entity in the way in which it does for Aristotle's Politics. Households, however many, do not aggregate into a village, nor villages, however large, into a polis, a city or a town that defines a political entity. No political role in the politics of this Judaism is assigned to the social entity constituted by either the village or the town. No political role is assigned to the householder because he forms the critical component of a social unit that itself is politically inert. The *élan vital* of this Judaism's Israel's politics is social, but society is other than Aristotle considers it to be.

The systemic message comes forth at points of differentiation: what the system-builders wish to sort out defines the focus of their interest and the medium of their systemic message.[51] And, in point of fact, the framers of the Mishnah scarcely differentiate among urban settings, between village or town or city, and hence the difference between the one and the other bears no systemic consequences. To see that point clearly, we have to gain perspective on the village and the town in the system of the Judaism of the Mishnah. What do we find in the Mishnah's repertoire? I discern remarkably few allusions to an urban setting in which distinctions as to the setting—*polis* or town as against village, town composed of villages made up of households, for instance—make much difference. For example, when peo-

---

[51] And, to the contrary, failure to differentiate within an entity signals the system's lack of interest in the entity: hence systemic inertia, and, in this context, political as well. But I do not wish to argue only from silence.

ple refer to a city on which it has not rained (M. Ta. 2:1), or a city
that has been taken in a siege (M. Ket. 2:9), there is no consequence
I can see for a larger theory of the difference between a village or
town and a city. On the other hand, when, at M. Qid. 2:3, we find a
clear reference to the difference between life in the one place and
that in the other, we do reach a point of some interest. The passage
has a man falsely swear to a prospective bride that he is a villager
when, in fact, he lives in the city, or *vice versa*. The unmet stipulation
nullifies the woman's agreement to become betrothed to him. A husband may not take his wife from a town to a city and vice versa (M.
Ket. 13:10D). So there a was a clear distinction. But why is the
difference that the distinction makes unspecified.[52] Clearly it involves
conditions of everyday life, with no bearing on any larger systemic
interests. Nor does the equivalent distinction make a difference at M.
Meg. 2:3.

Overall, moreover, I find no tendency to evaluate life in the one
place as better, or worse, than life in the other; the location is simply
a fact of life. The notion of dwelling together with gentiles in the
same city is a commonplace (e.g., M. Makhshirin 2:5). Likewise,
there are references to large and small cities (e.g., M. Erubin 5:8),
and these references produce no grounds to think sages held a higher
opinion of one than of the other or thought there were consequential
differences. A large city is defined as one in which there are ten men
of leisure (M. Megillah 1:3), and a small town, one in which there are
fewer than that number. The usage of KPR, small town, is unusual;
generally the framers of the Mishnah use the word for town, 'YR,
sometimes clearly meaning a large one, sometimes a small one, and
often with no clear intent.

That, sum and substance, is the whole story for the Mishnah.
There is clear and present distinction between city and town. but it
makes very little difference. Where it does make a distinction we
cannot say what that difference is. The simple fact is that the
Mishnah's authorship does not imagine a difference between village
and town or city, that is, for Aristotle, polis, and, more to the point,
that same authorship never conceives the village or town to form a
political unit. That is to say, when the authorship refers to political
issues, it does not invoke the category town, or village, and it further

---

[52] Nor have I found in the later commentaries a very plausible explanation of the
difference.

does not speak of the householder as a political, as well as an economic, building block.

The differentiation as to location was not village as against town as against city; it was Jerusalem as against everywhere else—and that does form a distinction that makes a considerable difference for the politics of this Judaism. Jerusalem was where the politics took place. And, I stress, that forms a fundamental fact of the politics of this Judaism, in contrast to the view of Aristotle, for whom the location of a given polis is irrelevant. Aristotle describes an ideal political community; while it must have certain physical characteristics, it does not have to be in this place or that, but can exist anywhere that meets certain conditions. By contrast, the politics of this Judaism is locative.

The difference, of course, is readily explained. Aristotle could speak of the polis, a mode of socio-economic and political organization to be replicated anywhere. But the Mishnah and the Torah spoke of only one city, Jerusalem, the metropolis of Judaism. Mother of cities, from its perspective there were no differences among its offspring. Jews inherited in Scripture a sizable corpus of images and myths associated with the heavenly city, poised as it was in heaven over the earthly Jerusalem. Certainly, all Israel hoped for the rebuilding of Jerusalem and the reestablishment of the Temple. The law itself made ample provision for life in Jerusalem. Whole tractates, such as Maaser Sheni, took up the definition of the city and of food that entered the sacred limits of the city. Others, such as Sheqalim, dealt with the officials of the city and the Temple and their work. So in the Judaism of the Mishnah, there is only one social entity that can correspond to the *polis* in the thought of Aristotle, and that is Jerusalem: the unique *polis*, the metropolis.

Jerusalem is the location of the temple, the king, the high court; it constitutes the political place par excellence. But it also was the only such place, and no other place situated itself in relationship to that place. So Jerusalem's critical status within the political structure of Judaism bore hierarchical, and also locative consequence. In relation with Jerusalem, everywhere was no-where in particular, and Jerusalem was above everywhere else. Then the politics of this Judaism served a larger hierarchical purpose of assigning a place in the social order to one place above all other places, and the focus of the politics upon Jerusalem made its statement as well. But that statement is made in a voice of silence for, after all, Jerusalem now was inaccessible. So the political structure and system of Judaism addressed an imaginary world; an Israel without a king, high priest, or even access to Jerusalem, called for a king to govern, a high priest to preside, a Jerusalem to form the center.

And here we gain perspective on the politics of this Judaism for, we now realize, this politics forms a mere chapter in a story with its own beginning and purpose. The system of Judaism before us formed an exercise in the study of sanctification and its effects, and therefore, for systemic reasons, Jerusalem was *the* "city," and its "city-ness" derived from its holiness.[53] And so far as "city" or "town" forms, for Judaism, the counterpart to *polis*, and the locus of power makes that a necessary comparison, then "city" formed a utopian and hierarchizing category, not a locative and political entity. To state the matter very simply, for the Judaic system Jerusalem served the hierarchizing purpose of distinguishing one place from everywhere else. And that distinction made no political differences whatsoever, because—let me stress—*only Jerusalem was empowered, and from Jerusalem all power flowed.*[54] Jerusalem formed an abstraction. But in the system the issue was not the concrete reality of the city or its abstraction and material inaccessibility. Systemically, Jerusalem stood for something else, something other, a social entity with no analogy down here in the village or town or city. It stood for some place, a center as against an undifferentiated periphery of no-places. And that standing made of Jerusalem an instrument of locative hierarchization.[55] The power of Jerusalem to hierarchize also defines the place of Jerusalem in this Judaism. Where the system-builders locate opposites, we find the critical message, and Jerusalem is holy in the way that uncleanness is unholy, point by point, stage by stage. Uncleanness is a matter of status, of hierarchy of what I may do or may not do if I am unclean, balanced against where I may go or may not go when I am clean.

Incidental to all this are the political classifications king, priest, scribe, which form epiphenomena of the hierarchization of all else, but do not themselves impose order or hierarchy on anything else, except as their systemic tasks permit. To hierarchization the matter of place is simply irrelevant, except for Jerusalem. But place, in Jeru-

---

[53] Compare Finley, *The Ancient Economy*, p. 123. I mean to emphasize that in the pages of the Mishnah we cannot distinguish town from country.

[54] The picture of appeal to the high court in the Temple seems to me adequate proof of this self-evident proposition.

[55] Within a system aimed at systematic hierarchization as a means of overcoming chaos—everything in proper place and classification, which is to say, everything in correct order, hence, once more, hierarchization.

salem, is not locative but an expression of the order of things. The
political structures and system the Mishnah's philosophers have in
mind find categories in the correspondence between Heaven and
earth which takes place at or over Jerusalem. And that is not a
locative conception; it is, by definition, utopian.[56] The politics of the
Mishnah's philosophers concerned power everywhere in general
but—as a matter of social fact then and there—no where in particular. The specificity of Jerusalem then hardly masks its utopian quality. To put matters very simply, in the politics of this Judaism, Jerusalem is not *about* place, not at all. For if, beyond Jerusalem, no
particular place is distinguished from any other, so that (in our case)
the politics works (or does not work) without regard to location, then
Jerusalem too hardly lays claim to take place somewhere in particular. As the cited passage of the Mishnah expresses the point, *Jerusalem
defines not location but relation.*[57]

So if Aristotle were to interrogate a sage about the *polis*, inquiring
where, precisely, the locative community figures in the politics of this
Judaism, what sort of answer would he get? The *polis*, a particular
community in a specified place, makes its appearance only once, so
far as I have noticed, in the political sector of the system of the
Mishnah. This occurs at M. San. 10:4: "The townsfolk of an apostate
town have no portion in the world to come." These people form part
of a catalogue of those who lose life beyond the grave because of
crimes or sins against God. A share in the world to come is something one gains as part of an entire community—the community of
all Israel—but one may lose that share also as part of an entire
community that is discerned as a community in relationship to God
in particular. Among the components of the political community that
has acted collectively and is to be subjected to collective sanctions, we
find a variety of castes or classes singled out for consideration—

[56] Jerusalem stands for something, but at the time and in the circumstance of the
composition of the Mishnah, took place solely within the theory of things, as much a
matter of imagination as king, high priest, and temple. But that is not critical to my
argument, as already indicated.

[57] Because there is Jerusalem and there is everywhere else, Jerusalem too is no-
where in particular, for no other place locates itself in relationship to Jerusalem. A
status, a focus, a medium for mediation—none of these political traits imputed to
Jerusalem define locative characteristics; in accord with not a single one of them can
we locate any other political entity, and there in fact is within the system no other
political entity anyhow. Consequently, as I said, Jerusalem is not a place but a state,
even, in context, a state of mind, and, it follows the politics of Judaism is not locative
but utopian in a very concrete and immediate sense indeed.

women, children, temporary residents, bypassers—but among them the householder does not appear.

And that fact brings us back to the striking absence of the householder, who really does have power, in the politics of this Judaism. At no point does the householder define a categorical imperative that is either the subject or the object of power. In the context of sanctions that pertain to a village/town/*polis* as such, he is not a presence, does not define a political category. Indeed, the householder occurs in the Mishnah only when the management of farms or estates plays a role. Why can the conception of the householder play no role whatsoever in the politics of this Judaism? Because the politics of this Judaism, to begin with, is not a dimension of location. It is not based on the land. Possession and management of the means of production, comprising a particular place or space, has no bearing upon politics. Why? The issues settled by legitimate use of violence are simply different from those worked out by the allocation of scarce resources—and economics is subordinated.[58]

Landholding, then, does not bear consequences for the politics of this Judaism. Controlling the irreducible unit of means of production bears no political weight; it does not help to define one political classification as against some other. Holding or not holding the land never defines the legitimacy of violence in a political circumstance. The case just now noted, concerning the apostate city, proves the opposite. Mere residence, not qualified by land-ownership, defines guilt. I cannot point to a single component of the theory of politics that appeals to possession of the land for definition of a categorical component of the system.[59] The politics of Judaism never appeals to enlandisement as a political category, that is, as the requirement for participation in the political process, in the way in which the economics defines the household as the farming unit but also ignores those farming units that do not comprise households. So clearly, control of means of production does not constitute the kind of power that the politics of this Judaism mediates. That fact is underlined by the discontinuity between the political institutions of the system as a whole—king, priest, sage—and the actual politics of the village or

---

[58] And would soon be redefined altogether, so that in the second phase in the unfolding of Judaism and the move from philosophy to theology, there would be no economics in the this-worldly sense at all, rather, a complete revaluation of what we mean by "scarce resources."

[59] Of course, agencies of the political system deal with possession of land, but that is not the same thing.

town. These rest in the hands not of king or priest, but only of sage. Sages are not represented as landholders or as employees of landholders. And the sages work, in the village, as *ad hoc* administrators, not being represented as part of a coherent politics of administered power.

These observations about the difference between a politics that omits reference to control of means of production and one that encompasses that form of power within a larger theory of the distribution of power draw us back to our basic work of comparison. The primary locus of power dictates, for both systems, the answer to the question of where politics takes place at all. Aristotle's premise is that power inheres in the community (*koinonia*), and the community finds its definition by the nature or natural condition revealed in the citizens, who encompass all landholders and therefore most householders.[60] So Mulgan:

> Aristotle begins his analysis of the *polis* by describing the *polis* as a community (*koinonia*), a concept which is fundamental for his political theory...communities should properly have morally valuable purposes,...and the true *koinonia* will pursue the true good....Another essential characteristic of any koinonia is that it involves...both friendship and justice...In politics the most important...principle is distributive justice which governs the distribution of goods and benefits to different members of the same group, and it is this aspect of justice which is an essential feature of every koinonia.[61]

Power, then, flows from the community to the individual, and the foundation of the politics is the community that comprises the *polis*. That is, the male, free citizens—all landholders, defined as householders—form the institutions of politics that all together comprise the *polis*.

For the politics of this Judaism, holy people, divided into castes of a hierarchical order, constitute the political entity; holy land, ordered in relationship to the holiest place, Jerusalem, constitutes the definitive locus. The power parceled out is the power of the sacred, and politics' task is to order all persons and classes of persons who are eligible according to appropriate taxic indicators with regard to their

---

[60] We have already noted that to own land one had to be a citizen, even though to be a citizen one did not have to own land. That accounts for the framing of matters here. All landholders were householders and were citizens, but not all those who possessed wealth and could have been householders in an economic sense were landholders.

[61] Mulgan, p. 14.

sanctification (that is, by caste, not by wealth). In such a system no place exists for the householder because the kind of power that concerns this politics is not the power he enjoys to allocate scarce material resources in a rational manner. This politics concentrates on the power to allocate holiness in a rational manner. So to politics the householder is simply irrelevant. What he governs has no bearing upon matters of consequence. The distributive economics of Judaism makes the important decisions upon materials goods and services; the issues of politics then concern entirely other matters. The hierarchization of all persons and places and things in proper place and order aims at the highest point, which is defined as the most holy. The householder in such a system is not subject to hierarchization at all, forming as he does no category that appeals for identification, standing, and status to taxic indicators of the sacred.

These distinctions flow from still more fundamental propositions about how things are by nature. What, specifically, do we mean by "nature"? For Aristotle, the answer derives from the teleology signaled by the natural traits of things, and for the Mishnah's sages, from their supernatural traits, signaled by the inherited qualities imputed by scriptural science.[62] Aristotle speaks of the this-worldly and given characteristics of the human being in general, yielding, as a matter of fact, the *polis*. The sages make up their politics in speaking of "Israel," that is, the holy people. What explains the formation of the political unit? For Aristotle, householders forming villages (villages making up towns or cities) frame the *polis*. That is, nature defines the social entity, defines how things are.

For sages, by contrast, "Israel" forms a supernatural category made up of people born to Israel the supernatural social entity. It comprises children of very particular persons, Abraham, Isaac, and Jacob. So birth—hence caste, or marriage into a caste for a woman —carries with it a supernatural definition signified by genealogy. And, as a matter of fact, that genealogy has its heaviest bearing upon caste arrangements ("priest," "Levite," "Israelite"). Once more a politics of hierarchization results. In it nothing is merely natural or ordinary; in the formation of the social entity governed by the politics of this Judaism, there are no givens, only gifts of grace—and the chief gift is one's place in the social order, one's caste-standing as to sanc-

---

[62] I use the word "science" very deliberately, to signal facts established beyond all doubt by appeal to irrefutable sources of truth, for the Mishnah's sages' Judaisms as for all other Judaisms—Scripture above all.

tification. Aristotle appeals to the natural as what promotes the human good. That is not what is at stake in the Mishnah's Judaism, and it predictably plays no role in Mishnaic Judaism's politics.

If I had to describe the most striking differences between the two political systems at hand, I should address more than the systems' disagreement on how to evaluate the political consequences of control of the means of production.[63] I would refer to Aristotle's striking power to take up questions of competition, control, political change, on the one hand, and the Mishnah's steady-state conception of politics on the other. Whereas constitutional change comprises a principle interest for Aristotle, issues of instability and disorder in the political context receive no attention in the Mishnah.[64] In Aristotle's mind, constitutional change can be contemplated. People can force change through violence (illegal means); they can gain power within an existing constitutional framework; as members of a governing body they can implement change peacefully by taking a deliberate decision to alter the rules. By contrast, the Mishnah includes no provision for constitutional change. Its silence with regard to the transfer of power and the revision of institutional structures differs strikingly from Aristotle's thoughtful treatment of these topics.

But then, for Aristotle, change forms part of his politics' topical program; it is something to be considered. For the Mishnah's fram-

---

[63] Other such differences may be noted briefly. The politics of Aristotle is abstract, general, accessible, that of the Mishnah concrete, particular, and recondite and arcane. We find in the Mishnah no conception of "the state," a category that is critical and ubiquitous for Aristotle. Modes of thought that for Aristotle yield analytical categories for the Mishnah's framers produce personifications of institutions. That is exemplified, in the fact that in the Mishnah's system there is no classification "community" (counterpart to *koinonia*, for instance). Unlike Aristotle's politics, in the Mishnah's I find no interest in questions of residence, possession of legal rights, e.g., the right of suing and being sued and the right to share in the administration of justice and in political office. (Indeed, by that criterion, the only citizens of the Jewish state are the king, priests, and scribes!). There is no consideration of a "constitution," such as Aristotle foregrounds. The distinctions among the things government does, e.g., executive judicial and legislative, was mine; it is not native to the Mishnah. Aristotle's conception of the constitution as "the arrangement which states adopt for the distribution of offices of power and for the determination of the sovereign and of the end at which the community aims" (Mulgan, p. 45), can mean nothing in the politics of Judaism, and his three elements of a constitution, deliberative, official or magisterial, and judicial, find no counterpart. Aristotle's whole discussion of "rule of the best men," oligarchy, aristocracy, has no point of intersection with the politics of Judaism. These are issues never discussed in the Mishnah, because it is taken for granted that the qualifications of government are genealogical or Torah-learning.

[64] Although as I shall argue, these define the generative problematic of the entirety of Mishnaic Judaism.

ers, I maintain, disorder is unthinkable, anti-systemic. A system that proposes to bring about order (to be defined in the coming chapter) will find only danger in change and reform of public institutions alike. And this accounts for the avoidance we see. But the main point of difference is that for Aristotle the household forms the point of departure for politics, and for Judaism, it does not. And from that one point of difference, we can account for all of the other differences just now catalogued. Let me state the upshot of this comparison with emphasis:

Aristotle works out a system that joins economics to politics by appeal to a single and uniform teleology. The Mishnah's philosophers set forth a system that distinguishes economics from politics by appeal to a single and uniform principle of classification.

Politics in each setting bears its share of the burden of the system, and from what the two systems have in common, we see only points of contrast and differentiation. Now, to accomplish the final task, we turn to the question, for this Judaism what requirement of the systemic message has provoked the invention of a politics? To answer that question, we must find a mode of analysis that serves for the Judaic and Aristotelian systems both. When a single manner of inquiry yields different answers for different systems, and we can therefore explain why this, not that, we have reached the end of our study.

V. *The Mishnah's Politics of Hierarchization*

The contrast between Aristotle's and Judaism's politics alerts us to two important points of difference. First the Mishnah's economics and its politics seem disjoined. The householder functions as the building block for the house of Israel, for its *economy* in the classic sense of the word—but the politics of the house of Israel does not know him.[65] Second Aristotle's keen interest in recognizing, explaining, and even controlling change contrasts vividly with the Mishnah's framers' apparent incapacity to recognize change at all. The one thing the Mishnah does not want to tell us is about change. It does

---

[65] But if there is a disjuncture between the generative metaphor of the Mishnah's economics and the one that is spun out in its politics, the systemic message is the same in both cases. The message of the document as a whole concerns order and stability, and that means, hierarchization of things and persons in proper place and order.

not encompass history as the story of how things come to be what
they are. Once more we commence with Finley:

> ...inquiry into the ancient state and government needs to be lowered
> from the stratosphere of rarefied conceptions, by a consideration not
> only of ideology, of 'national' pride and patriotism, of *der staat*, of the
> glories and miseries of war, but also of the material relations among the
> citizens or classes of citizens as much as those more commonly noticed
> between the state and the citizens.

M. I. Finley[66]

What do we learn from the difference between Aristotle's and the
Mishnah's politics about the Mishnah's system of the social order? At
stake is an account of what we may call the Mishnah's rationality, its
sense of how things are and are meant to be. Accordingly, when we
compare the politics of this Judaism with that of Aristotle, we find
ourselves moving beyond the boundaries set by the topic before us.
Our question concerns no longer principal components of systems,
but generative conceptions thereof. It addresses the basic sense for
the fittingness, the logic, the right ordering of things. When we can
identify the rationality of a system, then at the deepest layers of
perception we can compare that system with some other. And that is
the right way to conclude, for at stake in politics, for both Aristotle
and Judaism, is not politics at all.

As a matter of fact, both Aristotle and the philosophers represented in the Mishnah utilized politics to make a point that in each
system far transcended the subject at hand.[67] That point, in the case
of the politics of this Judaism, addresses the relations among classifications of persons and the relationships among those classifications.[68]
These relations, while transcending the matter of legitimate violence,
encompassed politics within a larger frame. That fact tells us, why
the Mishnah's particular Judaism also invoked politics in making its
larger statement. The system required a politics because an important part of its message in the system-builders' judgment could come

---

[66] M. I Finley, *Politics in the Ancient World* (Cambridge: Cambridge University Press,
1983), p. 49

[67] This is precisely the question I treat in my *Economics of Judaism*: why did this
Judaism work out an economics at all? And, in the same way, I asked Aristotle for
perspective by inquiring why, for his philosophy, economics proved so central.

[68] I avoid the word "classes," because that bears meanings hardly demonstrated to
be present here. Finley's writings on class and class-structure in antiquity seem to me
the model to be followed.

to expression only in a politics.[69] The question therefore becomes, "what was that message," and "why was politics, in particular, the correct medium for stating it?"

True, the Pentateuch itself set forth a politics, and so the choice of politics as a mode of spelling out the systemic message can hardly present any surprises. The character of the Pentateuchal system assuredly found definition in the establishment of an "Israel" that was fully empowered, and fully enlandised as well. But framers of other Judaisms and Christianities did not appeal to a politics to set forth their systemic compositions, not at all. As a matter of fact, other Judaisms and Christianities set forth their systemic program in entire indifference to the issues of politics. And this point requires serious consideration so that the issue before us—why a politics at all?—will gain its rightful weight.

The topical program of the Mishnah, when compared with the themes deemed urgent by other system-builders of some of the Judaisms and Christianities of the time, seems singular in its sustained and systematic interest in civil law and government.[70] For example, the writings of apocalyptic Judaisms scarcely include any counterpart to the design for an everyday and functioning political structure and system (all the more so for an economics, it goes without saying). The Judaism of the Essene community of Qumran designed a political structure and system mainly for itself; it rejected the prevailing politics and assigned to its community the sole legitimate politics and also, of course, the sole standing as authentic Israel. Whether this be deemed a counterpart to the Mishnah's politics requires attention in its own terms; I am inclined to doubt it. Finally, the Judaism that would emerge in the writings that would continue the Mishnah, the two Talmuds in particular, recognized the existence of institutions of power for the Jews without encompassing those institutions within its politics as legitimate and important components of the legitimate use of power. The exilarch in Babylonia and the patriarch in the Land of Israel in no way form counterparts in the politics of the two Talmuds to the king and high priest of the politics of this Judaism.[71] So in the context of other Judaisms, the interest in

---

[69] Just as I asked, why does this system invoke also economics in making its larger systemic statement?

[70] Singular, but not unique, since Philo showed keen interest in setting forth a whole politics in the context of his larger structure and system.

[71] I return to these questions in projected studies of the second and third layers in the unfolding of the Judaism of the dual Torah.

political structures and systems of the one before us should not be regarded as merely characteristic of any Judaism because of the Pentateuchal precedent.

The profoundly political character of this Judaism becomes still more astonishing when we look at the writings of early Christian figures, at the Gospels and the Letters of Paul, for instance. There we search in vain for any political discourse that might bear implications for political institutions and their operation. Jesus is represented as having been perceived by the Romans as a political figure, but the Gospels formulate no political structure or system in his name, and the entire range of politics—appeal to legitimate use of violence, whether natural or supernatural—finds its boundaries at the limits of the church-communities. The conception of a Christian state is beyond imagining. True, to Jesus are attributed sayings that respond to political facts, but none that will frame such facts; and Paul is utterly apolitical. Indeed, sayings cited in Jesus's name argue against any Christian politics whatsoever.

And that conforms to a familiar fact, that the earliest writings of Christianity hardly contain the raw materials for political theory of any kind; the exercise of power lies beyond the imagination of the Christian system-builders and thinkers even after the advent of Constantine. From the formation of the Mishnah, ca. 200, two centuries would pass before a Christian writer would set forth a political theory of ambition and weight. But the parallel with the politics of post-Temple Judaism even then is inexact, for Augustine, the first Christian political thinker, did his work well after Christianity had gained the standing of a political power, when Christian emperors and bishops had wielded power and enjoyed the right of exercising legitimate violence in its name for more than a century.

If a system of Christianity such as Augustine set forth encompassed a politics, it was because Christianity by nature of its institutional position formed a political power within the Roman empire. That did not make it necessary for Augustine to think up a politics for his Christianity, but it made it plausible and natural for him to do so.[72] By contrast, the authorship of the Mishnah, even though remembering a Jewish state perhaps, never knew what it meant to put a person to death for a felony, to take away peoples' property in the name of

---

[72] I do not claim that that is why he did so. My intent is only to contrast Augustine's situation with that of the Mishnah's authorship.

collecting taxes, to beat, to maim, to expel and send into exile, in the name of the legitimate rule of the law enforced by the legally-constituted and just state. Augustine was a bishop; he knew what power was about; the sages of the Mishnah, if they held any power at all, were at best local busybodies. From the perspective of competing figures, they seemed mere meddlers and no-accounts and bunglers, pretending to make up their minds and bear weighty opinions about matters concerning which, in point of fact, they utterly lacked experience. So why a political Judaism?

To answer that question we must address it to philosophy: why is it that a philosophy that attends, also, to politics? The task of identifying the role of politics in the systemic composition, and defining the unique message that was assigned to politics by the system, seems to me quite clear. Having identified Aristotle as our guide and model, we turn back to the position and systemic tasks of politics in his philosophy, and with that perspective as our guide, we shall return to the Judaism at hand. We do well to begin with the judgment of the great M. I. Finley: "In the *Politics* Aristotle defined man as a *zoon politikon*, and what that meant is comprehensible only in the light of his metaphysics; hence correct translation requires a cumbersome paraphrase—man is a being whose highest goal, whose telos (end) is by nature to live in a *polis*."[73] It follows that sustained and cogent thought on politics, in particular, formed a critical component of Aristotle's larger thought on the nature of humanity. Political science encompasses all other areas of learning:

> Now since political science uses the rest of the sciences, and since, again, it legislates as to what we are to do and what we are to abstain from, the end of this science must include those of the other sciences, so that its end must be the good for man.[74]

If Aristotle wishes to discuss "the whole of human good," he must address a politics and, as Mulgan states at the outset of his exposition, "An account of Aristotle's political theory must therefore begin with his conception of human good."[75]

Let us dwell for a moment on how politics delivers the systemic message concerning human good. Aristotle starts with a definition of "human good" meaning "the good life." What are the traits of hap-

---

[73] M. I Finley, *Politics in the Ancient World* (Cambridge: Cambridge University Press, 1983), p. 25.
[74] Mulgan, p. 3.
[75] Mulgan, p. 3.

piness? "The happy man will be someone who values the philosophical contemplation of eternal truths above all else and will devote a
considerable amount of his time to it...."[76] And again, Mulgan states,
"The subject matter of political science is human action."[77] Aristotle's
main purpose in the *Politics* is "...to provide a handbook of guide for
the intending statesman"; "political science" is also "statesmanship."[78] Aristotle writes primarily for the ruler, the statesman or legislator who will be making important political decisions, rather than
for the ordinary citizen; his political science is statesmanship not
civics."[79] And what does Aristotle wish to accomplish through his
political philosophy? "The overtly practical purpose of Aristotle's
political science explains the close dependence of the Politics on his
conception of human good. Political decisions must be based not
only on knowledge about the workings of politics but also on some
view of the ends of goals which the community ought to be pursuing."[80] So the goals which the statesman ought to achieve constitute
Aristotle's starting point; next come generalizations or rules about
how these goals can be achieved in different types of political situation; finally, Aristotle applies the rules to actual situations.[81] The role
of political thought in the definition of human good therefore is
critical:

> The happy man will be someone who values the philosophical contem
> plation of eternal truths above all else and will devote a considerable
> amount of his time to it....This conception of the good life provides the
> background and inspiration for most of Aristotle's political theory. The
> connection between his ethical ideals and his political science is most
> clearly expressed in the last chapter of the Ethics, where, having com
> pleted his account of the good life, he raises the question of now it is to
> be implemented. People are unlikely to become good unless the govern
> ment and the laws are directed toward the achievement of human good.
> The complete 'philosophy of human nature' must therefore include the
> study of laws and constitutions and how best to frame them.....The
> influence of Aristotle's ethics on his politics will be most apparent in his
> discussion of the nature of the polis and in his account of the ideal state
> which is intended to implement the ethical ideal.[82]

---

[76] Mulgan, p. 6.
[77] Mulgan, p. 8.
[78] *ibid.*
[79] Mulgan, p. 9.
[80] Mulgan, p. 9.
[81] Mulgan, pp. 10-11.
[82] Mulgan, p. 6.

Evidently, Aristotle attends to political science because he is interested in the nature of the human being and especially in human action.

This fact explains why politics forms a medium for the expression of Aristotle's larger system of thought on the nature of the human being and human society:

> The overtly practical purpose of Aristotle's political science explains the close dependence of the *Politics* on his conception of human good. Political decisions must be based not only on knowledge about the workings of politics but also on some view of the ends or goals which the community ought to be pursuing.[83]

The principal point is that the politics of Aristotle forms part of a larger inquiry into how things are by nature. In this connection we rapidly review what formed the centerpiece of our inquiry into the role of the household in Aristotle's *polis*. Aristotle's philosophical program, we remember, is to investigate what accords with nature or exists by nature. In this context the correct mode of thought derives from the discovery and classification of the traits and characteristics of things by nature.

So Mulgan states: "Because this world is constructed according to a coherent and rational pattern, it is proper...that each species should develop and exercise its own natural characteristics. By doing so, it realizes its 'essence' and performs its work of function."[84] The appeal to nature, beginning with biology and ending with the political community, then accounts for the place of the politics in the larger system, to which politics likewise proves natural and necessary. The subject-matter accounted for, the message delivered through this topic as through many others spelled out, we may now turn to the counterpart for the initial Judaism.

When we come to Judaism and ask "what is the message of politics, and why does politics serve as a particularly appropriate medium for the message?" we do best to begin not with similarity but with difference, for having established grounds for comparison, we can now explore the incongruities of the two systems. Seen in this light, each system will then serve through the outline of its shadow to highlight the indicatively different systemic traits of the other. To understand the message for which politics served as a medium, and

---

[83] Mulgan, p. 9.
[84] Mulgan, p. 18.

to explain why that particular medium uniquely served the purposes of the system-builders, we return to our discussion of the systemic myth, spun out of the facts of power in its most brutal political form, from which, after all, all else flows.

Why a political Judaism? And what message did this Judaism find possible to express uniquely, or most powerfully, in the medium of a fabricated political structure and system? The principal message of politics in the system of Judaism derives, we recall, from our capacity to differentiate among the applications of power by reference to the attitude of the person who comes into relationship with that power. We remember that if the deed is deliberate, then one institution among the set of politically-empowered institutions exercises jurisdiction and utilizes supernatural power. If the deed is inadvertent, another political agency exercises jurisdiction and utilizes the power made available by that same supernatural being. Why does this seem to me of such fundamental importance? *Because where a system differentiates, there it delivers its critical message.* So the point at which the system tells us why this, not that marks its exegetical fulcrum. And that, we recall, lies in the systemic identification of the two powers that do conflict, God's and the human person's. The entire politics works out the issues of power that to begin with are generated out of that conflict. And, by the way, the politics then identifies political agencies to deal with the several distinct types of conflict between those two wills.

The system's entire message stands within that resolution of the power of will that is implicitly and tacitly contained within the labor of hierarchization, beginning at the very foundations of all being. As I shall now explain, the question answered by the politics for the system, and by the system as a whole, is this: what happens when God's will, which is supreme, confronts conflict ("rebellion," "sin," "disobedience") with the human will, which is subordinate? The answer is, God's will be done. And this—this politics—is how. Why a politics? Because the system recognizes that the human will does constitute power. It is, moreover, a power to be reckoned with, taken into account, deemed legitimate even in its violent confrontation with God. And therefore—because of its very legitimacy—the power formed of the human will is to be met with equal, and equally legitimate violence that the political system, acting in God's behalf, effects. The hierarchization of power sets forth the systemic problem, and the theory of the politics of this Judaism defines the self-evidently valid solution.

The conflict worked out by politics then is between God's will, expressed in the law of the Torah, and the human being's will, carried out in obedience to the law of the Torah or in defiance of that law. Here, as we noted in the beginning, we find a reprise of Eden's politics and of all the other mythic formulations of the conflict between God's power and humanity's, between God's commandment and humanity's freedom to obey or to disobey. The politics of Judaism emerges as a reprise, in stunning detail, of the story of God's commandment, humanity's disobedience, God's sanction for the sin or crime, and humanity's atonement and reconciliation. When Adam and Eve or Moses and Aaron exercise their own will and defy God, they set their power, free choice to obey or disobey, against God's power, his capacity to command—without coercion. And because of God's limitation, we have here a conflict of human and divine wills that stand in equal contest with one another.

This again precipitates the systemic question, how are equal powers ordered? The power of the will of the one against the strength of the will of the other (a will limited by self-restraint, to be sure) forms not so much the theme of the system before us as its problematic. That, in my view, accounts for the system's profound engagement with issues of hierarchization. The dynamic of the system derives from the capacity of human attitude and intention to define culpable action, and, as I said, that central theme draws us back to the myth of Adam and Eve in Eden. Once more we note the principal message: God commands, but humanity does what it then chooses. In the interplay of those two protean forces, each a power in its own right, the sanctions and penalties of the system apply.

Let me then say why I think this Judaism found a politics necessary, a political statement integral. And let me define the statement that this Judaism made through its politics. Politics served the critical systemic task of differentiation: why this, not that. It proved necessary because it sorted out the effects of the human will among three media of divine intervention: the Heavenly court above, earthly court below, Temple altar in between. Power, as we noted earlier, works its way in the interplay between what God has set forth in the law of the Torah and what human beings do intentionally, inadvertently, obediently or defiantly. Accordingly, a politics was necessary, a political statement integral to Judaism. And given the subject-matter of politics, the legitimate uses of coercion, we may hardly find astonishing the inclusion, in the initial Judaism, of a politics.

But what was the shape of the particular statement that emerged? To answer that question, we turn from the myth to the method: how, precisely, did the sages of the Mishnah work out their politics? When we know the answer to that question, we shall understand the character of the system's details, just as, when we know the main purpose of Aristotle's system, we can also account for the character of his fictive politics. This is why the answer to our question draws us to an account of Judaism's counterpart to Aristotle's thesis about the priority of the natural over the conventional, his insistence upon the principle—prior to all propositions—that both political and non-political institutions derive from the very nature of things. This quality enables them to realize the potential that is inherent in that nature, that is justified by the traits of human nature. Accordingly, here we shall juxtapose and compare things that, when we began this inquiry, could not have appeared to us to be congruent or—as we shall see in a moment—even related. Since, in my view, one of the marks of an analysis' success is the possibility it raises for us plausibly to juxtapose and compare what to begin with appeared utterly incomparable, we seem to have made some progress.

Knowing Aristotle's mode of thought, and therefore his fundamental purpose in making his system, we can account for his topical program in general and the particular relevance of politics within that program. That is, if only after the fact, we can account for his uses of politics. But can we identify within the method of the Mishnah's sages an equivalently fundamental method or mode of thought? To answer that question, we turn from generalities about myth to the concrete cases at hand. When the framers of the Mishnah speak, it is only in and through detail. But if, as I maintain, their statement is systematic and forms a system, then how they treat any detail of any substance should indicate how they think about all details. From that indication, consequently, we should be able to generalize about the methods and modes of thought at hand. And once we can describe how the system-builders think, we can identify what is the generative tension and critical concern of the system as a whole, a tension worked out, a concern expressed, also in the realm of politics.

For that purpose we move, as we did before, from the myth of power to the institutions thereof. When the Mishnah's sages address the description of institutions, what do they want to know about them? That is to say, given a topic, they will have a particular pro-

gram of inquiry they propose to follow. From a scarcely-limited corpus of facts, they will want to find out or invent answers to one set of
questions rather than to some other. A particular aspect of the facts
will attract their interest. This aspect I term a generative problematic,
for it generates the problems the system-builders identify and propose
to solve. In the case at hand, we turn to the two most consequential
matters, to the political structures and sanctions which, together,
constitute the formation of coercive power that defines a politics—
any politics.

And this inquiry draws us to two issues, the relationship between
king and high priest, and the catalogue of judicially-inflicted penalties. These issues seem utterly unrelated, yet they yield a single mode
and method of thought and produce results that fall within a single
classification. Specifically, they compare and contrast and therefore
hierarchize. In the matter of institutions, exemplified by the treatment of the king and the high priest, we find silence about questions
that engage us. For example, the authority and role of king and high
priest in the administration of the everyday affairs of particular locali-
ties, and the way in which people leave and enter office, do not
appear. But we do learn in exquisite detail the relative position of the
high priest and the king (the king stands higher in the hierarchy of
power and authority than the high priest). The Mishnah's framers
want to accomplish the hierarchization of these two important loci of
power, so they compare the king to the high priest and in detail make
explicit the standing imputed to each. By consequence, as I said, the
high priest is shown to be a subordinate figure, the king an auto-
cephalous authority.

The entire politics is a politics of hierarchization. At stake are the
right arrangements, the proper and correct positions, for all persons
and all things. The questions that delineate the hierarchy cover who
is on top, who underneath, and who comes first, who next? Just as
Aristotle everywhere seeks the answer to one question, systematically
worked out in diverse areas, so do the sages of Judaism. Aristotle
consistently wishes to know what is good for humanity, a question he
answers by appealing to the natural traits of persons and things to
answer the question; similarly, the philosophers of the Mishnah want
to answer their question. And they too answer their question by
appealing to the natural traits of persons and things, traits that they
work through inductively in quest of the pertinent rule or generalization.

Aristotle, we recall, appeals to the capacity of humanity to speak, and this forthwith forms a fact of nature that dictates a trait of politics as well:

> Nature...does nothing without some purpose, and for the purpose of making man a political animal, she has endowed him alone among the animals with the power of reasoned speech. Speech is something different from voice...speech serves to indicate what is useful and what is harmful, and so also what is just and what is unjust"

The same mode of thought—appeal to the traits of things in search of generalization—accounts for the hierarchical positions assigned to king and high priest. So we juxtapose the sentences of Aristotle beginning, *"Nature...does nothing"* with those of the Mishnah that declare, *"A high priest judges and others judge him, the king does not judge, and others do not judge him."* Aristotle's thinking about the political implications of the natural trait of humanity to be able to speak forms the counterpart to the Mishnah's authorship's thinking about the comparison of the king and the high priest. Incongruous? Only if we do not grasp the systems and what is at stake in them. The Mishnah's sages dealt with politics because they wished to address fundamental issues of power, and they imposed upon politics the generative problematic of hierarchization, because that defined their mode and method of thought. What they wanted to find out, in the description of the social order, was the right ordering of things, and what they managed, then, to say, through politics in particular, was that God disposes of the effects of human freedom.

That is not to suggest that all Israelites were conceived to be equal and to stand in the same relationship to Heaven within the grid of sanctification. The contrary is the case. Although a system of hierarchization by definition concerns itself with the opposite of the equalization of relationships, proposing to show how persons (things, places, conditions as to cultic cleanness—just about anything!) are not equal, in the politics at hand, the upshot of hierarchization is that diverse castes are unequal, but all male Israelites may overcome the hierarchical structure imposed by caste by entering the category of sage. The sage, after all, truly possesses and manipulates power, for power comes from God, and the sage is the master of the message of Heaven.

Now that we have the Mishnah's modes of thought in hand, let me conclude with a reprise of the main conceptions on which this politics of Judaism rests. The framers of religious systems that concern themselves with the structure and order of society answer urgent questions set for them in the life of society, questions of economics, philosophy, and politics. To these issues of the social order, governing the material and intellectual foundations of the social entity and the proper administration, through sanctions, of its collective life, they respond with what are to them self-evident answers. The religious system, then, comprises identification of the urgent question and the composition, out of accounts of the ethics, ethos, and politics dictated (commonly) by Heaven of final solutions to that critical problem. The Judaism provides one striking example of how people in writing set forth the ethics, ethos, and ethnos that all together comprise a Judaism, how they give a cogent answer to an urgent question. Since in this Judaism we deal with a social entity that in the minds of its inventors also constitutes a political entity in particular, we here consider how in their imagination intellectuals proposed to sort out issues of legitimate violence. For the political entity, "Israel," in this Judaism exercises the form of coercion that consists of the power to tell people what to do and then to make them do it.

In describing, analyzing, and interpreting the politics of this Judaism we have dealt with high abstractions. But we cannot permit matters to conclude with so theological a judgment of what is at stake. Remembering the words of M. I. Finley that stand at the head of this chapter, we have to ask how the politics of this Judaism sorted out "the material relations among the citizens or classes of citizens as much as those more commonly noticed between the state and the citizens." The answer is that this politics did not sort out the material relations among citizens or classes of citizens. This is a politics that appealed to indicators of an other-than-material order when it classified persons, social entities—all living things—within an order and a hierarchy. Independent variables, in the imagination of the system-builders, derived from other considerations than the control of the basic means of production. Perhaps it would be more to the point to say the system-builders thought that the systemically interesting means of production were not those that produced material things. What mattered was holiness, and how holiness ("the holy" or "the sacred") was defined would then indicate who produced it, that is, who sanctified whom, and how.

So the systemic issues of hierarchization dealt with the ordering of different things on the basis of different traits from those things that are signified by the indicators of material productivity, and that explains why, if Marxians can identify with their views the politics of Aristotle, they cannot similarly appropriate the politics of this Judaism. Only in that light can we take into account an economics that utterly ignores most of the actual economy and a politics that treats as null such obviously puissant classes as are comprised of householders. Now we see the full meaning of the simple fact that sages ignored when treating politics what proved the critical and central component of their thought when treating economics. When sages in the Mishnah set forth a politics, they concerned themselves not with material relations at all, but with power relationships, and these, they conceived, flowed not from the relationships among classes of citizens but from that between all Israelites and God. So the distinctions are between like entities—yet signal vast differences.

From their intellects, the Mishnah's system-builders have composed a world at rest, perfect and complete, made holy because it is complete and perfect. In mythic terms, the Mishnah confronts the fall from Eden with Eden, with the world on the eve of the Sabbath of Creation: "Thus the heavens and the earth were finished and all the host of them. And on the seventh day God finished his work which he had done, and he rested on the seventh day from all his work which he had done. So God blessed the seventh day and hallowed it, because on it God rested from all his work which he had done in creation" (Gen. 2:1-3). The Mishnah's framers have posited an economy embedded in a social system awaiting the seventh day, and that day's divine act of sanctification which, as at the creation of the world, would set the seal of holy rest upon an again-complete creation. There is no place for action and actors when what is besought is no action whatsoever, but only unchanging perfection. There is room only for a description of how things are, for the present tense, for a sequence of completed statements and static problems. All the action lies within, in how these statements are made. Once they stand fully expressed, when nothing remains to be said, nothing remains to be done. There is no need for actors, whether political entities such as king, scribes, priests, or economic entities, householders.

The Mishnah's principal message, expressed through the categorical media of economics and politics alike, the message that makes the Judaism of this document and of its social components distinctive and cogent, is that man stands at the center of creation, at the head of all creatures upon earth; he corresponds to God in heaven in whose image he is made.[85] Who this man is—whether householder in economics, whether priest, monarch, or sage in politics—shifts from topic to topic, but the priority of the human (male's) will and attitude in the disposition of important questions everywhere forms the premise of discourse. The way in which the Mishnah makes this simple and fundamental statement by imputing to man the power to inaugurate and initiate those corresponding processes which play so critical a role in the Mishnah's account of reality, sanctification and uncleanness. The will of man, expressed through the deed of man, is the active power in the world. Will and deed constitute the operators in creation working upon neutral realms subject to either sanctification or uncleanness. They affect the Temple and table, the field and family, the altar and hearth, woman, time, space, transactions in the material world and in the world above. An object, a substance, a transaction—even a phrase or a sentence—although inert, may be made holy when the interplay of the will and deed of man arouses or generates its potential to be sanctified. Conversely, each may be treated as ordinary or (where relevant) made unclean by neglect of the will or by an inattentive act of man.

We conclude with the obvious point about utopia, that it exists no where in particular, to whom it may concern. The politics of Judaism began in the imagination of a generation of intellectuals who, in the aftermath of the Jerusalem government's and Temple's destruction (70) and the military defeat Jews suffered three generations later (132-135), had witnessed the end of the political system and structure that the Jews had known for the preceding millennium. Initially set forth in the Mishnah, a second-century philosophical treatise in the form of a law-code, the political theory of Judaism laid out political institutions and described how they should work. In that way these intellectuals, who enjoyed no documented access to power of any kind and who certainly seem unable to coerce many people to do very much, sorted out issues of power. They took account, in mind at least, of the issues of legitimate coercion within Israel, the holy people, which they considered more than a voluntary association, more than a community formed around a cult.[86]

Their Judaism encompassed a politics because through politics

---

[85] Woman is subordinate and dependent. Man is the norm and the normal. That is why I can say only "man," rather than, in this context, "the human being."

[86] The power exercised by gentiles, e.g., the Roman government, never entered the picture since it was not a legitimate politics at all.

they found it possible to express their systemic message, one that put everything in its proper place and order, correctly differentiating, compellingly hierarchizing. And that systemic message explains why their system's social entity, that is, their Israel, formed a political entity as well. Their "Israel" was supposedly able to govern in its holy land through the exercise of coercive power, not merely through a voluntary community that persuaded compliance. The setting was an age of endings and, consequently, beginnings. Everyone knew what was now behind. Within the half-century before the time of the authorship of the document, the Temple of Jerusalem had been destroyed, together with the political structures based upon it, and a major war meant to recover the city and reinstitute an autonomous, even independent, Jewish state had been lost. But no one could anticipate what would now happen.

Whatever politics had been beforetime now had no call upon the future, unless the coming generations restored the now-lost structure and system. And the founders did not. Instead, they made up a system for which, in concrete, historical time, no counterpart had actually existed in the world and age of which sages had first-hand knowledge. Indeed, whatever the political facts deriving from Israel times past—or from Roman practice in their own day, for that matter—the authorship had in hand, they were drastically reworked. All received information and fabricated conceptions served equally to form the essentially fresh and free-standing structure and system that sages made up. From the mid-second-century to the end of that same century, the work of rethinking the politics of this Judaism went forward. And, therefore, embedded within the religious system represented by the Mishnah and correlative and successor writings was set forth a politics that would define the reference-point of Judaism from that time to the present. But that does not mean the politics of this Judaism in its initial statement ever attained realization in the structure of actual institutions and in the system of a working government.

The system of the initial Judaism, while influential for nearly two millennia, never actually dictated how people would do things at all. By the time the systemic document made its appearance a new politics had gotten under way, one that accorded to holy Israel in the holy land, that is, to Jews in Palestine, limited rights of self-government that were mainly focused upon matters of no interest to the provincial authorities (e.g., issues of personal status, transactions of petty value, ritual and cultic questions that meant nothing to anybody who mattered). But that new politics, with its jurisdiction over things of no account and its access to power of no material weight in no way corresponded to the formidable conceptions of legitimate violence, exercised through enduring institutions, a well-organized bureaucracy, and appealing to a sustaining political myth, that are set forth here. Nor in the realities of Jews' limited self-administration in the third and fourth centuries, down to ca. 400, do we find actual examples of the workings of the passion, responsibility, and proportion and balance of a concrete system of political life, such as the document's authorship has made up for itself. But the one trait that would characterize all subsequent systems is the one dictated by the initial system. Politics would require the working out of issues of hierarchization, and sages would dictate the composition and construction of Israel's social order—or so they thought.

INDEX